How to Read Your Way to Heaven

VICKI BURBACH

HOW TO
READ
YOUR WAY TO
HEAVEN

A SPIRITUAL READING PROGRAM
for the Worst of Sinners, the Greatest
of Saints, and Everyone in Between

SOPHIA INSTITUTE PRESS
Manchester, New Hampshire

Sophia Institute Press
Box 5284, Manchester, NH 03108
1-800-888-9344

www.SophiaInstitute.com

Sophia Institute Press® is a registered trademark of Sophia Institute.

Library of Congress Cataloging-in-Publication Data

Names: Burbach, Vicki, author.

Title: How to read your way to heaven : a spiritual reading program for the worst of sinners, the greatest of saints, and everyone in between / Vicki Burbach.

Description: Manchester, New Hampshire : Sophia Institute Press, 2017. Includes bibliographical references.

Identifiers: LCCN 2016048458 ISBN 9781622823604 (pbk. : alk. paper)

Subjects: LCSH: Books and reading — Religious aspects — Christianity. Christian literature — History and criticism. Christians — Reading interests. Christians — Books and reading. Catholic Church — Doctrines.

Classification: LCC BR117 .B87 2017 DDC 248.4/6 — dc23 LC record available at https://lccn.loc.gov/2016048458

For my mother, Donna Wilson,
who always encouraged my love for reading

CONTENTS

·—— PART I ——·
A Proper Approach to Spiritual Reading

·—— PART II ——·
How the Program Works

PART III

Pillars of Joy: A Complete Spiritual-Reading Program

APPENDICES

Acknowledgments

My heart is full of gratitude for Father C. John McCloskey, who was kind enough to respond ten years ago to an e-mail from yours truly about my comprehensive idea for a spiritual-reading program, for which his Catholic Lifetime Reading Program was the impetus. Through the years, he has responded to question after question in an amazingly generous and timely manner.

It was Father McCloskey's recommendation nearly five years ago that I contact Dan Burke and offer to write an article about spiritual reading for the *National Catholic Register* that put our book club on the map. I cannot thank Dan enough for his deep faith and never-ending mission to draw hearts and minds to Christ and for the opportunity to share such amazing works with Christians around the globe each and every week. Without Dan's encouragement, this reading program would still be housed in its crude, copy-shop spiral binding, where it originated for my personal use.

Thanks to my "book club partner" at Spiritual Direction.com, Sarah Reinhard, who was kind enough to share her experience with me when I began asking questions. Sometimes all you need is a simple example to get you started.

Thanks to Charlie McKinney and Nora Malone of Sophia Institute Press, who have made my first book-publishing experience a complete joy through their kindness, professionalism, and availability every step of the way.

I would like to thank all those friends from Holy Family Homeschoolers who listened to my passionate ideas way back when. A special thanks to Joan Gilmore. At the very beginning of this journey, she—along with a few other brave souls—tested this reading program and offered invaluable feedback.

Thank you also to Meghan Cunningham, Kate Ziegerer, and most especially my mother, Donna Wilson, for their mountains of love, support, and feedback throughout this project.

For every writer there is one invaluable person without whom nothing would get written. This person offers an ear, an eye, and is available during the late-night hours and in the early-morning haste—a voice of encouragement and motivation. For me, that person is Linda Ochs, a great friend and confidant for whose patience, availability, and intelligent feedback I am very grateful. Thank you so much for all your help. I couldn't have finished this book without you.

To my husband, Dale, I offer my undying gratitude for encouraging me to pursue this project through the years, taking care to make our house a home even when I was hidden away with my computer and a stack of books.

A special thank you to Christian, Caleb, Emma, Noelle, Elias, and Marlena, who have patiently endured my absence often these past months, even caring for one another on those few occasions when Dad, too, has been gone in the evening. Some of you have been my cheerleaders. All of you have been my joy.

Mostly, I am thankful to Christ, my Savior, who plucked me out of a life of materialism and self-indulgence, introduced me to His Church, and placed me where worldly values can most readily be stamped out—united with my husband, at the helm of a family.

Acknowledgments

A special thanks to those who contributed to the amazing reading lists provided in this book:

Bishop James Conley

Charlotte Ostermann

Dan Burke

Danny Abramowicz

Diana von Glahn

Father C. John McCloskey

Father Mike Schmitz

Father Timothy Gallagher

Jason Evert

Jennifer Fulwiler

Karl Keating

Lisa Hendey (catholicmom.com)

Marcy Klatt (The Catholic Book Lady)

Mike Aquilina

Patrick Coffin

Patti MacGuire Armstrong

Paul McCusker

Peter Kreeft

Sam Guzman (The Catholic Gentleman)

Sarah Reinhard

Steve Ray

Tim Gray

Tim Staples

Trent Beattie

Trent Horn

Note to the Reader

Dear Reader,

Wouldn't it be wonderful if we *could* read our way to heaven? If going to heaven were as simple as curling up with a good book—with *the* Good Book, a cup of coffee, and maybe a candle for a little atmosphere? We'd open to page 1 full of hope and wonder, but still feeling the filth and grime of our sinful natures and those pesky bad habits. But page by page, we'd feel the smut fall away. No effort would be necessary, other than the methodic turning of the pages as words would rise to our intellects and descend to rest softly upon our souls. No pain; no suffering. And when we'd reach the last page, we'd have our one-way ticket to the Promised Land. Voila! Virtually instant sanctification.

As nice as that sounds, we all know that sanctifying grace does not come to us from a book. Nevertheless, spiritual reading *is* critical to our development as Catholics, and ultimately as saints. The information in a book travels directly from intellect to intellect, from soul to soul. Because of this, a book's words can often sink in without encountering the barriers we tend to construct, even subconsciously, to protect ourselves from the judgment or criticism of others. Often books provide an impetus for profound change in our lives. They can have a dramatic impact on our decisions, our habits, and our relationships and can even cause a complete paradigm shift in our hearts and minds, changing the way we see the world as a whole. Great saints, such as Augustine and Ignatius, experienced profound conversions through books.

Although dedicated spiritual reading can have a great impact on our lives and on our ability to share Christ's light with the world, the world often demands so much time and energy from us that we often fail to take the time to fill ourselves spiritually before running off to face each day's challenges.

Most likely you are familiar with the story of Martha and Mary. But for the sake of discussion, let's read it again now:

> Now as they went on their way, he entered the village; and a woman named Martha received him into her house. And she had a sister called Mary, who sat at the Lord's feet and listened to his teaching. But Martha was distracted with much serving; and she went to him and said, "Lord, do you not care that my sister has left me to serve alone? Tell her then to help me." But the Lord answered her, "Martha, Martha, you are anxious and troubled about many things; one thing is needful. Mary has chosen the good portion, which shall not be taken away from her." (Luke 10:38-42)

The truth is that many of us long to spend more time at the feet of our Lord, obtaining the "good portion" sought by Mary, but our lifestyles much more resemble Martha's—yes, even you men. Serving families, careers, and communities often leaves little time for precious contemplation and spiritual reading.

With some guidance and a little organization, however, each of us can obtain the good portion.

The flexible one-, three-, or five-year reading program in these pages will lay out for you a schedule for fifteen to thirty minutes of prayerful spiritual reading and study, five days a week, structured around the four pillars of the Faith as described in the *Catechism of the Catholic Church*: the Profession of Faith, the Celebration of the Christian Mystery, Life in Christ, and Prayer. The key is to set aside time each day and to remain faithful to that special one-on-one time with our Lord. By scheduling a little spiritual reading each day, you will be amazed at what you can accomplish over time.

Note to the Reader

It is my prayer that by the time you finish this book, you will be prepared and even excited to embark on a purposeful spiritual-reading program as a way to build a more prayer-filled, Christ-centered life.

In Christ,
Vicki

How to Read Your Way to Heaven

My Spiritual Journey with a Stack of Books at My Side

The primacy of the spiritual means that there is nothing in
the world that really matters except the salvation of our soul,
and that in its salvation the spiritual must reign over the
temporal, the soul over the body, grace over nature, and God
over the world. Religion means this or it means nothing.

—Archbishop Fulton Sheen, *Moods and Truths*

Books played a significant role in my life long before I found my way
home to the Catholic Church more than twenty years ago. In addition
to my attraction to the truth and beauty of a great novel, I've always
believed that whatever questions life proposes, and however challenging,
the answers can always be found in a book. Whether I wanted to earn
better grades, find the right job, clean my house, or be a better parent,
there was a book that promised to teach me what I wanted to know.

No matter what we desire to learn, most of us seek wisdom from the
experts—people who have learned a thing or two that can make our
experience more successful. Nowhere is seeking advice from an expert
more valuable than in our Faith life.

As apologist Frank Sheed so aptly put it in *Theology for Beginners*, "Truth is light." And one of the beautiful things about being Catholics is that we need not scrounge around all alone in the shadows, hoping to grasp some spark of brilliance. We have brothers and sisters wielding flashlights and candles extending back more than two thousand years, so we need not waste time feeling our way through the darkness.

When I converted to the Faith, it was as though I had become a card-carrying member of the most amazing and far-reaching library in the world! And I was quick to take advantage of my good fortune. After reading *Rome Sweet Home* by Scott and Kimberly Hahn, I embarked on a quest to learn everything there was to know about the Catholic Church. I became a huge fan of Scott Hahn and Peter Kreeft. In addition to reading several of their works, I read *This Is the Faith* by Rev. Canon Francis Ripley, *Catholicism and Fundamentalism* by Karl Keating, *Where We Got the Bible* by Henry Graham, *The Spirit of Catholicism* by Karl Adam, *The Great Heresies* by Hilaire Belloc, *The Spirit and Forms of Protestantism* by Louis Bouyer, and many others.

Having lived twenty-four years of my life outside the Catholic Church, I had a lot of catching up to do. During those early days, I hadn't the first clue as to how to *be* Catholic, how to walk the walk and talk the talk. I had no idea what a day in the life of a devout Catholic should look like. So, in addition to trying to fill my brain with centuries of wisdom about the beauty of Christ's one, holy, catholic, and apostolic Church, I was also trying to learn how to sit correctly in the pew. I felt as if everyone thought I wasn't *really* Catholic, but rather just a Catholic wannabe who sneaked in the side door when no one was looking. (Don't get me wrong. Everyone I met in the Church was very kind to me and I knew my self-consciousness was irrational.)

To address my discomfort I once again turned to a book—or rather, several of them. Despite my research, I didn't feel more at home during the Mass right away, and going to Confession continued to be awkward. (I've since learned that, as with anything new to us, repetition is the key. This is an issue all the books in the world cannot solve—more on that later.) But my research revealed an array of Catholic customs and traditions that I wanted to practice at home. After all, if I was going to be Catholic, I wanted to do things *right*! (Are you sensing a theme here?)

For a time I believed that to be a *good* Catholic meant that I should *know every single thing* Catholics believe and *do every single thing* Catholics do. My well-meaning but wrongheaded passion made me a poster-child for Protestants who claim that the Catholic Church makes Christianity much too complex. While my heart was bursting with desire, my head was bursting with knowledge. There were Morning Offerings, the Rosary, the Angelus, holy-water fonts in the home, guardian angels, novenas, feast days, baptismal days, holy cards, advent wreaths, and an overwhelming number and selection of medals, scapulars, litanies, chaplets, devotions, consecrations, postures, gestures ... I found my head spinning over the depth and breadth of practices within the Catholic Faith. And I believed that I should know, understand, and practice all these things if I wanted to be a *good* Catholic. It goes without saying that I felt unbelievably inadequate, yet despite all the self-inflicted pressure, my faith never wavered. I knew that God had made all these things available to me, and He would help me to understand them in His time.

I struggled this way for a while; but over the years, I learned that, like reading a book about baseball without playing the game, I was learning about the Faith without really *experiencing* it. Yes, I loved God. And yes, I loved His Church. But for type-A me, it had become a head game. As I was introduced to other authors, I came to realize that the question wasn't so much how to *be* Catholic as how to get to heaven; how to live the life of Christ and share His light with the world. I began to read the writings of the saints, as well as Pope John Paul II and Pope John XXIII (neither of whom had been canonized at the time), Frank Sheed, Deitrich and Alice von Hildebrand, Elisabeth Leseur, Father Lawrence Lovasik, and many others who have illustrated the sheer beauty and intricately woven plan that Christ has passed down for our holiness and edification. These writers provided keen insight on how to know, love, and serve God in my daily life. Our Church has a tremendous amount of insight to share with us on that point. There is no self-help book that can beat the wisdom of the ages. We have at our fingertips the answers to life's most important questions—those answers lovingly passed down to us by our older and wiser brothers and sisters in Christ. And often those answers run completely counter to the self-obsessed culture in which we live.

Of course, with all this great insight bouncing around in my head, I was desperate to get it out. My desire to *know* was surpassed only by a need to *share*. Needless to say, for a few years I was probably *not* the person you wanted to chat with at the neighborhood picnic! As I've shared in blog posts, whatever the topic of conversation, I could always find a segue into whichever book I was reading.

For example:

Friendly acquaintance at a mothers' group: So, are you keeping warm this week? I heard on the radio that we've been having the coldest temperatures on record!

Me: Actually, yes—I've been cozying up with the most amazing book—*Trustful Surrender to Divine Providence*. It's unbelievable! With every page, I realize more and more the meaning of that song "He's Got the Whole World, in His Hands." He really does! And no matter what happens, God's holy will has allowed it either through His active or passive will, and I can be joyful even if someone brutally attacks me! If that doesn't keep you warm inside, I don't know what would!

Often, these conversations ended abruptly because the friendly acquaintance spotted her sister's babysitters's mother's best friend across the room and just *had* to rush over and say hello or risk being rude.

After several years of this—which, as you can tell, allowed very little opportunity for two-way discussion—I started a Catholic book club. At least in this venue, I was able to meet with four or five like-minded friends once a month and discuss the latest book. Truth be told, we were often lucky if two of us showed up because we were all busy mothers with several children whose extracurricular activities came before book club. (Book clubs are great but are often inconvenient in a time-consuming and scheduling sort of way.)

Eventually, after moving to a new state where we knew very few people, I came up with the idea for an online spiritual-reading club — in which readers could step in or out depending on what life sent their way. The thought was that this would solve scheduling problems while still allowing readers to interact and discuss all these amazing works the Church has to offer. Just a few months after its inception, our book club was invited to join SpiritualDirection.com. After four years, by God's grace, the website has grown to include hundreds of thousands of readers worldwide and has proven to be a great way for readers to share in their spiritual growth. Together we have read books such as Father Walter Ciszek's *He Leadeth Me*, Saint Augustine's *Confessions*, *The Secret Diary of Elisabeth Leseur*, and Lorenzo Scupoli's *Spiritual Combat*.

The Introduction of Order

As you can see from my meandering spiritual journey, I am no expert on spiritual reading or on our Faith. In fact, it took me about fifteen years to make my way from theology to the sacraments and the writings of the saints. Far from being a scholar, I'm just a Catholic wife and mother who loves to read and loves to share the amazing truths I've found over the years.

As I mentioned earlier, at some point in my spiritual journey, it occurred to me that my goal is heaven. In case you think this should be obvious, please remember that my Protestant background taught me that heaven is pretty much a foregone conclusion. Understanding the need for my cooperation with God's grace in the innermost recesses of my heart took quite a bit of time and a whole lot of prayer.

Once I recognized my need to submit my life to Christ in a tangible way, I wanted to create a spiritual-reading environment that would help me accomplish that goal. One of the books that I most wanted to read over the years was the *Catechism of the Catholic Church*. Everywhere I turned, it was recommended that Catholics should read this book from cover to cover and not merely use it as a reference guide. So I saw this resource as a guide to help me grow in every possible way in my relationship with Christ. But, as much as I enjoy reading, every time I opened the book, I found each paragraph so profound that I had to meditate on it for a while before moving on. Rather than read a chapter per day, I could read only a paragraph or two. Consequently, it never failed that the *Catechism* was lost by the wayside as I moved on to other books that I wanted to read.

In addition, my reading of Sacred Scripture—which, from reading the saints, I knew was critical for my relationship with Christ—was intermittent because I didn't have much time to read on any given day. Once I read and prayed over Scripture, there was time for little else. Consequently, I would read the Bible for a month or so before setting it down in favor of another spiritual book. To complicate matters, each time I picked up the Bible or the *Catechism*, I felt a compulsion to start over so I could read them from cover to cover; needless to say, I never got very far. So for years I rotated between Scripture, a spiritual book, and the *Catechism of the Catholic Church*. My spiritual life felt disorganized, to say the least.

Thankfully, all this frustration resulted in a bit of solution seeking. First, I felt that I should be reading Sacred Scripture much more routinely. Additionally, over time, I began to notice that my spiritual reading aligned itself with the pillars of the Faith as described in the *Catechism*. I found that organizing my spiritual reading around those pillars helped me to discern which books to read among the thousands of choices. I wanted a system that would let me read Sacred Scripture, the *Catechism*, and a spiritual book every day, yet not require me to spend all day reading to accomplish my goal.

I organized a schedule that would allow me to spend fifteen to thirty minutes per day, five days per week, on prayerful spiritual reading and study. This spiritual-reading program has served me well over the years. I offer it here because I think it will offer other busy men and women a plan that can be incorporated into the tightest schedule. If you can find thirty minutes per day for spiritual reading and reflection (and you *can*—more on that later), if you desire to learn your Faith, find greater meaning in the Sacraments, meditate on the lives of the saints, and develop a deeply spiritual prayer life, then this program will serve you well too.

What Will You Accomplish?

This program will allow you to:

+ meditate daily on Sacred Scripture
+ read the *Catechism of the Catholic Church* in its entirety (following the five-year program), focusing on one section each year
+ read some of the greatest Catholic books ever written—books that offer great wisdom for modern times and get right to the heart of the purpose of life

In the pages ahead, I will share with you five important lessons about spiritual reading that I've learned over the past several years. From there, we'll move on to discuss the makeup of the program, including the four pillars of the Faith as described in the *Catechism*, as well as the types of writing that should be included in any spiritual-reading program. I will also discuss other important considerations such as how to pursue spiritual reading in order to reap the greatest rewards, where and when to read, and how to keep a spiritual-reading journal.

It is said that any new activity can become a habit, provided that we stick with it for at least thirty days. So, at the end of the written portion of this book, I will challenge you to stick to an organized reading program for at least thirty days. Once you've committed to a month of devoted reading, you'll find that the benefits will far outweigh any challenges you encounter along the way. It is my prayer for you that at the end of our journey together, you will adopt some form of an intentional, organized spiritual-reading program that will enrich, illuminate, and perhaps even revitalize your lifelong journey of intimacy with your Father in heaven.

After all the advice and all the discussion, in part 3 we get down to the nitty-gritty. This is where you will find a complete, hands-on, day-by-day spiritual-reading program with specific assignments for five years of reading fifteen to thirty minutes per day, five days per week. In case five years sounds daunting, you will also find instructions for using the same plan to achieve a one-year or three-year program.

I've also included two helpful lists that you can use for a lifetime of spiritual reading. In appendix 1 you will find a list that in itself should make this book well worth your while. It contains book recommendations from some of the most well-known and respected Catholics in the Church today—persons to whom many look for instruction, direction, and inspiration, such as Dr. Peter Kreeft, theologian extraordinaire; atheist-turned-Catholic Jennifer Fulwiler; Lisa Hendey (Catholicmom.com); Sam Guzman (aka, the Catholic Gentleman); Mike Aquilina; Father Timothy Gallagher; and Tim Staples, to name just a few. In appendix 2 you will find Father C. John McCloskey's famed *Catholic Lifetime Reading List* (the impetus behind this reading program), which he has graciously permitted me to include.

You've heard the saying "Never put off till tomorrow what you can do today." This could not be truer than with respect to our relationship with our Lord and Savior. We must be purposeful about our time spent at the feet of Christ if we desire to obtain the *good portion* enjoyed by Mary.

READING READINESS

Before you turn the page, find your calendar and schedule thirty minutes per day, five days per week, over the course of the next month. Don't simply record it on a list of items you hope to complete. Schedule time on your calendar—preferably in the morning. Over the next few weeks, use that scheduled time to read this book and prayerfully ponder your spiritual life, considering how an organized reading program might serve to enrich it. Seek guidance from the Holy Spirit as you consider the topics discussed in the following pages.

What If I'm Not Catholic?

Whether this book found its way into your hands by accident, or you are actively exploring the Catholic Church, I welcome you with open arms. Nothing in this book should make it inappropriate for a non-Catholic. There was a time when I was not Catholic. In fact, I wasn't a Catholic when I first read some of the texts included in this book. The fact is that spiritual reading is about seeking God's Truth and applying it to our lives. There is not a Catholic truth and a non-Catholic truth. There is only God's Truth. While my commentary in this book refers on occasion to my personal journey from Protestantism to the Catholic Church, the many books offered for your spiritual edification were not written for the purposes of propaganda or slander. They were written in pursuit of or in an attempt to share some truth about

God, about His Church, or about our Faith. So if you are not Catholic, please join me on this journey toward a more intimate union with our Lord Jesus Christ, the Way, the Truth and the Life.

PART I

A Proper Approach
to Spiritual
Reading

Chapter 1

Spiritual Reading Arms Us for Battle

What do you say? The reading of these good books does not concern you? But I find this duty more incumbent on you, than on those living in the security of the cloister. For you who sail on the open sea, whether you will it or not, are beset by a thousand occasions of sin. Thus the aid of spiritual books is for you a necessity. A religious cannot be wounded, because she is far from the combat. But you who are in the midst of battle, must protect yourself with the buckler of holy thoughts drawn from good books.

Saint John Chrysostom, Discourse 3

For the past twenty years, I've been doing my best to commit to daily spiritual reading. Some days have gone better than others. In fact, some years have gone better than others. But I have done my best to stay the course. In that time, I've learned a few things about the process. I've learned some basic things, such as how hard it is to make the time for spiritual reading, but how good it makes me feel when I've done it — kind of like jogging for the soul. I've also noticed that spiritual reading is better for my psyche than any motivational book. It helps me to grow in faith and to deepen my relationship with God, which in turn has strengthened every other area of my life. And although at first I thought that my spiritual growth would come mostly by studying theology, I've found that there is also a great intellectually and emotionally challenging component to reading other spiritual material, such as biographies of saints and books on prayer.

But in addition to these basic lessons, I've learned a few other things that run a little deeper than the obvious. We'll look at those here and in the pages ahead.

Life in the Trenches

One need only watch the news for five minutes to know that this world has become a bastion of paganism more and more emboldened in its persecution of those who choose to follow Christ. Everywhere we turn, secularism is the new religion. Worse, the world is fast becoming, not merely secular, but *anti*-God — and not only anti-God, but anti-everything-that-even-remotely-relates-to-God.

Daily we are bombarded from every angle with messages that are clearly designed to remove us one step further from our Faith or to cripple us within it. Whether social situations at work or school, the news, television shows, movies, books, advertising, or — the ultimate temptation — social media, the influences on our daily lives do virtually nothing to draw us closer to our calling as Christians to live the life of Christ.

The only way to shield our hearts and minds from the lies of a hostile culture is to fill them with reinforcements before we head out to battle each day. Additionally, the more we fill our hearts with the love of Christ, the greater the light we bring to the darkness around us. Spiritual reading arms us for all those daily battles with negativity, temptation, and sin, filling our minds, hearts, and souls with truth, building us in Christ, and strengthening us for combat.

Spiritual reading brings us closer to Christ and provides a peace and joy that the world can never offer. Of course, prayer and the sacraments are also critical to our interior life. Unfortunately, although time in prayer is wisely spent, many claim that they spend hour after hour in prayer and it does no good. They may attend Mass, pray the Rosary, offer up many rote prayers, and even speak from their heart to our Lord; but they often complain that their efforts are to no avail, and they still feel alone in the world.

Sitting (or kneeling) in a room, praying our hearts out, while laudable, can be like sitting on one end of a telephone just talking away, with no input from the other side. But couple that time with spiritual reading from some solid books, and our faith and joy will improve exponentially. Spiritual reading offers God's perspective. This is obviously true with regard to Sacred Scripture; but it is also true when we read from any of the countless books written by those with great wisdom and grace whose hearts and minds are united with the Magisterium of the Church.

Spiritual reading provides us with a Person to know; a Person with whom to communicate; a Person to whom we can listen in prayer because, with a better understanding of who He is, we can actually hear His voice when he speaks to us. Saint Alphonsus Liguori, in his *On Spiritual Reading*, quotes Saint Jerome as saying, "When we pray we speak to God, but when we read, God speaks to us." And Saint Isaac the Syrian asserts, "From reading the soul is enlightened in prayer."

Spiritual reading helps us to build a relationship with Christ. Reading Sacred Scripture and the classics helps us to know and to love a God who actually trod the ground we tread, who suffered the things we suffer, who ate and slept just as we do.

We know that spiritual reading can keep us grounded because we have many brothers and sisters in Christ who have been through what we're going through, fought the same battles we face, and would recommend to us the same solution I'm here to recommend: spiritual reading. Although we have neither time nor room to discuss every friend of Christ who endured an environment hostile to his faith, it seems fitting to examine the lives of two such individuals, one who lived far from us in time, but perhaps not so far in spirit; and another who, like many Catholics today, endured hostility toward her faith even in the sanctuary of her home.

Both of these amazing people would credit their perseverance to God's grace and the openness of their hearts and minds to the wisdom offered through spiritual reading.

Saint John Chrysostom[1]

We live in a world where Christ is ridiculed and laughed at, even despised and spat upon. Often, we wonder how our Judeo-Christian heritage could have fallen so far. But ours isn't the only era to experience such derision. Saint John Chrysostom lived in the fourth century, shortly after Constantine converted and turned Rome into a Christian nation. John's father died when he was only an infant; devoted to her only child, his mother "felt she was called of God to devote herself wholly in the training of her son and to shield him from the contaminating influences of the pagan city of Antioch."[2] As a young boy, her son received the best education available. As a young man, he lived as a hermit, separating himself from the secular hostility of his culture. He spent this time committing the entire New Testament to memory. This practice served him well throughout his life. Eventually, he returned to society and was ordained a priest. Shortly after his ordination in Antioch, he gave a series of eloquent sermons to fearful crowds who worried about the possibility of retribution from Emperor Theodosius after they had demonstrated against a new tax. John's popularity grew, but so did the alliances forming against him.

After twelve years in Antioch, where he gained great popularity because of his speaking ability and his command of Sacred Scripture, John was appointed bishop of Constantinople, enduring great opposition from the powers that be. He was continually the victim of intrigue, lies, and

---

[1]   From Fr. Christopher Rengers, O.F.M. Cap., *The 33 Doctors of the Church* (Charlotte, NC: TAN Books, 2000), pp. 101-107.

[2]   Won Sang Lee, *Pastoral Leadership: A Case Study, Including a Reference to John Chrysostom* (Eugene, OR: Wipf and Stock, 2015), pp. 97-98.

defamation of character. He was accused of supporting one side of feuding clergy over another and was eventually exiled from Constantinople by the emperor Arcadius. His banishment was short-lived, however, as the public threatened to burn the royal palace down unless he was allowed to return.

But John faced exile again for denouncing pagan practices among the ruling class, including the wife of the emperor. In fact, much of his world was affected by pagan practices, against which he preached repeatedly in his homilies.

Throughout his service, John continued to preach that people needed to know the Faith and to practice it. In Eastern Orthodoxy, he is called the Great Ecumenical Teacher because he spoke so profoundly on both the Old and New Testaments while thundering against pagan practices and pastimes. He is known as the Father of Catechesis because he spent much time teaching people the Faith and guiding them to practice spiritual reading, so that they might ward off temptations, particularly those temptations encountered by Christians in a pagan culture.

Here are just a couple of his admonitions:

> Moreover, if the Devil does not dare to enter into the house where the Gospel lies, much less will he ever seize upon the soul which contains such thoughts as these, and no evil spirit will approach it, nor will the nature of sin come near. Well, then, sanctify your soul, sanctify your body by having these thoughts always in your heart and on your tongue. For if foul language is defiling and evokes evil spirits, it is evident that spiritual reading sanctifies the reader and attracts the grace of the Spirit. (Homily 32 on John)

> This is the cause of all evils, the not knowing the Scriptures. We go into battle without arms, and how are we to come off safe? (Homily 9 on Colossians)

This advice should be applicable to each and every one of us, struggling to keep our bearings as we face a pagan culture day after day.

Elisabeth Leseur[3]

Unlike John Chrysostom, Elisabeth Leseur did not benefit from a high-class education. She came from an upper-middle-class family and had a moderately Catholic upbringing, having attended Catholic school and received the sacraments as a girl. As a young lady, she married Felix Leseur, a well-educated, well-to-do doctor, in 1889 after a brief engagement. Shortly before their marriage, Elisabeth learned that Felix was no longer a practicing Catholic. In fact, he was a self-proclaimed atheist and became well known in Paris as the editor of a newsletter that promoted atheist and anticlerical beliefs.

Although he promised that he would respect Elisabeth's Faith, Felix set about almost immediately to destroy it, and he nearly succeeded. For a time, Elisabeth even stopped attending Mass. Fortunately, at the height of his influence against her Faith, Felix handed his wife a book that made her think twice about the arguments it offered. Rather than be influenced by the poverty of such a book, Elisabeth turned to masters of Catholic thought. Here is what her husband says of her in his "In Memoriam":

> To counterbalance my anti-Christian library, she gathered together one composed of the works of the great masters of Catholic thought: Fathers, Doctors, mystics, St. Jerome, St. Thomas Aquinas, St. Francis de Sales, St. Teresa of Avila and many more. Above all she read and reread the New Testament, the Gospels, the Acts, the Epistles; she never passed a day without meditating upon some passage from it. She thus acquired a reasoned and substantial faith. Knowing the opposing arguments, possessing her own replies to them, and strengthening perpetually the foundations of her belief, by the grace of God she established her faith indestructibly.[4]

---

[3] From *The Secret Diary of Elisabeth Leseur* (Manchester, NH: Sophia Institute Press, 2002).

[4] *The Secret Diary of Elisabeth Leseur*, p. xxiii.

More than just reading books, Elisabeth took great pains to apply what she read to her life. She never spoke to her husband about her Catholic Faith. She did not try to convince him of the truth. Rather, she offered all to God, who helped her to *live* the truth. The beauty within her became evident to everyone she met.

That is exactly what we desire to do: to live our Faith. To experience the peace of knowing that we are not of this world but are to spend this life sharing the light of Christ with others. Elisabeth was so successful in that vein that, after years of offering up her suffering silently and making sacrifices for her husband, she offered her very life to God for his salvation. Upon her death, her husband not only returned to Catholicism but also became a Dominican priest!

Elisabeth armed herself each day to do battle in her own home—not with arguments or smugness, but with love. There was no more effective weapon she could have found to help her win the war.

Arming for Battle: The Church Militant

We may not feel called to memorize the entire New Testament like St. John Chrystostom, but meditating daily on Sacred Scripture will provide us with the strength we need to face the enemy. Saint Paul tells us:

> Put on the full armor of God, so that you can take your stand against the devil's schemes. For our struggle is not against flesh and blood, but against the rulers, against the authorities, against the powers of this dark world and against the spiritual forces of evil in the heavenly realms. Therefore put on the full armor of God, so that when the day of evil comes, you may be able to stand your ground, and after you have done everything, to stand. Stand firm then, with the belt of truth buckled around your waist, with the breastplate of righteousness in place, and with your feet fitted with the readiness that comes from the gospel of peace. In addition to all this, take up the shield of faith, with which you can extinguish all the flaming

arrows of the evil one. Take the helmet of salvation and the sword of the Spirit, which is the word of God. (Eph. 6:11-17).

We need to be armed for battle. At all times, and especially during these crazy times in this vale of tears, we need to lay our foundation in Christ Jesus. I pray that spiritual reading plays a part in helping you build and strengthen that foundation.

READING READINESS

Spiritual reading will help arm us for battle with all that impedes our relationship with Christ. Take time today to consider prayerfully which activities would be better removed from your day. For example, is there a television show that promotes values that are in direct opposition to your Faith? Are there groups to which you belong or places you go where your Faith is subverted or demeaned, even at a subliminal level? Consider abandoning these activities. Not only will you free up more time to read, but you'll also remove one more barrier to your relationship with Christ.

Chapter 2

Spiritual Reading Keeps Our Self in Check

We must in no way be surprised to find self-love in us, for it never
leaves us. Like a fox it sleeps sometimes, then all of a sudden leaps
on the chickens; for which reason we must constantly keep watch
on it, and patiently and very quietly defend ourselves from it.

— Saint Francis de Sales, Letter 17, to a Young Lady

In addition to battles that come to us from the outside, there is a much greater battle that faces us in the darkest recesses of our minds and hearts. We all know that the thoughts that run rampant through our heads and the passions that stem from deep within us can be much more dangerous than the onslaught from our environment. And, of course, it is important to note that the two are closely related, as influences in our environment can either impede or encourage our self-obsessed natures.

Despite our greatest efforts to remain grounded in faith and truth, we cannot help but define our worth somewhat in terms of the venomous culture in which we live. We begin to believe we have a *right* to do what we like, whether enjoying some quiet time or controlling our money. Spiritual reading reminds us that everything has been given to us, to be shared on our journey back to Him who is the greatest Giver.

There is nowhere in the culture that we can turn to obtain an accurate picture of the value of *self*. But spiritual reading leads us to the fresh waters of humility, to the concepts of selflessness, self-examination, self-effacement, self-gift.

Unfortunately, we hate to be called out on our interior struggles to control self. At least that has been true for me. When I began reading spiritual classics, I was a little put off by what I considered to be a directive issued in some spiritual books to "hate" myself. After all, I've always considered myself to be a decent person. I kept thinking, "I'm not perfect, but I try to be kind to others; I do what I can for friends and family. I certainly wouldn't consider myself evil, so why would I *hate* myself?" I felt the writers who made mention of this idea were a little over the top, to say the least. Here is an example of what I considered extreme talk from the classic *Spiritual Combat*, by Lorenzo Scupoli:

> The essence of the spiritual life does not lie in any of those things to which I have alluded. It consists in nothing else but the knowledge of the divine goodness and greatness, of our own nothingness and proneness to evil; in the love of God and the hatred of self; in entire subjection, not only to God Himself, but, for the love of Him, to all creatures; in giving up our own will and in completely resigning ourselves to the divine pleasure; moreover, in willing and doing all this with no other wish or aim than the glory and honor of God, the fulfillment of His will because it is His will and because He deserves to be served and loved....
>
> But if you aspire to such a pitch of perfection, you must daily do violence to yourself, by courageously attacking and destroying all your evil desires and affections. In great matters as well as in small, it is necessary, then, that you prepare yourself and hold yourself in readiness for this conflict, for only he who is brave in the battle will be crowned.[5]

---

[5] Lorenzo Scupoli, *Spiritual Combat* (Manchester, NH: Sophia Institute Press, 2002), p. 9.

When I read this passage, the alarms went off. Of course, it makes sense that we are to love God and subject ourselves entirely to Him. But I was taken aback by the harshness of the words "hatred of self" and "doing violence to yourself." These concepts were alien to everything I had been taught to believe. I mean, words like these could wreak havoc with my *self-esteem*! Not to mention my *self-regard*, *self-worth*, *self-identity*, and *self-ishness*. They certainly put a huge dent in my efforts at *self-aggrandizement*! And they even made me recognize all the *self-pity* I had felt since reading that passage.

When God created everything, didn't He say that it was "very good" (Gen. 1:31)? And what about the fact that God made me in His image and likeness (Gen. 1:26)? If that is true, I wondered, why must I *hate* myself?

After I took some time for prayer and contemplation, I remembered a children's book that I've read to my kids every Lent for the past several years. The book is called *The King of the Golden City: An Allegory for Children* by Mother Mary Loyola (which I strongly recommend for children and adults alike — particularly the version with pictures: it's beautiful!).

The King of the Golden City explains the passage from Scupoli's *Spiritual Combat* in terms that even a seven-year-old can understand. And frankly, in order to digest such concepts, I often need to approach them as a young child would, because they are so foreign to everything I've been taught.

Chapter 5 in *The King of the Golden City*, "A Troublesome Partner," is a great lesson in self-mortification. Following are a couple of excerpts from this chapter:

> All the men, women and children each had a comrade who was always with them, from the time they came into the Land [of Exile] till the time they went out, and forever after. The name of this partner was Self. The two were never separated. They walked, worked, went to sleep and woke together. But the owner of the hut was — or ought to have been — master or mistress there. Self was the sub- or under-partner. So it was not what Self liked or disliked that mattered, but what the King wanted and what was

good for the owner of the hut. This lesson Self had to learn, and, as a rule, it was learnt very slowly.[6]

If allowed to become master,

Self showed himself a cruel tyrant. He made a slave of the hut-owner who should have taught him better, and treated him so badly that life was a misery to him. No: the only way to secure any kind of peace was to keep this unruly comrade in his place and put him down firmly when he gave himself airs.[7]

I am certainly not a theologian (as demonstrated by my use of a children's book to make sense of a passage from Scupoli's *Spiritual Combat*), but in light of this description quoted above, I understand Self as almost separate from Me. It reminds me of the old cartoons where a person, when contemplating an action, has a little devil on one shoulder and a little angel on the other. Perhaps this detestable "Self" being described by Scupoli is the result of *concupiscence*. According to the *Catechism of the Catholic Church*, concupiscence is "an inclination to sin" that we all inherit as a result of the Fall of Adam. The *Catechism* assures us that while "it is left for us to wrestle with, it cannot harm those who do not consent but manfully resist it by the grace of Jesus Christ."[8]

After reading *The King of the Golden City* and the *Catechism*, I understand that *Self* must be trained to be subject entirely to God's will. How can I love God above all things if I love my Self and wish to please my Self above all things? There should be no Self but that which is completely in union with God. And to the extent that Self is not completely subject, it should be *hated* and *viciously attacked*, or else. That said, through the grace of Christ, it can certainly be overcome.

---

[6] Mother Mary Loyola, *The King of the Golden City: An Allegory for Children* (Twain Harte CA: Little Way Press, 2004), p. 27.

[7] Ibid., pp. 27-28.

[8] CCC 1264; St. Irenaeus, *Dem ap*. 3:SCh 62,32.

Self-Control

Spiritual reading can help us tame Self. Just as the wisdom of the ages helps us keep all the messages from the world in check, it can remind us to keep Self in check as well.

Spiritual reading allows us to separate the wheat from chaff. It helps us to ensure that we promote the fruitful parts of ourselves and have disdain for those whispers of entitlement. Only to the extent that we unite our wills to Christ's are we good. Christ is the perfect God-man. Any deviation from His will is a flaw in our character, in our makeup, a cancer to be carved out — not just a little, but completely, so that what remains may not spread and do more damage than the initial tumor threatened.

The bottom line is that to love Christ is not to be "good enough." It is not to listen to the world when it claims, "I'm okay, you're okay." To love Christ is to let go of one's self and give all to God, so that, like Saint Paul, we can say, "It is no longer I who live, but Christ who lives in me" (Gal. 2:20). To love Christ is to become a saint. Spiritual reading provides us with a map to sanctification.

READING READINESS

It is almost impossible to list all the ways we are motivated by self-interest. Think of some particular ways that you find your Self dominating in your day-to-day life. What do you cherish as yours? What is something that will seriously compromise your day if you don't have it? A cup of coffee in the morning? A special snack during the day? Alone time? What is something that, if you are denied it, makes you say, "At the very least I deserve ..."? Spend time in prayer today asking God to rid you of your feelings of entitlement. Ask Him to help you in your reading to discern which areas Self has taken too much control of and to give you the courage and strength to release those areas to Him.

Chapter 3

Spiritual Reading Makes Saints

Don't neglect your spiritual reading. Reading has made many saints.

— Saint Josemaría Escrivá, *The Way*

Shortly after I became a Catholic, I stumbled upon a book that highlighted traditions of the Faith that had been followed for some centuries. Some were small-*t* traditions, and others large-*T* traditions. My husband is a cradle Catholic, but there were a lot of things I was reading about Catholic traditions that didn't ring a bell with him. Regardless, I dove in head first. I began to attend daily Mass. I read books by the stack, trying to make up for lost time as a Catholic. I created a prayer routine and went to Confession monthly. As we had children, we celebrated baptismal days and feast days. We had our home blessed, and I began to sprinkle holy salt around the bedrooms. We began to make the Sign of the Cross more reverently. We read Bible stories, sang religious songs, watched videos about the Faith, and hung a holy-water font near the front door. I took great pains to dot all the *i*'s and cross all the *t*'s in our little domestic church. Our little ones loved all the celebrations. But I became stressed in my zeal.

This was the point at which I realized something was missing. I was learning the hows and the whys. But there was little connection between my head and my heart.

Countercultural Messages

In the spring of 2004, I walked into a little Catholic bookstore, and my interest was piqued by two books that were jointly featured on every endcap in the store. Little did I know at the time that Blessed Gianna Beretta Molla was to be canonized within weeks. I had never heard of her. But as I made my way around the store, I was met at every turn with her biography and a companion book called *Love Letters to My Husband*. Something about the joy in her eyes and her captivating smile attracted my attention, and I picked up the book of her love letters. I was fascinated by the genuine love and concern this woman showed for her husband. I was able to surmise through skimming that she had young children and a husband who traveled—as I had at that time. I was a stay-at-home mom with three children under the age of four, and my husband traveled almost weekly. So I purchased both books and began reading the love letters that night. This was the first book I ever read that provided an intimate look into the mind and heart of a saint.

I found a letter Gianna wrote to her husband when he was out of town. Although I didn't mind my husband's traveling, I must admit I was a bit jealous of all the "alone" time I imagined he was getting in his hotel room. Of course, he complained about this time as being *lonely*, but I could not even imagine the thought as I stood amid the mess and chaos of little people twenty-four hours a day, desperately longing for silence. Reading Saint Gianna's letter gave me an entirely new perspective. She showed me that my consideration had been more for my own comfort than for my husband's. This was the first time I saw what it looked like to have a truly generous heart toward one's spouse. Saint Gianna showed me that I could reach for something higher than myself:

> It's about 10:30 pm and our beautiful little ones are sleeping tranquilly after enjoying the sunshine almost all day long. I say "almost" because it rained for a little while this afternoon. It's calm and clear now, though, and I can see the beautiful starry heaven. Adelaide, Cecco, and Zita left half an hour ago, happy after spending

a lovely day with beloved nephew and niece. I'm thinking of you traveling right now, your heart here with us. Dear Pietro, it would be so wonderful to be able to be together, united, all of the time. Luckily, your vacation begins in only ten days: what joy![9]

In another letter, she talks about their little son, Gigetto, and his sister, and then follows up with her concerns for her husband's welfare:

He's as lively as ever, as is Mariolina. They couldn't sleep last night because of the storm—peals of thunder, torrents of rain, wind—it sounded like the end of the world.

They couldn't go outside today either, because of the bad weather. Patience....

Ciao, Pietro, take care of yourself and don't tire yourself too much [10]

When I first read her letters, I admit that I found them a bit over the top. *Who thinks like this?* But after mulling them over for a while, I realized how unbelievably self-centered my concerns had been. When my kids were "as lively as ever," I often considered them unruly. And when my husband was away for a few days to a week, I was jealous. I wanted to head off to a hotel for a few days and sit in business meetings while he took care of the kids!

And frankly, the culture backed me up on that. According to the culture, I was sacrificing my livelihood, my career, to raise my children. My husband enjoyed the fun and excitement of the children while still pursuing a career! I should back up and clarify that my husband and I had agreed to this choice. In fact, I was even the more dominant voice in the conversation. My mother worked, and I always felt that when I had children, I'd like to be home to raise them myself when they were young. I'm not condemning mothers who choose to work, but I felt this

---

[9] Gianna Beretta Molla, *Love Letters to My Husband* (Boston: Pauline Books and Media, 2002), p. 80.

[10] Ibid., pp. 92-93.

to be my firm calling as a mother. That said, it's impossible to describe the strain caused by the juxtaposition of my passion for raising my children with the bitter undertones that made their way into my thoughts and even began to cast a shadow over my soul.

The culture advised me, "You have a right to a career! You, too, have gifts to offer to the world! Your husband has the easy job. He's living the good life while you slave over the house!" I didn't feel good about having conflicted feelings. But, frankly, my bitterness was condoned and validated at every turn.

That is, until I read Saint Gianna's letters. Here was an educated woman who basked in the privilege and joy of motherhood. She loved and supported her husband and believed that they were truly one unit, working together to obtain the same goal — heaven.

This woman turned what I considered the loneliness of raising my children with a traveling husband into a family adventure full of grace and purpose!

I wanted her joy.

And it occurred to me that clinging to all that bitterness was a choice. I could live my motherhood as a martyr, as an unappreciated victim, or I could *choose* to love my children and my husband and to live my life accordingly.

To this day, I am so thankful that God allowed me to have a little peek into the heart and soul of such a lovely woman. And His timing could not have been better. Through Saint Gianna's example, I was completely transformed as a mother. Not to say that I haven't fallen here and there, but my perspective was changed through my experience with Saint Gianna — and through the time I've spent with numerous saints since.

There are many saints who had the benefit of being mentored by a close friend, relative, or colleague who was a saint. Think of Saint Augustine, who was transformed through the influence of Saint Ambrose. Or Saint Clare, who was graced with the friendship of Saint Francis.

Most of us aren't lucky enough to be personally mentored by a saint, but we can seek guidance through spiritual reading.

Saints Are Often Influenced by Those Who Have Gone Before Them

Saint Alphonsus Liguori writes extensively about the fruits of spiritual reading:

> How many saints have, by reading a spiritual book, been induced to forsake the world and to give themselves to God! It is known to all that St. Augustine, when miserably chained by his passions and vices, was, by reading one of the epistles of St. Paul, enlightened with divine light, went forth from his darkness, and began to lead a life of holiness. Thus also St. Ignatius, while a soldier, by reading a volume of the lives of the saints which he accidentally took up, in order to get rid of the tediousness of the bed to which he was confined by sickness, was led to begin a life of sanctity, and became the Father and Founder of the Society of Jesus — an Order which has done so much for the Church. Thus also by reading a pious book accidentally and almost against his will, St. John Colombino left the world, became a saint, and the founder of another religious Order. St. Augustine relates that two courtiers of the Emperor Theodosius entered one day into a monastery of solitaries; one of them began to read the life of St. Anthony, which he found in one of the cells; so strong was the impression made upon him, that he resolved to take leave of the world. He then addressed his companion with so much fervor that both of them remained in the monastery to serve God. We read in the Chronicles of the Discalced Carmelites that a lady in Vienna was prepared to go to a festivity, but because it was given up she fell into a violent passion. To divert her attention she began to read a spiritual book that was at hand, and conceived such a contempt for the world, that she abandoned it and became a Teresian nun. The same happened to the Duchess of Montalto, in Sicily. She began also by accident to read the works of St. Teresa, and afterwards continued to read them with so much fervor, that she

sought and obtained her husband's consent to become a religious, and entered among the Discalced Carmelites.[11]

And there are many more stories. Venerable James Duckett[12] was a Protestant bookseller in London when a friend lent him a Catholic book. As a result, he converted and in the process was imprisoned twice for missing Protestant services. So moved was he by the power of the written word to enlighten the human heart that he began to distribute Catholic literature to as many as would receive it. He was so passionate that he risked and suffered imprisonment and death as a result of sharing the truths of his Faith.

We also have the conversion story of Blessed John Henry Newman,[13] once an Anglican preacher who had been raised to believe that the Catholic Church was the anti-Christ. He became known for his expertise in early Church history and eventually read his way into the Catholic Church. He is famous for saying, "To be deep in history is to cease to be Protestant."[14] He claimed, "Catholicism is a deep matter—you cannot take it up in a teacup."[15]

And then there's Elisabeth Leseur, whom we discussed in the previous chapter. Her spiritual reading transformed her from a common French woman to a wholly devout and captivating person who inspired her atheist husband to become a priest after her death!

St. Thérèse of Lisieux was known to keep a copy of *The Imitation of Christ* with her at all times, and she referred to the book often in her

[11] Saint Alphonsus Ligouri, "The Importance of Spiritual Reading," posted at Catholic Apologetics Information, http://www.catholicapologetics.info/morality/general/read.htm.

[12] "Ven. James Duckett," New Advent, http://www.newadvent.org/cathen/05182b.htm.

[13] Pat McNamara, "Newman's Road to Rome," Catholic Education Resource Center, www.catholiceducation.org.

[14] John Henry Newman, *An Essay on the Development of Christian Doctrine*, pt. 1, introduction.

[15] John Henry Newman, *Letters and Diaries*, vol. 11.

autobiography.[16] Saint John XXIII, who was devoted to daily spiritual reading, read a chapter of *The Imitation of Christ* every day.[17]

These stories are just a few examples of people who have been inspired through spiritual reading to turn away from their past lives and embrace *the Way* of Christ. You may have your own story in this regard. And if not, I've no doubt you'll be able to tell one soon!

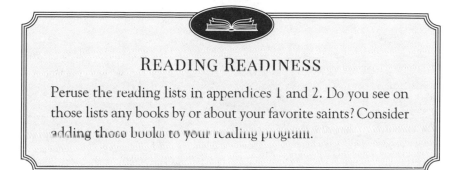

READING READINESS

Peruse the reading lists in appendices 1 and 2. Do you see on those lists any books by or about your favorite saints? Consider adding those books to your reading program.

[16] Saint Thérèse of Lisieux, *The Story of a Soul* (Washington, DC: ICS Publications, 1996), pp. 68-69.

[17] *The Journal of a Soul: The Autobiography of Pope John XXIII* (New York: Doubleday, 1980), p. 5, "Every Day," nos. 3, 10.

Chapter 4

SPIRITUAL READING IS A MEANS TO AN END

Head knowledge is worthless, unless accompanied
by submission of the will and right action.

— ARCHBISHOP FULTON J. SHEEN, *LIFE OF CHRIST*

There are many who argue that we need not study our Faith. They claim
that holiness is available to the lowliest and least educated of peasants,
as demonstrated throughout Church history.

Some of the greatest saints were considered rather dim-witted
in most circles. As a young man, Saint Joseph of Cupertino could
barely read or write, and he seemed unable to perform the most basic
of jobs. After he failed as a shoemaker and was sent away from the
Franciscans and the Capuchins because he was deemed incapable, his
mother, at her wits' end, sent him to serve at a Franciscan convent.
They considered him unfit for anything but cleaning stables and caring for the animals. Joseph grew in humility and gentleness, and over
time his great holiness was revealed. Despite his inability to retain
much in the way of his studies, Divine Providence allowed him to
become a priest. If that weren't enough, Joseph began to levitate in
states of ecstasy. He became so well known for his miracles that he

had to stay out of public view so that he didn't become a distraction to Christian worship.[18]

Would that we all could be so blessed. But according to Frank Sheed:

> While it is obvious that an ignorant man can be virtuous, it is equally obvious that ignorance is not virtue; men have been martyred who could not have stated a doctrine of the Church correctly, and martyrdom is the supreme proof of love. Yet with more knowledge of God they would have loved him more still.[19]

Sheed argues that knowledge can help us love God better. The *Baltimore Catechism* tells us that God made us to know Him, love Him, and serve Him in this life and to be happy with Him forever in heaven. Now, it stands to reason that it is difficult to love or serve someone we don't know. According to Sheed:

> Knowledge does serve love. It serves love in one way by removing misunderstandings which are in the way of love, which at the best blunt love's edge a little. For example, the fact of hell can raise a doubt of God's love in a man who has not had his mind enriched with what the Church can teach him, so that he is driven piously to avert his gaze from some truth about God in order to keep his love undimmed. But knowledge serves love in a still better way, because each new thing learned and meditated about God is a new reason for loving Him.[20]

Saint Augustine says that knowledge is essential for faith: "Who does not see that knowledge precedes faith? Nobody believes unless he knows what to believe."[21]

---

[18] "St. Joseph of Cupertino," Catholic News Agency, September 18, 2016, http://www.catholicnewsagency.com/saint.php?n=598.

[19] Frank Sheed, *Theology for Beginners* (Cincinnati: Servant Books, 1981), p. 5.

[20] Ibid., p. 5.

[21] Quoted in *Catholic Encyclopedia*, vol. 13 (New York: Robert Appleton, 1912), p. 604.

If that is true, then we also have an obligation to know the Faith. We live in a world of spiritual starvation. The gospel has been lost for many. Within Catholic circles, the numbers are staggering. According to Pew Research,[22] for every one person who is brought into the Catholic Church, six leave her. While Christianity as a whole is on the decline, the Catholic Church is losing more members than any other denomination.

According to Sheed, the Catholic laity are the last bastion of hope for the Church in the world. We must be able to feed the Truth to our loved ones, to our friends, to anyone with whom we come in contact, so that they, too, might grow in faith. For without faith, the world will starve. His words are compelling, particularly in today's pagan world:

> If spiritual starvation is to be relieved, it must be the work of the laity, who are in daily contact with starvation's victims. We must come to an understanding of the great dogmas, so that we know them in themselves and in their power to nourish; we must begin every effort to mastering their utterance. Only thus can we relieve the starvation that now lies all about us. Once we see it, we see that we must set about it—primarily and overwhelmingly for the sake of these others, since it is intolerable that men should be perishing for want of truth that we could bring them.[23]

Knowledge Is Not Spiritual Growth

Although there are many reasons to understand our Faith in a more comprehensive way—most importantly, to help us in our mission to love and to serve God—we must resist the temptation to allow our spiritual reading to be about merely an acquisition of knowledge and thus an end in itself.

[22] "America's Changing Religious Landscape," Pew Research Center, May 12, 2015, http://www.pewforum.org/.

[23] Sheed, *Theology for Beginners*, p. 6.

When done with the head only, spiritual reading is a fruitless endeavor. For reading to be *spiritual* at all, it must involve the heart as well as the mind. It should be an act of love, not merely a duty. And it must be done for the purpose of change. All the wisdom of a book means nothing if we fail to respond by approaching every word in a spirit of prayer and thereby surrendering to God's will in our daily lives.

The most important reason to embark on a spiritual-reading program is a desire for heaven. Many of us long for a relationship with God; to that end, we seek to know Him through the pages of a book, as we should. But simply having a desire to *know* for the sake of knowledge will not lead us to heaven. Knowledge will do little for us if we fail to put it into action. According to the Venerable Fulton J. Sheen: "Knowledge without love leads to conceit, intolerance and selfishness."[24]

Father P. Lejeune offers a warning about reading for knowledge alone:

Some read solely with their minds. They treat the Science of God as a human science. Their one aim is to satisfy their need of knowledge and instruction. If you, my daughters, should attempt spiritual reading with this end in view, it would be just as well, I must avow, to lay down your book. You would only waste your time.[25]

Father Lejeune cites *The Imitation of Christ* to explain:

The author of the *Imitation* tells that there are two kinds of knowledge. One resides solely in the mind; it is cold and sterile. The other resides in the heart, and having partaken of its warmth, is warm itself and luminous. It is this latter knowledge, impelling us to action, self-reform, and the practice of good deeds, that we must have in view when making our spiritual reading.[26]

---

[24] Fulton J. Sheen, *Thoughts for Daily Living* (Garden City, NY: Garden City Books, 1955), p. 27.

[25] Monsignor P. Lejeune, *Counsels of Perfection for Christian Mothers*, trans. Francis A. Ryan (Harrison, NY: Roman Catholic Books, n.d.), p. 103.

[26] Ibid.

Knowing God better so that we can love Him better requires an inti-mate knowledge — not an intellectual knowledge. With this in mind, it's easy to see why reading must be done with our hearts as well as our minds.

You may be thinking, "This sounds great, but how exactly do I read with my heart?" I'm glad you asked. Reading with your heart means reading seriously and slowly; it means rereading a passage several times, if you feel called to do so. It means meditating on your reading. It means taking your time. You should not sit down with the goal of reading ten pages per day, fifty pages per week, and getting it done, by golly, even if you have to get up at 4:30 a.m. to do it! *More* reading does not equal *better* reading. The key is to approach your reading in a prayerful spirit, with a will to grow and change.

The Risk of Making Knowledge Your Goal

A word of warning. There are many Catholics (I used to be one of them) who are so concerned with the letter of the law that they forget the Source of the law. They are busy meting out justice but have no concept of God's infinite mercy. In the Bible, those people who were meticulous about the letter but not the spirit were called Pharisees.

Archbishop Fulton Sheen expounds on this subject in his *Life of Christ.* In describing the adulteress who was brought before Jesus, he says:

> A rusty old shield one day prayed, "O sun, illumine me"; and the sun answered, "First, polish yourself." Should, therefore, this woman be judged by men who were guilty? It was a solemn affir-mation that only the sinless have a right to judge. If on this earth, there is anybody really innocent, it will be found that his mercy is stronger than his justice.[27]

Now, I know that no one who begins a spiritual-reading journey is out to become arrogant and judgmental. There is nothing in our goal to

---

[27] Fulton J. Sheen, *Life of Christ* (New York: Image Books, 2008), p. 255.

become better Christians that warns us of the temptation to look with disdain at our pew-mates chitchatting away in the nave of the church; or the self-righteous indignation we experience as we see our neighbors show up late for Mass and leave early, and we think, like the Pharisee, "God, I thank thee that I am not like other men" (Luke 18:11).

We do not want to pursue spiritual reading in a way that makes us pass judgement on our fellow Christians or on those who have yet to recognize the light of Christ in the world. If we respond to spiritual reading in that way, we will have failed ourselves and our Lord, for rather than drink in the humility of Christ so that we might extend ourselves in love and mercy to our fellow man, we will have filled ourselves with pride, which will extend Christ's love to no one:

> We would willingly have others perfect, and yet we amend not our own faults. We would have others severely corrected and will not be corrected ourselves. The large liberty of others displeases us, and yet we will not have our own desires denied us. We will have others kept under by strict laws, but in no sort will ourselves be restrained. And thus it appears how seldom we weigh our neighbor in the same balance with ourselves.[28]

As a bent rudder cannot properly guide a boat, a judgmental response toward others will only steer them away from the truth and beauty you so desperately long to share with them.

Connecting the Dots

Although knowledge must not be an end in itself, spiritual reading can connect the dots between the heart and the head. By focusing our reading efforts on the four pillars of the Faith, we can develop a greater understanding of what Christ teaches us through His Church; we can develop

---

[28] St. Thomas à Kempis, *The Imitation of Christ* 1, 16, 2-3.

a greater appreciation for the sacraments; we can be inspired to a deeper prayer life and greater devotion. Finally, through those who went before us we can learn how to walk better with Christ.

Father Lejeune passionately explains the importance of spiritual reading in the pursuit of sanctity:

> Why have the saints so highly extolled the advantages of spiritual reading? Why have they exalted it—almost to a level with prayer?... It arises from the fact that spiritual reading is one of the principal sources whence we draw light.
>
> Have you ever reflected, my daughters, how important light is for us in our relations with God? From certain maxims or passages taken at random from spiritual writers, it would seem that mortification and sacrifice are the sole means of approaching nearer to God. Thus the author of the *Imitation* exalts reaction against our evil inclinations. He declares that the success of our struggle against nature is always the measure of our progress towards perfection.
>
> Certainly this principle is true and it would ill become us to complaisantly modify it. On the other hand, we must remember that energy in sacrifice is dependent upon clear-sightedness. We are energetic in sacrifice only when we see clearly the object of that sacrifice. It is the office of the intelligence to point out the path to the will. The will itself would remain inert, if motives of action and sacrifice did not stimulate it. A strong and vigorous will is always accompanied by an enlightened intelligence. Must we not conclude, then, that a solid knowledge of the principles of the spiritual life is a potent aid to the soul in its striving towards good? Hence, we must appreciate the value of spiritual reading since it furnishes us with the principles of the science of the saints, as well as with practical counsels, and precious examples.[29]

[29] Lejeune, *Counsels of Perfection*, pp. 96-97.

Saint Isidore of Seville, a Doctor of the Church, tells us:

The conscientious reader will be more concerned to carry out what he has read than merely to acquire knowledge of it.... Learning unsupported by grace may get into our ears; it never reaches our heart. It makes a great noise outside but serves no inner purpose. But when God's grace touches our innermost minds to bring understanding, his word which has been received by the ear sinks deep into the heart.[30]

READING READINESS

Spend some time in prayer today, preferably before the Blessed Sacrament. List the goals you have for spiritual reading. What are you trying to attain? Consider not necessarily what is the "right" goal but why you would embark on a spiritual-reading journey. Be honest with yourself. Do you have a desire to gain knowledge? To understand your Faith better? To live your Faith better? To develop a closer relationship to Christ? Are you motivated a little by each of these things? Recognizing your motivations will help you to adjust them if necessary, or at the very least to engage our Lord in prayer, asking that He guide your reading in a way that will best serve your growth in sanctity.

---

[30] Saint Isidore, *Book of Maxims* 3, 8-10.

Chapter 5

Syntopical Reading Can Reap Great Rewards

Help yourself during this troubled period by reading holy
books. This reading provides excellent food for the soul and
conduces to great progress along the path of perfection.

— Saint Pio of Pietrelcina, *Letters*, vol. 2

Now that we know why spiritual reading is valuable and what kind of
knowledge we are seeking, it is incumbent upon us to understand how
we can obtain the greatest good from what we read. The number of great
spiritual books available to us is vast. If you're like me, you've lost count
of all the books you've read over the years. Many of us approach spiritual
reading as we approach reading for entertainment: we'll read any book
as long as it looks good, someone recommended it, we like the author,
or we have an interest in the subject matter. For all the reading we do,
there is often no rhyme or reason to our selection of books.

This was the case with me. I read books on prayer, the saints, theology,
particular virtues, life issues, and more. But I didn't feel as if I was retaining
much of anything I read, much less applying it. I went from subject to subject so fast that my intentions regarding one book were lost as my excitement for the lessons contained in the next book grew. And the information

was gone just as quickly. Of course, somewhere in the back of my mind, I knew I had read about a particular subject, such as the profound nature of the Mass, but I was not equipped to discuss it with anyone. I retained the feelings of excitement I had when reading the book but could recount few insights shared by the author. This is where syntopical reading comes in.

What Is Syntopical Reading?

Syntopical reading, for the purposes of this book, is reading more than one book on the same topic either simultaneously or in succession. I first read the word *syntopical* in Mortimer Adler's 1940 classic, *How to Read a Book*. Adler speaks of syntopical reading as reading several *passages* from different books on one topic either at the same time or in succession. In this spiritual-reading program we will read not only passages but also complete books as we focus on one theme for a year (or even two years). Reading successive books in a general subject area, such as *prayer*, in addition to reading a couple of paragraphs per day in the *Catechism* on the same topic provides much greater insight into that pillar of the Faith.

Our spiritual leaders recognize the value of focus and concentration. In recent years, popes have declared the Year of the Family, the Year of Faith, and the Year of Mercy. The Holy Father does this in order to dedicate a full liturgical year to the prayer and study of a particular subject. Every one of these liturgical-year dedications is meant to encourage us to spend additional time and concentration growing in that area through prayer, education, and personal action in our daily lives.

Ultimately, focusing similar energy in the area of spiritual reading can reap great rewards in our spiritual lives. That is why our spiritual reading is better done in a *syntopical* fashion.

The Benefits of Syntopical Reading

Albert Einstein is thought to have said, "If a person studies a subject for fifteen minutes a day, in a year he will become an expert. In five years, he will be a national expert." Whether Einstein said this, or whether the statement is true, I'll leave to your imagination. Thankfully, when it comes to spiritual reading, *expertise* is not our goal. But there are benefits to organizing reading around a particular subject:

Focused reading offers greater breadth and depth of knowledge and understanding. We're not so concerned about being able to sound like experts to our friends and family (although a little expertise doesn't hurt when it comes to evangelization, provided it's wrapped in humility), but knowing and understanding our Faith better will help us to live it out more fully.

Different authors offer unique perspectives and insight into the same subject. There is a depth to our Faith that is better grasped through the perspectives of various teachers, provided they all adhere to the teaching of the Magisterium (more on that later).

By reading several books about Mary by several authors, I am bound to come away with a much fuller understanding of her as a person as well as her role in salvation history. As another example, say I want to learn more about living my *life in Christ* (one pillar of the Faith), which could include a book about Mary. But I could also decide to read the life of Saint Gianna Berretta Molla to learn how she reflected Christ's light to the world. Although learning what Saint Gianna did might give me great wisdom, reading about Mother Teresa in tandem is bound to help me see similarities between the two saints, as well as how Christ's light shines uniquely through each precious soul. Witnessing the truth reflected through the varied lives of the saints is like seeing a prism with light bursting forth from every angle, each ray creating a different color.

And then I could read Father Lawrence Lovasik's *Hidden Power of Kindness*, a wonderful, thorough look at what is meant by kindness, which is demanded by God, if we would be His disciples. "Love one another, as I have loved you" (John 15:12). By reading this book in succession with books about two amazing saints, I am bound to see Father Lovasik's insights about kindness illustrated in light of the lives of these unique women. Essentially, by reading several books in tandem that relate to living the Christian life, we can see what kindness looks like in a tangible way, in a sacrificial way. And we can better emulate these examples than we could if we read, say, one book on love and then another about prayer.

Focusing on one area of the spiritual life allows for greater application of what we learn. I don't know about you, but when I read a book on, say, prayer, I do my best to apply what I learn. While reading, I am highly motivated to change. But before any changes can become habits, I move on to the next book, which might be on the papacy or on a saint or a sacrament. While the information in that book might be just as valuable and just as good, such random reading leaves me little time to focus on improving my spiritual life in one area before moving on to the next. Syntopical reading allows for long spans of prayerful focus in a particular area. In this program, you will spend a full year improving your prayer life, little by little, day by day. This offers time for much greater reflection and meditation and time for habits to change. With syntopical reading, our actions can catch up with our intentions. In other words, syntopical reading helps us to apply what we read to our everyday lives, which is what we're going for; living out our relationship with Jesus Christ is our ultimate goal.

Retain What You Read

All this brings up an important point. Will reading from various sources about a particular subject help us to remember what we read? Yes and no. Reading from a variety of sources and perspectives helps us to ground the information more securely in our minds. Different angles and varied activities stimulate the brain differently.

That said, merely reading is not a good way to remember anything. We tend to remember things better when we immerse ourselves in them, when we practice them, when they are repeated in different ways, in varying contexts, over and over — essentially, when we *live* them. According to scientists Henry Roediger III and Mark A. McDaniel in their book *Make It Stick: The Science of Successful Learning*,[31] learning is directly correlated with how strongly you relate to the new concepts and information, as well as whether you can link new knowledge to knowledge you already have. In other words, reading is one thing. Practice, application, and context make it stick. A different perspective, practice added to reading, taking notes, doing practice problems from various sources, teaching what you've learned — all these things help to solidify information in your memory.

I propose that you use at least four of those tools to help you retain what you read, starting with syntopical reading: read about related topics from a variety of sources, take notes on what you read, pray over what you've learned, and put what you've read into practice each day, either with others or within your own heart and mind.

That means that if you read *In Silence with God* by Benedict Bauer and follow it up with *Little Talks with God* by St. Catherine of Siena, aspects of the second book would validate and solidify information you took from the first, and vice versa. If you also read one or two paragraphs on prayer in the *Catechism* per day, each of the three books would build on the other two. Now tie Sacred Scripture in with the others, and this foundation book would become the backbone of every grain of truth in the other sources you've explored. Finally, and arguably most important, you would incorporate concepts from your reading about prayer into your everyday life. Imagine praying over profound words in the *Catechism* as it relates to other reading material. Imagine keeping a journal on that subject and making it come alive by initiating what you've learned into your own prayer life? Imagine spending an entire year focused on prayer alone? Not a month on Confession and another month on Saint Augustine and another month on the papacy, but an entire year focused on strengthening your prayer life?

If we approach our spiritual reading with a learning heart, how can we not come away enlightened intellectually? And, provided we approach

---

[31] Peter C. Brown and Henry L. Roediger, *Make It Stick: The Science of Successful Learning* (Cambridge, MA: Belknap Press, 2014), p. 100.

our reading spiritually, of course, that depth of understanding will help to deepen and strengthen our spiritual lives as well.

READING READINESS

Have you ever read more than one book on the same topic in succession or at the same time? Did you find any reward in that experience? Did multiple perspectives help you to understand the subject matter better? Did you keep that subject in mind longer through syntopical reading? Can you imagine the possibilities inherent in reading about the same topic from multiple sources in your spiritual reading? Prayerfully ask God today to help you grow through this method.

PART II

How the Program Works

Chapter 6

The Four Pillars of the Catholic Faith

It is well always to have at hand some good devotional works,
such as those of St. Bonaventure, Gerson, Denis the Carthusian,
Blosius, Grenada, Stella, Arias, Pinelli, Da Ponte, Avila, *The
Spiritual Combat*, the *Confessions* of St. Augustine, the Epistles
of St. Jerome, and other such, and to read some portions daily,
counting them as letters from the Saints in heaven intended to
show you the road thither and give you courage to follow it.

— Saint Francis de Sales, *Introduction to the Devout Life*

When we think of a pillar, we think of someone or something of foundational importance. A pillar of a community plays an important role in that community. The pillars of a building hold the building up; should the pillars collapse, the entire building would crumble into an unrecognizable heap. A building's support is a necessary component of its structure.

Our spiritual-reading program is built on the pillars of the *Catechism*: the Profession of Faith, the Celebration of the Christian Mystery, Life in Christ, and Prayer. Each of these pillars of our Faith is critical to the life of a Catholic. If we disregard even one of them, we risk allowing our Faith to crumble into an unrecognizable heap. On the other hand, if you spend time strengthening each of these pillars through catechesis and the reading of Sacred Scripture, you will be amazed at the growth you see in your spiritual life.

THE PROFESSION OF FAITH (WHAT WE BELIEVE)

At the heart of every Catholic, cradle and convert alike, there is a deep-seated sense of identity, a feeling of family and belonging that words cannot express. But sometimes we take that family for granted. We rest on our laurels, going through the motions without realizing the profound gift we've been given. Converts tend to hold on a little tighter. Sometimes cradle Catholics are surprised by the excitement and passion they express. But whether they joined the Church after spending a lifetime away, or they were raised in the Church and left for a time before returning home, converts tend to be actively thankful and even passionate about what they have. Frankly, they know what it's like to be without.

Rather than get all deep and theological about what some converts think about the Faith and why they want to know everything there is to know (and why they want everyone else to know everything there is to know), I'm going to share a profound revelation I experienced.

Preserving Truth, Promoting Beauty

I was introduced to my husband's entire family on Christmas Eve at his parents' home on the dairy farm where he was raised. We had become engaged the night before—December 23—and the welcome and excitement I experienced from his parents, eight siblings, their spouses, and their kids was breathtaking. I had already been taken with his parents months before. And I knew and loved two of his sisters who lived in the same college town. But to encounter the family as a whole was incredible. Words cannot express how moved I was to become part of it a few months later.

My infatuation may sound silly to you, but I came from what is commonly referred to as a broken home. My parents divorced when I was ten years old, and my siblings and I didn't grow up together. When I first met my husband's family—two parents who at the time had been married for nearly forty years, eight siblings, and their spouses, who were all the best of friends—I was in awe, not only of the mass of people, but of the love each one displayed. Joy poured forth when they were together and nourished anyone they touched.

More than twenty years later, every time we have a family get-together, I am still excited to visit the small town in Northeast Nebraska where my husband grew up. I've written posts about my mother-in-law and her goodness, and the work ethic of my late father-in-law. I gush over the kindness and the loyalty of all my in-laws. Don't get me wrong. I love my own family. But there is something about the cohesiveness of my husband's family that demonstrates in a profound way what God intended when He created the *family*.

And yet, despite all my awe and wonder, my husband tells me that until he met me, he never realized what he had taken and, to some extent, still takes for granted. To him, "It's family." Sure, he loves them all. But he doesn't get all philosophical about it. Nor is he overwhelmed with the beauty of the eternal union they all share together. I, on the other hand, have spent our entire married life trying to understand what it was about their parents that makes their family so successful. I mean, my husband and I have been married almost twenty-two years—we were the second-to-last couple of nine to marry—and to date, by God's grace, there has not been one divorce in the group. In this world, that's nothing short of miraculous. To my husband and his family, *it's just life*.

Why do I share that story? Well, those of us who are new to the Church, or who have come back after being estranged for any reason, recognize the profound nature of the family to which we belong. We want to understand everything there is to know about Christ through His Church. We want to wrap ourselves in the Church's history and her truth. We are so unbelievably excited to be *grounded* in the family of God. And we want to pass our heritage along to our children, hoping to infuse their precious hearts with the truth and beauty that is inherent in this great family, encouraging them to take great pride in the legacy that has been handed down to them and to hand it down to their children. But before we can pass along our Faith, we must *know* it. That is why we study it.

The Passionate Embrace of Truth

When we think about the great mystery that is our God, the grandeur of beauty and the complexity of truth in our Faith, it is difficult to fathom why we wouldn't take great pains to spend a lifetime becoming more intimately familiar with every detail of every mystery that our minds and hearts can comprehend.

Every Sunday at Mass, we profess our Faith. What we believe as a people is integral to who we are as individuals and is deeply ingrained in our thoughts, words, and actions. Of course, we must take steps to continue to grow in the knowledge and understanding of our Faith.

God has placed in each of us a natural desire to seek answers to the meaning of our existence. Saint John Paul II expressed this concept eloquently at the outset of his encyclical *Fides et Ratio* (*Faith and Reason*):

> Faith and reason are like two wings on which the human spirit rises to the contemplation of truth; and God has placed in the human heart a desire to know the truth — in a word, to know himself — so that, by knowing and loving God, men and women may also come to the fullness of truth about themselves.

This truth that we all seek can be found by studying the more than two thousand years of wisdom offered by the Church for our enlightenment. We are not orphans left to wander the earth, seeking meaning and a kind of grounding mechanism in the things around us. We have something far greater. We share a creed of beliefs with family members stretching back more than two thousand years. We are all one in Christ.

To the extent that we can share that history, our family will begin to grow again, because truth is sought by all. The desire to *know* is written in our hearts, and once we learn the truth, its beauty is downright irresistible.

READING READINESS

Spend about ten minutes combing through the appendices for books on theology that address particular questions you may have about the teaching of the Church. Try to discern which two or three God may be calling you to pursue. Note them here or highlight them in the appendices.

The first pillar of the *Catechism* is the Profession of Faith. In section 2 of the Profession of Faith, the *Catechism* highlights the Apostles' Creed, which summarizes the Faith of the apostles, a Faith that has been preserved and transmitted from the earliest Church, uniting Christians to this day under the one true God, in His one, holy, catholic, and apostolic church. Take some time today to ask our Lord to help you come to know Him better through His holy Church. Ask Him to guide you as you embark on an organized spiritual reading journey. Conclude your prayer with the Apostles' Creed, professing your faith in the Triune God and His precious gift to us in Holy Mother Church:

The Apostles' Creed

I believe in God, the Father almighty, creator of heaven and earth, and in Jesus Christ, His only son, our Lord, who was conceived by the Holy Spirit, born of the Virgin Mary, suffered under Pontius Pilate, was crucified, died, and was buried. He descended into hell; the third day He rose again from the dead. He ascended into heaven and is seated at the right hand of God, the Father almighty; from thence He shall come to judge the living and the dead. I believe in the Holy Spirit, the holy catholic Church, the communion of saints, the forgiveness of sins, the resurrection of the body and life everlasting. Amen.

The Celebration of the Christian Mystery

If I had to boil my conversion to Catholicism down to one thing, I'd have to say it's my complete and utter awe for the transformative grace available in the liturgy and the sacraments. Comments made by Felix Leseur in his tribute to his late wife, Elisabeth, speak to God's hand in my life:

> It is always wonderful and impressive to contemplate the action of God's grace, and to see how sweet and strong—and at the same time how simple and human—are the means He employs to guide a man to the path designed for him from the beginning.[32]

And so it was with me. In hindsight, the fact that God Himself escorted me home to His Church is so obvious. And yet the crumbs that marked my path were so well dispersed that I never discovered His hand until one day, when I glanced back in awe, I recognized in full the trail that led me straight to Him.

A Introduction to the Church

At the age of five, I was given my first glimpse into the arms of heaven by what would seem a natural escort—my grandmother. But Grandma Sam

---

[32] *The Secret Diary of Elisabeth Leseur*, p. xiii.

was no ordinary cookie-baking, apron-wearing stereotypical specimen. Spunky and fun-loving, she preferred a cigarette and an ice-cold bottle of beer. As tiny as a peanut and quicker than the flutter of a hummingbird's wings—always busy, never still—my grandma worked for many years as a barmaid in South Minneapolis. In fact, she met my grandfather in that bar. As a young widow, she worked nights trying to raise four young children when he stopped in for a drink as he was passing through town. It didn't take long before she swept him off his feet and he planted himself in Minnesota, stepping in to raise her family as his own.

I remember the home of my grandparents as one big, happy hoopla. On a typical Friday night when we pulled into town, I recognized my grandparents' house, not by the rod-iron porch rails framing the front door, not by the narrow facade or the tan stucco or the neatly manicured lawn, but by the sound of old country music and the sight of people mingling in the backyard and piling into the house. Ash trays were featured throughout the property, smoke wafted through the air in thick clouds, and the beer was flowing.

Not necessarily a place one would expect to be rolling in sanctity.

But one morning after a night of music and revelry, I was given a window into the source of my grandmother's joy and energy. Grandma Sam liked to go for walks, and she and I trucked up and down just about every street in her neighborhood when I came to visit. So on that fateful morning I had no way of knowing this particular walk had a destination. Together we strolled down Twenty-Fifth Avenue all the way to 42nd Street, and from there, we wound our way around to find—to my great surprise—a church nestled amidst the hundreds of houses in her South Minneapolis neighborhood. I learned as an adult that my grandmother had always been a Catholic. But as a young girl, I didn't even know what *Catholic* meant. This moment was my first and only peek at Catholicism until my senior year in high school. What I experienced upon entering St. Helena's was the grandness enveloping me. The beautiful stained-glass windows ran a story high, and the nave offered the profound intimacy of a whispered conversation while feeling as colossal and as packed as

Grand Central Station. I don't exactly remember the Mass. But what I do remember can be summed up in one word: reverence.

When I was really young, I had thought that people flocked to my grandparents' home for the weekend parties. But as I grew older I realized that my grandmother had a huge heart for everyone she met, and her kindness was reflected in the size of the crowds in her home. At Thanksgiving and Christmas, she would invite to dinner the indigent people she'd met around the bar where she worked. She treated everyone with equal dignity, whether black, white, rich, or poor. All who came relished the friendly atmosphere of her home. Not until years later did I make a connection between the grace she extended and the grace she received on a weekly basis.

For all the excitement found in their home, my grandparents were the one constant in my life. They represented stability. My maternal grandparents were divorced before I was born, and my parents divorced when I was ten. But my father's parents remained a symbol of unity, even from a distance. They were the one fixture in my life that would always remain the same.

Even my grandparents' *house* held great significance for me. They lived in the same house until they both passed away, my grandmother first, of a slowly suffocating, drawn-out emphysema, brought on by many years of inhaling first- and second-hand smoke.

God brought me back to them in her last years, just months before my wedding. In the summer of '94 I was offered a full-time summer internship in downtown Minneapolis and had the privilege of living with an aunt and uncle just a few blocks from my grandparents. In those months, I watched my strapping grandfather handle his frail shell of a wife with great delicacy. Their love and devotion, particularly in those later years, mirrored the cross. In my heart, God had secured the memory of a five-year-old girl, introduced to the arms of heaven on that bright morning years ago, and in His providence He brought me back all those years later as I spent that summer attending the same church with both my grandparents, meeting their friends, and sharing coffee with them after Mass.

Their witness to the cross was a profound source of inspiration for me as I prepared to come home to the Catholic Church just a few months later.

Encounters with Catholics

In the intervening years between my first introduction to and my entrance into the Church, God did not leave me to my own resources. Rather, He whispered in my ear every step of the way. Throughout my life, our Lord quietly placed Catholics in my path in a way that beautifully illustrated the sacredness of marriage.

In high school, many of my friends attended CCD classes. Their antics in class were often discussed in our social circles. Theirs was a shared experience that I envied, although I didn't know why. Around that time, I dated a guy who took me to Mass before our senior prom and before our high school graduation. I knew that the Mass was an important part of his life and that of his family. In fact, my great respect for his family seemed connected somehow to St. Malachy's. My experience in Mass led me to link *family* with Catholicism.

In college, my best friend used to stop by my apartment all dressed up and full of joy on Sundays after she went to Mass. Of course, she was joyful most of the time—her middle name, in fact, is Joy. To this day I don't think she could possibly comprehend how amazed and inspired I was that she *voluntarily* went to church. I just couldn't imagine anyone doing something like that unless her parents forced her to. Over time, I got to know my friend's family as well, and we still keep in touch. There was something attractive and compelling about her family even way back then, and somewhere deep down, I just *knew* it had something to do with that Church.

While in college my future husband and I worked together at a hotel and had become friends. I was usually stressed about school; but one day, he noticed that I was particularly distraught about a certain class. In our conversation, he very casually asked if I had ever considered going to church. I was dumbfounded. What did *church* have to do with this thing that had me so upset? To be honest, I don't remember where that conversation ended, but I can tell you that his question resonated with me. It certainly elevated my opinion of him, as, it seemed to me, he risked something to ask me about God. As you can imagine from my comments in the previous chapter, meeting his family further strengthened my opinion of the Church.

Faith and Family

All those encounters with the faithful through the years culminated in my receiving First Communion, two days before my wedding. I was overjoyed by the profound meaning of the Church's liturgy and her sacraments. They are the vehicles by which we develop and strengthen our relationship with Christ, our means of gaining the grace necessary to carry on in a world that promotes values diametrically opposed to our Faith. The more I read, the more I realized the intricate depth and beauty linking all the sacraments together, enabling us to share in the light of Christ.

For me, the association between marriage, family, and the Catholic Church was a powerful revelation. As a child of divorce, I spent my adolescence watching *Little House on the Prairie*, believing that this television family reflected all that a family should be. I was fascinated by the beauty of this family's sacrifice, by their love and devotion to one another. I wanted that. And I thought that, if there was a God, He must have intended that too. Once I began looking into the tenets of the Church, I believed I had struck gold. In the Catholic Church was a plan for marriage, a plan for family, a plan that was *founded* on sacrifice! Unlike the Protestantism with which I grew up, the Catholic Church did not teach that divorce was acceptable in this or that circumstance. In the twentieth century, the Catholic Church was still teaching that in marriage, the two spouses become one — literally; that love for one's spouse should reflect Christ's death on the Cross; that the more the spouses' commitment was united to the Cross of Christ, the more perfect it would be. *Nowhere* else had I heard this! But when I read about it, I knew that it was true. In *Familiaris Consortio*, Saint John Paul II eloquently describes the intimate relationship between the family and Christ's Church:

> The Eucharist is the very source of Christian marriage. The Eucharistic sacrifice in fact represents Christ's covenant of love with the church, sealed with his blood on the cross. In this sacrifice of the new and eternal covenant, Christian spouses encounter the source from which their own marriage covenant flows, is interiorly structured and continuously renewed. As a representation of Christ's love for the church, the Eucharist is a fountain of charity. In the Eucharistic gift of charity the Christian family finds the foundation and soul of its "communion" and its "mission": By partaking in the Eucharistic bread, the different members of the Christian family become one body, which reveals and shares in the wider unity of the church. Their sharing in the body of Christ that is "given up" and in his blood that is "shed" becomes a never-ending source of missionary and apostolic dynamism for the Christian family. (no. 57)

Our lives are bound up in the liturgy and the sacraments. We are able to live out fully the love of Christ only in the context of these gifts. We must not walk through them mindlessly, showing up for Mass on Sunday and leaving no different from when we walked in, or merely existing in marriage and going through the motions of Confession. We must learn about the liturgy and the sacraments to appreciate their beauty and to gain a meaningful respect for God and a newfound gratitude for His gifts. And we must — with great passion — pass them along to our children.

The Church was made manifest to the world on the day of Pentecost by the outpouring of the Holy Spirit.[33] The gift of the Spirit

---

[33] Cf. SC 6; LG 2.

ushers in a new era in the "dispensation of the mystery"—the age of the Church, during which Christ manifests, makes present, and communicates his work of salvation through the liturgy of his Church, "until he comes."[34] In this age of the Church Christ now lives and acts in and with his Church, in a new way appropriate to this new age. He acts through the sacraments in what the common Tradition of the East and the West calls "the sacramental economy"; this is the communication (or "dispensation") of the fruits of Christ's Paschal mystery in the celebration of the Church's "sacramental" liturgy. (CCC 1076)

As Christians, we are called to something higher than human existence—not only once we reach heaven—if we reach heaven—but within the world as well. Reading prayerfully about the mysteries of our Faith will allow us to live them more fully and to be transformed so that we can then transform the world around us.

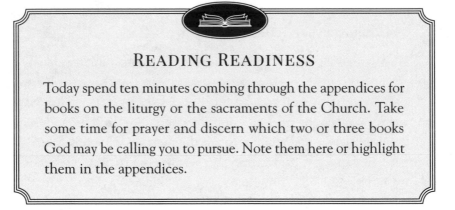

READING READINESS

Today spend ten minutes combing through the appendices for books on the liturgy or the sacraments of the Church. Take some time for prayer and discern which two or three books God may be calling you to pursue. Note them here or highlight them in the appendices.

---

[34] 1 Cor. 11:26.

LIFE IN CHRIST

In years past, it would have been an absolute disgrace to besmirch one's family name in any way. A person's behavior reflected well or poorly on his parents and grandparents. People felt a great commitment to uphold the good reputation developed through generations of their elders. In this day and age, we seem to have trouble with understanding the concept of the "family name" and our obligation to uphold it. With broken families and the virtual disappearance of the connected extended family due to job location and the prioritization of the individual over the family unit, we've come to think of ourselves as lone entities in the world. We are adrift on our own reputations. And even then, as independent entities, we often don't even think in terms of reputation. Each decision seems to be made in a vacuum, concerned only with immediate circumstances as opposed to long-term consequences. But this notion of rugged individualism has a grave impact on our lives as Christians.

When we think only about ourselves and our personal interests, it becomes challenging to think in terms of a "family name" of any kind. And yet, as Christians, our every move must be considered in light of our new lives in Christ:

> Christian, recognize your dignity and, now that you share in God's own nature, do not return to your former base condition by sinning. Remember who is your head and of whose body you are a member. Never forget that you have been rescued from the power of darkness and brought into the light of the Kingdom of God.[35]

These words of St. Leo the Great are as true for us today as they were in the fifth century. As part of the body of Christ, we are a new creation in Him. We are called to set ourselves and our interests aside and allow

---

[35] St. Leo the Great, *Sermo 22 in nat. Dom.*, 3:PL 54,192C, quoted in CCC 1691.

Christ to live through us. This is the ultimate in placing family interests above our own. The saints were permeated with this concept.

Saint Thérèse of Lisieux said, "Let us be one with Jesus.... May all moments of our life be for Him alone."[36] This sounds so easy on its face. Just hand over the reins to Christ, and all will go well. But most of us have grown up listening to the gospel of "If it feels good, do it," and we simply aren't equipped to set our interests aside to become something better. The lives of the saints can help us in that regard. Instruction from those brothers and sisters in Christ who have gone before us can remind us of who we are in Christ and how we can respond to that identity.

The *Catechism* quotes Saint John Eudes, followed by a quote from Saint Paul:

> I ask you to consider that our Lord Jesus Christ is your true head, and that you are one of his members. He belongs to you as the head belongs to its members; all that is his is yours: his spirit, his heart, his body and soul, and all his faculties. You must make use of all these as your own, to serve, praise, love, and glorify God. You belong to him, as your members belong to their head. And so he longs for you to use all that is in you, as if it were his own, for the service and glory of the Father.[37] (CCC 1698)

> For to me, to live is Christ.[38]

The amazing thing is, once we acknowledge this reality and pursue a life in Christ, the rewards we reap will be found not only in heaven but on earth as well. Our joy will be palpable. And just as our sin spreads beyond us, poisoning family and community and multiplying its dire effects, our joy affects everyone we meet, bringing light and freshness and

---

[36] Letter 65, to Céline.
[37] St. John Eudes, *Tract. de admirabili corde Jesu* 1, 5.
[38] Philemon 1:21.

filling the earth with Christ's beauty. St. Seraphim of Sarov said, "See, this kingdom of God is now found within us. The grace of the Holy Spirit shines forth and warms us, and is overflowing with many and varied scents into the air around us, regales our sense with heavenly delight, as it fills our heart with joy inexpressible."[39]

We are creatures of habit. To change our habits, we need constant reminders. To live in Christ and to disavow our deeply ingrained selfishness, we must constantly remind ourselves who we truly are. What we encounter in books that reflect the life of Christ, and what we read in the *Catechism*, can profoundly change the trajectory of our lives. According to the *Catechism*, the change we seek requires catechesis:

> Catechesis has to reveal in all clarity the joy and demands of the way of Christ.[40] Catechesis for the "newness of life"[41] in him should be:
>
> + A *catechesis of the Holy Spirit*, the interior Master of life according to Christ, a gentle guest and friend who inspires, guides, corrects, and strengthens this life;
> + A *catechesis of grace*, for it is by grace that we are saved and again it is by grace that our works can bear fruit for eternal life;
> + A *catechesis of the beatitudes*, for the way of Christ is summed up in the beatitudes, the only path that leads to the eternal beatitude for which the human heart longs;
> + A *catechesis of sin and forgiveness*, for unless man acknowledges that he is a sinner he cannot know the truth about himself, which is a condition for acting justly; and without the offer of forgiveness he would not be able to bear this truth;

---

[39] Quoted in Ronda De Sola Chervin, *Quotable Saints* (Oak Lawn, IL: CMJ Marian Publishers, 2003), p. 175.
[40] Cf. John Paul II, CT 29.
[41] Rom. 6:4.

✦ *A catechesis of the human virtues* which causes one to grasp the beauty and attraction of right dispositions towards goodness;

✦ *A catechesis of the Christian virtues* of faith, hope and charity, generously inspired by the example of the saints;

✦ *A catechesis of the twofold commandment of charity* set forth in the Decalogue;

✦ *An ecclesial catechesis*, for it is through the manifold exchanges of "spiritual goods" in the "communion of saints" that Christian life can grow, develop, and be communicated. (CCC 1697)

The catechesis we seek can certainly be found in this spiritual-reading program. In fifteen to thirty minutes per day, we can make life-changing progress in our spiritual lives. In fact, there will come a time, by God's grace, when we can speak the words of Saint Paul: "It is no longer I who live, but Christ who lives in me" (Gal. 2:20). And to the extent that we can speak those words, opening ourselves to live and breathe Christ Jesus, we can find eternal happiness in Him.

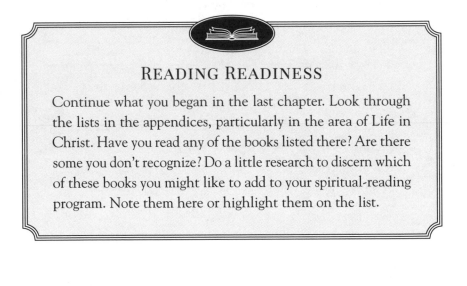

READING READINESS

Continue what you began in the last chapter. Look through the lists in the appendices, particularly in the area of Life in Christ. Have you read any of the books listed there? Are there some you don't recognize? Do a little research to discern which of these books you might like to add to your spiritual-reading program. Note them here or highlight them on the list.

PRAYER

Did you know that a newborn can copy your facial movements? I had read this, so I asked the doctor about it as I sat holding my firstborn son. *Absolutely true*, he confirmed and demonstrated some gestures my husband and I might want to make to test the concept. The two of us sat transfixed with astonishment as I stuck out my tongue and my precious two-hour-old infant followed suit!

Why do I mention newborns and silly facial expressions in a discussion about prayer? Because I think this natural instinct may have something to do with the challenges that prayer brings to our lives. *We are born copycats!* From our very first hours we have been imitating those around us, observing how the world is run so that we might survive and thrive in it. But prayer? According to the *Catechism*, prayer is, at its core, a relationship (no. 2564). And while it is a key component of a life lived in Christ, it is also the most interior action of our soul. That means that, try as we may, we cannot imitate prayer. Yes, we can imitate the words. But prayer is not, by definition, simply about words or gestures. We know this intuitively. Imagine kneeling before the Blessed Sacrament beside Pope John Paul II (now Saint John Paul II) in Saint Peter's Basilica. If we were determined to learn to pray as he prayed, we might repeat every word we heard him speak. We might imitate his posture, his reverence, and his calm. But I am nearly certain that we would leave there believing that something deeper was going on between our Lord and Saint John Paul II on an interior level that we would be hard-pressed to emulate, despite our best efforts to do so.

In his book *Saint John Paul the Great: His Five Loaves*, Jason Everett notes how people described the pope while in prayer:

> When visitors arrived to join him for Mass, they would always find him kneeling in prayer. Some said, "he looked like he was speaking with the Invisible." One of the masters of ceremonies added, "it seemed as if the Pope were not present among us." Bishop Andrew Wypych, who was ordained to the diaconate by Cardinal Karol Wojtyła, added, "You could see that he physically was there, but

one could sense that he was immersed in the love of the Lord. They were united in talking to each other."[42]

Is there anyone who believes they could replicate this intimate conversation merely through imitation?

On a more personal level, we experience this same frustration in our daily lives. Most of us know at least one person whom we consider to be holy. By our observation, this person seems to thrive on a fulfilling and fruitful prayer life, but we just can't figure out how he does it. When we ask him, he can't explain. When this happens often enough over time, frustration sets in, and eventually we begin to believe that we must be the problem. When the prayer gene was handed out, we must have been out to lunch, because there is just nothing there.

Thankfully, all that frustration, while understandable, is simply not warranted. If there is a prayer gene, we all have it. Our very desire to speak with God demonstrates a disposal toward communication with our Creator. That desire to pray, and even our frustration with its apparent futility, is, in a way, a prayer in itself. According to Saint Ignatius of Loyola, "Everything that one turns in the direction of God is a prayer."[43] "Everything" includes our frustration with the challenges we encounter in our prayer lives. And we must see our desire to improve in this pillar of our Faith as progress in the spiritual life. We must recognize God's hand on our shoulder as we continue to travel the road. Most certainly, we can persevere. The bottom line is that as Christians, we must learn to pray through *practice*, through conversing with God in our hearts.

We can read a prayer just as easily as we can follow a cake recipe in a book. But an expert baker, after much practice in the kitchen, becomes almost one with the very process of baking, elevating his creations to

---

[42] Jason Everett, *Saint John Paul II: His Five Loaves* (Lakewood, CO: Totus Tuus Press, 2014), p. 127.

[43] Quoted in Carol Kelly-Gangi, *365 Days with the Saints: A Year of Wisdom from the Saints* (New York: Wellfleet Press, 2015), p. 147.

levels unimagined by a novice. So, too, through daily prayer that involves our hearts and minds, the process of prayer can become an extension of our very selves. We can experience prayer as a conversation and feel our Lord's presence in our lives.

Prayer is therefore something that we must *do* in order to learn, but apprenticeship is the fastest way to make progress, both in the kitchen and in the spiritual life. In fact, we have much to learn from those who have mastered a craft, or, in our case, have developed a relationship with God that allows them to converse with Him as their closest friend. The saints have plenty to say about prayer and can surely help us in our efforts. Saint Thérèse of Lisieux is particularly known for her words on prayer:

> Prayer is an aspiration of the heart; it is a simple glance directed toward heaven, it is a cry of gratitude and love in the midst of trial as well as joy; finally, it is something great, supernatural, which expands my soul and unites me to Jesus.[44]

While our personal relationship with Christ will be just that—personal—the words of the saints and others who have gone before us can certainly guide and inspire our prayer lives. They do a beautiful job of defining prayer. They can instruct us on the ins and outs of prayer. And some have even expressed in writing their innermost thoughts and prayers, so that we might witness at an intimate level what fruitful prayer looks like.

There are many fabulous resources available to help us deepen our prayer lives. Reading about prayer can help us to find time to pray, to dispose our hearts and minds to a conversation with Christ, to improve our ability to listen during our prayer time, to create a prayerful environment, and more. It is true that we cannot know or replicate the relationship between another person and Christ. But rather than allow this to frustrate us, let us recognize that each of us will develop a distinctive, remarkably personal form of conversation with our Lord. Your relationship with Christ

---

[44] Saint Thérèse of Lisieux, *The Story of a Soul*, chap. 11.

will be as uniquely defined as the intricate ridges of your fingerprint. What could be more amazing and beautiful than that?

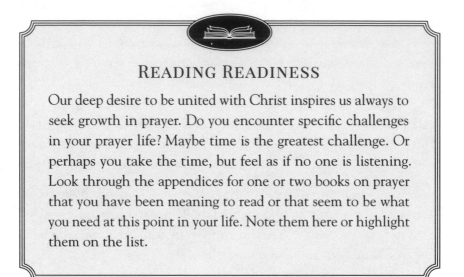

READING READINESS

Our deep desire to be united with Christ inspires us always to seek growth in prayer. Do you encounter specific challenges in your prayer life? Maybe time is the greatest challenge. Or perhaps you take the time, but feel as if no one is listening. Look through the appendices for one or two books on prayer that you have been meaning to read or that seem to be what you need at this point in your life. Note them here or highlight them on the list.

Chapter 7

READING SACRED SCRIPTURE

The Emperor of heaven, the Lord of men and of angels, has sent
you His epistles for your life's advantage—and yet you neglect to
read them eagerly. Study them, I beg you, and meditate daily on
the words of your Creator. Learn the heart of God in the words
of God, that you may sigh more eagerly for things eternal, that
your soul may be kindled with greater longings for heavenly joys.

— POPE ST. GREGORY I, *LETTERS* 5, 46

I hope we agree that spiritual reading should be a part of your everyday
routine. So the next question is, what to read? There are three categories
of reading you should do regularly: *Sacred Scripture*, the *Catechism of the
Catholic Church*, and *great spiritual works*. Let's look at Sacred Scripture first.

If you've started reading the Bible in Genesis and set it aside a few
pages into Leviticus, you are not alone. For years, I tried reading the
Bible but just could not get into it. It wasn't until I went through Jeff
Cavins's *Great Bible Adventure* Bible study that it all began to make sense.
To recognize Sacred Scripture as the story of salvation history was a huge
eye-opener for me. Until then, I had just read a lot of what I thought
were marginally related stories about Adam and Eve, Abraham, Noah,
Elijah, and others in various Bible-story books without knowing why
these stories were highlighted.

In my spiritual reading I have found that most authors agree that we should begin with the Gospels when reading the Bible. It could be because they are most familiar or because they tell the story of the life of Christ, the Second Person of the Blessed Trinity, the Way, the Truth, and the Life. The birth, death, and Resurrection of Christ as described in the Gospels are the greatest and most monumental events in all of history and the most discussed in all circles related to Christianity. But as Catholics, we recognize that the New Testament is a fulfillment of the Old Testament; that is, in understanding the Old Testament, we can better understand the New. As we learn in 2 Timothy 3:16, "All scripture is inspired by God and profitable for teaching, for reproof, for correction, and for training in righteousness."

But for those reasons mentioned above, the Gospels do hold a special place in our Faith and in the liturgy of the Catholic Church. Many saints read and meditated on a chapter from the Gospels every day. Elisabeth Leseur mentions Gospel reading in her diary. In *Theology for Beginners*, Frank Sheed recommends that one "start with the Gospels and then perhaps the letters of Paul." Unlike some portions of the Bible, the Gospels read like a story—a story with which we are familiar. And their format is understandable.

The Word Is the Word

Sacred Scripture should be a key component of any spiritual-reading program. Through Scripture, God whispers intimately to each and every one of us. There is no substitute for that sacred communication. The Word of God is a love letter from our Father in heaven. Saint Ambrose says that we speak to God when we pray and we listen to Him when we read the Scriptures.[45]

According to the *Catechism of the Catholic Church*:

---

[45] St. Ambrose, *De officiis ministrorum* 1, 20, 88.

In Sacred Scripture, the Church constantly finds her nourishment and her strength, for she welcomes it not as a human word, "but as what it really is, the word of God."[46] "In the sacred books, the Father who is in heaven comes lovingly to meet his children, and talks with them."[47] (CCC 104)

As beloved children of God, we are privileged to have a Father in heaven eager to share the wonderful stories of our family history, as well as the love and wisdom embodied in the very Person of His Son. More than merely memorizing Bible verses, our quest is to steep ourselves in Sacred Scripture. Throughout Church history, *Christ* has been synonymous with *Sacred Scripture*. In the beginning of his Gospel, Saint John refers to Christ as "the Word." This is an Eternal Word, for Christ is the Word of God, wholly and completely. How better to unite ourselves with Christ than to immerse ourselves in the Word of the Scriptures? On this the *Catechism* quotes Saint Augustine, stating:

> Through all the words of Sacred Scripture, God speaks only one single Word, his one Utterance in whom he expresses himself completely:[48] "You recall that one and the same Word of God extends throughout Scripture, that it is one and the same Utterance that resounds in the mouths of the sacred writers, since he who was in the beginning God with God has no need of separate syllables; for he is not subject to time."[49] (CCC 102)

No Substitute for the Real McCoy

There is a tendency in the hurried pace of our society to place ourselves one step away from true wisdom. Rather than read the classics in an

---

[46] 1 Thess. 2:13; cf. *DV* 24.
[47] *DV* 21.
[48] Cf. Heb. 1:1-3.
[49] St. Augustine, *En. in Ps.* 103, 4, 1:PL 37,1378; cf. Ps. 104; John 1:1.

unabridged form, we read summaries or watch the movie. As you know if you have read any classic and then watched the corresponding movie, the movie never adequately tells the story.

When it comes to Sacred Scripture, there are countless commentaries, summaries, abbreviated stories, and devotionals. All these resources were created for our edification and to help us to understand salvation history better. But unless we are reading Scripture itself, we are doing ourselves a grave disservice.

There is no substitute for drinking in His life-giving words. Reading anything else without reading Sacred Scripture is like having your sister tell you how much your mother loves you. That may be nice, but it pales in comparison to hearing the words from your mother herself.

Although Sacred Scripture was written by fallible men, those men were inspired by the Holy Spirit, and by His divine hand, their words reflect His story and pave the way to His very heart.

This is why the foundation of all spiritual reading should be Sacred Scripture. Other reading should supplement Scripture, but never replace it.

> For sacred scripture is not like other books. Dictated by the Holy Ghost, it contains things of the deepest importance, which in many instances are most difficult and obscure. To understand and explain such things there is always required the "coming" of the same Holy Ghost; that is to say, His light and His grace.[50]

By virtue of the Holy Trinity, to know Sacred Scripture is to know Christ: "All sacred Scripture is but one book, and this one book is Christ, 'because all divine Scripture speaks of Christ, and all divine Scripture is fulfilled in Christ'"[51] (CCC 134).

Reading Scripture can be transformative. By prayerfully reading from the Gospels every day, we can develop an intimate relationship with

---

[50] Pope Leo XIII, *Providentissiumus Deus* (November 18, 1893), no. 5.
[51] Hugh of St. Victor, *De arca Noe* 2,8:PL 176, 642: cf. ibid. 2, 9:PL 176, 642-643.

our Lord, opening ourselves to His suggestion in our lives, ripe for the transformation of our character, our habits, our very lives. The Scriptures are so influential that Saint Josemaría Escrivá advises in his book *The Way*: "May your behavior and your conversation be such that everyone who sees or hears you can say: This man reads the life of Jesus Christ."

Lectio Divina

Because reading Sacred Scripture can be a stumbling block for us, there are many resources available to help us in this endeavor. No doubt you've seen study Bibles and Scripture-related commentaries; or you've read along with the liturgy using a resource such as *Magnificat*. Maybe you belong to a Bible study or have taken a course on the Bible like Jeff Cavins's *Great Bible Adventure*. Or perhaps on a retreat you've learned about the Ignatian Method, lectio divina, or other means of contemplating the Gospels.

Any of these can help you to read the Bible prayerfully. Because of the way the Bible readings are laid out in this program, however, you may find lectio divina to be the most useful method available. Even its name makes it appropriate for *Reading Your Way to Heaven*, for *lectio divina* means "divine reading." What better reading could there be?

This tradition of prayer extends back to the monastic period[52] but has been reemphasized and encouraged by our Holy Fathers in recent years. Pope John Paul II noted the great strides that have been made in biblical study and catechesis since Vatican II, but he expressed a need to delve deeper by using lectio divina:

> Ever since the Second Vatican Council underlined the pre-eminent role of the word of God in the life of the Church, great progress has certainly been made in devout listening to Sacred Scripture and attentive study of it. Scripture has its rightful place

---

[52] Douglas J. Leonhardt, S.J., "Praying with Scripture," http://www.ignatian spirituality.com/.

of honour in the public prayer of the Church. Individuals and communities now make extensive use of the Bible, and among lay people there are many who devote themselves to Scripture with the valuable help of theological and biblical studies. But it is above all the work of evangelization and catechesis which is drawing new life from attentiveness to the word of God. Dear brothers and sisters, this development needs to be consolidated and deepened, also by making sure that every family has a Bible. It is especially necessary that listening to the word of God should become a life-giving encounter, in the ancient and ever valid tradition of lectio divina, which draws from the biblical text the living word which questions, directs and shapes our lives.[53]

Pope Benedict further encouraged lectio devina:

In this context, I would like in particular to recall and recommend the ancient tradition of "lectio divina": "the diligent reading of Sacred Scripture accompanied by prayer brings about that intimate dialogue in which the person reading hears God who is speaking, and in praying, responds to him with trusting openness of heart (cf. *Dei Verbum*, n. 25). If it is effectively promoted, this practice will bring to the Church—I am convinced of it—a new spiritual springtime.

As a strong point of biblical ministry, "lectio divina" should therefore be increasingly encouraged, also through the use of new methods, carefully thought through and in step with the times. It should never be forgotten that the Word of God is a lamp for our feet and a light for our path (cf. Psalm 119 [118]: 105).[54]

---

[53] John Paul II, *Novo Millennio Ineunte* (January 6, 2001), no. 39.

[54] Benedict XVI, address to participants in the international congress to commemorate the fortieth anniversary of *Dei Verbum*, Castel Gandolfo, September 16, 2005.

In his encyclical, *Evangelii Gaudium*, Pope Francis further promoted lectio divina, detailing the living encounter we can experience as well as possible temptations that arise when approaching God's Word through this method:

There is one particular way of listening to what the Lord wishes to tell us in His Word and of letting ourselves be transformed by the Spirit. It is what we call lectio divina. It consists of reading God's Word in a moment of prayer and allowing it to enlighten and renew us....

In the presence of God, during a recollected reading of the text, it is good to ask, for example: "Lord, what does this text say to me? What is it about my life that you want to change by this text? What troubles me about this text? Why am I not interested in this?"

Or perhaps: "What do I find pleasant in this text? What is it about this word that moves me? What attracts me? Why does it attract me?"

When we make an effort to listen to the Lord, temptations usually arise. One of them is simply to feel troubled or burdened, and to turn away.

Another common temptation is to think about what the text means for other people, and so avoid applying it to our own life. It can also happen that we look for excuses to water down the clear meaning of the text. Or we can wonder if God is demanding too much of us, asking for a decision which we are not yet prepared to make.

This leads many people to stop taking pleasure in the encounter with God's Word; but this would mean forgetting that no one is more patient than God our Father, that no one is more understanding and willing to wait.

He always invites us to take a step forward, but does not demand a full response if we are not yet ready. He simply asks that we sincerely look at our life and present ourselves honestly before Him, and that we be willing to continue to grow, asking from Him what we ourselves cannot as yet achieve.[55]

With a spiritual reading program, our goal is to be guided every step of the way by the Holy Spirit. The wonderful thing about lectio divina is the very involvement of the living, breathing Holy Spirit in our reading. In lectio divina, we give Him permission to speak to us, to guide us, to help us grow.

How to Use Lectio Divina

Entire books have been written about lectio divina. But for the purposes of this book, we will focus on the method itself, with little commentary. Much of what I relate here was taken from Dan Burke's book *Into the Deep: Finding Peace through Prayer*.[56] Please read his great book for a more in-depth look at this method of prayer.

Into the Deep relies heavily on tradition but reveals a simple, memorable, powerful five-step approach to praying with Scripture:

Read (*Lectio*)

First, select a passage from the text. On five days each week, if you follow the schedule in part 3, you will have assigned chapters, from which you can choose any portion on which to reflect. You needn't use the entire passage. In fact, you might reap more fruit by selecting a bite-size portion on which to reflect for this divine conversation.

Next begin to read the passage very *slowly* and gently — vocally (out loud) is always best, seeking to absorb the words themselves

---

[55] Francis, apostolic exhortation *Evangelii Gaudium* (*The Joy of the Gospel*), November 24, 2013, nos. 152-153.

[56] Dan Burke, *Into the Deep: Finding Peace through Prayer* (North Palm Beach, FL: Beacon Publishing, 2016), pp. 43-55.

along with any related ideas and images that surface from each word. Reading aloud is best because it stimulates your senses and your body in general (your vocal cords, your hearing, your mouth) and thus helps you to focus on God and better avoid distractions. It also helps you to slow down and increase mental engagement.

When a particular passage or word strikes you, pause to consider it more fully. As you pause, you will then naturally move into the reflecting step. If you don't seem to progress in the way suggested by the method, simply continue reading slowly and even re-read the passage.

As a general rule, each selected short portion of Scripture (as short as possible) should be read aloud slowly three times before you move on to the next section. Each of us moves at our own pace, however. The goal is not to mechanically execute the method, but to honor and seek God.

This first step of reading slowly cannot be overemphasized. When you read at your natural or normal pace, you are reading for information. But this prayerful reading is meant to help you encounter Jesus, listen to His voice, and follow His leading. If you read at the normal pace, you might miss the quiet call of God to venture into deeper waters.

Note. At the end of this chapter you will find suggested resources to help you understand the meaning of particular passages from the perspective of the writer, as well as important ideas and concepts in the text. Which supplement you use — or whether you choose to use one at all — may depend on the amount of time you have available.

Reflect (*Meditatio*)

In this second step, you engage with the details, words, places, visual images, attitudes, and insights of the passage, seeking to fully absorb and understand it, and then to apply it to your own life.

Gently and peacefully ponder what you have read, visualizing it and listening carefully for the Holy Spirit's prompting or guidance. Look for the deeper spiritual meaning of the words as you place yourself in a Gospel scene as one of the participants, or simply hear God speaking directly to you as you read the words.

What does it mean to place yourself in the Gospel scene? Use your imagination to see yourself as a particular person in the setting or as part of the crowd surrounding the scene. For instance, you might see yourself as the Samaritan woman at the well who meets and talks with Jesus to the astonishment of His disciples in the fourth chapter of St. John's Gospel. You might put yourself in the place of the prodigal son in the fifteenth chapter of St. Luke's Gospel. You might consider the temperature, the movement of the wind, the clothing of the people, the dust, the smell, the heat, and the look of the surrounding elements. The more you can slow down to consider these things, the more you will be able to enter into the passage and engage with the life-changing truths presented, and the more you will *discover* about yourself and about God's love and calling for you.

Regardless of the passages you chose, don't rack your brain to understand or exert extreme intellectual effort as you reflect. Simply engage and allow the words and related images to penetrate your heart and mind, and follow wherever God leads you through the text.

It is important to avoid a scientific or excessively intellectual examination of Scripture as if you were preparing to teach a course or explain it to someone else. Instead your goal is to listen carefully for God's leading. The prayerful understanding you seek should only go as deep as is necessary to keep your attention on the person and work of Christ as He engaged those around Him and as He desires to engage you.

To slow the process down and avoid slipping into the habit of reading at your normal pace, it can be helpful to briefly pause after each word before going on to the next one. As you do this, you will break out of your normal reading pattern, and you will make room for silence and careful listening. Your goal is to disrupt the normal, frantic pace of life in order to be attentive to God, as you would with your most intimate companion.

As you begin to gently respond to or converse with God about your encounter with Him, you'll be ready to move into the next step.

Respond (*Oratio*)

As you are drawn into a particular passage, begin to converse with God about what you are reading, and seek to respond with your heart. Remember, God has revealed Himself as person. In the Gospels He revealed Himself in and through His Son who lived and died as a full expression of His humanity and His love for you.

Thus, your conversation should be as natural as it is with someone you deeply love, respect, and desire to know better. In whatever manner you are led, based on what you have reflected on or what comes to mind as a result of your prayerful reading, you can ask for forgiveness, you can thank Him and praise Him, or you can ask Him for the grace to be changed by what you have read. You can ask Him to help you more fully realize what He wants you to be, and you can ask for his help in applying His moral, spiritual, or practical guidance to your life.

As you engage with Him, God may choose to call you to go deeper; you might become lost in a heavenly dialogue with Him that moves beyond words. For those of us who tend to be very talkative in life and prayer, it might be important here to minimize our own words and be attentive to Christ and His movements in our soul rather than focused on what we want to say. From here you may then find yourself being drawn by God into the next step on this ladder to the heart of God, *resting*.

Rest (*Contemplatio*)

Allow yourself to become absorbed in God's words as He invites you into a deeper kind of prayer, one that will bring you into His presence in ways that purely mental exercises could never achieve. You may not experience this kind of absorption as you initially explore this kind of prayer. It can take time to get familiar enough with the method so that it fades into the background and this approach becomes a normal expression of your heart. Regardless, God will give you exactly what you need, even if it is not what you desire or expect.

If you give yourself to God in this way He will satisfy your ultimate thirst, your deepest needs, as the Holy Spirit prays with you, in you, and through you. Sometimes you'll be able to recognize this work in your heart; sometimes it will merely be a matter of faith that God is with you, imparting His life-changing grace to you. However, you can always be sure He is at work within you as you seek Him in prayer. He has promised that His Word "never returns void" (Isaiah 55:11), and as St. Paul says, "Faith comes from hearing the word of God" (Romans 10:17).

Given that this phase of prayer is not always tangibly sensed, be careful to manage your expectations. In fact, for those who are more advanced in the interior life, it may be a time of dryness and a dark silence or a simple place of wordless, imageless peace. No matter what, we know by faith that God is true to His word. If you seek Him, you will find Him, even if He is found in ways that are difficult to understand or very different than you anticipated.

Dr. Tim Gray tells us:

In terms of effort, contemplation is as different from the first three stages as an elevator is to a ladder. In the labor of lectio-meditatio-oratio we toil for a harvest; in contemplation the Master of prayer comes to us and serves us, giving the grace of contemplation as pure gift. The first three stages are active, the last passive. In the first three we, like farmhands, take up a task, while in contemplation we are taken up ... by love.

Spiritual writers compare meditation to rowing a sailboat and contemplation to sailing, carried on by the wind of the Spirit. The first three steps up Jacob's ladder require arduous effort, whereas the last rung gives rest and repose.[57]

According to Dr. Gray, this step takes time to master. Just as an athlete trains to reach the top of a mountain, we are climbing a spiritual mountain and as such must exercise patience and perseverance to reach the summit.

Resolve (*Actio*)

This is where you take *action*. What virtue were you going to strengthen? How might that best be done? How can you take steps to eradicate that vice and replace it with its corresponding virtue? Is God asking that you spend more time with Him? That you get a handle on your materialism? Does He want you to hang up the vestiges of your pride and pursue humility with a vengeance? Whatever it is, take time to figure out some steps you can take in the right direction, and begin to take them. This final step will help you avoid a dangerous trap in the spiritual life: encountering God and doing nothing in response. One of the great spiritual masters of the Church said this about how we should respond when God reveals something to us in our time of prayer:

When you rise from meditation, remember the resolutions you have made, and, as occasion presents itself, carefully reduce them to practice that very day. This is the great fruit of meditation, without which it is not only unprofitable, but frequently hurtful: for virtues meditated upon, and not practiced

---

[57] Tim Gray, *Praying Scripture for a Change: An Introduction to Lectio Divina* (West Chester, PA: Ascension, 2008), p. 100.

often puff up the spirit, and make us imagine ourselves to be
such as we have resolved to be. This, doubtless, would be true
if our resolutions were strong and solid; but how can they be
really such, but rather vain and dangerous, if not reduced
to practice? We must, therefore, by all means, endeavor to
practice them, and seek every occasion, little or great, to
put them into execution. For example: if I have resolved, by
mildness, to become reconciled with such as offend me, I will
seek this very day an opportunity to meet them, and kindly
salute them; or, if I should not meet them, at least speak well
of them, and pray to God for them.[58]

Each time you sit down with Sacred Scripture, spend some time using
this method of prayer. You'll be amazed at how life-giving this process
can be, as God guides you toward greater union with Him.

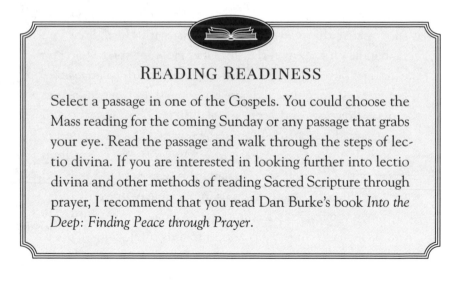

READING READINESS

Select a passage in one of the Gospels. You could choose the
Mass reading for the coming Sunday or any passage that grabs
your eye. Read the passage and walk through the steps of lectio divina. If you are interested in looking further into lectio
divina and other methods of reading Sacred Scripture through
prayer, I recommend that you read Dan Burke's book *Into the
Deep: Finding Peace through Prayer.*

---

[58] Francis de Sales, *An Introduction to the Devout Life* (Dublin: M.H. Gill
and Son, 1885), pp. 56-57.

Resources

Here are some resources I've used for guidance and instruction on reading and understanding the Bible with the mind of the Church:

The Bible Timeline: Story of Salvation (*Great Adventure* Bible Study Series) by Jeff Cavins, produced by Ascension Press

The Ignatius Catholic Study Bible by Scott Hahn and Curtis Mitch

The Navarre Bible (available in the Old Testament and the New Testament or in expanded form, with seven Old Testament and twelve New Testament volumes)

Introduction to the Bible by Fr. John Laux

A Practical Commentary on Holy Scripture by Bishop Frederick Justus Knecht, D.D.

Renowned biblical scholar and convert to the Catholic Church Scott Hahn has made it his life's work to help us to better understand the Bible. His St. Paul Center for Biblical Theology offers independent online Bible studies at no cost. Visit the center's website for other resources as well (https://stpaulcenter.com/). Scott Hahn also has an extensive list of resources recommended for Bible study available at Scotthahn.com/tools-for-bible-study.html.

Chapter 8

READING THE *CATECHISM OF THE CATHOLIC CHURCH*

Sacred tradition, Sacred Scripture and the teaching authority of
the Church, in accord with God's most wise design, are so linked
and joined together that one cannot stand without the others, and
that all together and each in its own way under the action of the
one Holy Spirit contribute effectively to the salvation of souls.

— *DEI VERBUM* 10

Although most people recognize that Sacred Scripture is essential to our
relationship with God, many regard the *Catechism of the Catholic Church* as
mere reference material for instruction or understanding of various doctrinal issues. But the *Catechism* is where Sacred Scripture and Sacred Tradition
meet. Archbishop Fulton Sheen referred to the importance of tradition:

Never once did Our Lord tell these witnesses of His to write. He
Himself only wrote once in His Life, and that was on the sand.
But He did tell them to preach in His Name and to be witnesses
to Him to the ends of the earth, until the consummation of
time. Hence those who take this or that text out of the Bible to
prove something are isolating it from the historical atmosphere

in which it arose, and from the word of mouth which passed Christ's truth.[59]

When we set aside Church teaching, which is comprehensively taught via the *Catechism*, we neglect the summation of our Faith. It draws on Sacred Scripture, works of the saints—particularly the early Church Fathers—and Church documents among other writings to present the truth of our Faith in all its beauty and fullness. The *Catechism* was developed by bishops throughout the world, in coordination with Pope Saint John Paul II, who says in its opening pages:

> The project was the object of extensive consultation among all Catholic Bishops, their Episcopal Conferences or Synods, and of theological and catechetical institutes. As a whole, it received a broadly favorable acceptance on the part of the Episcopate. It can be said that this Catechism is the result of the collaboration of the whole Episcopate of the Catholic Church, who generously accepted my invitation to share responsibility for an enterprise which directly concerns the life of the Church. This response elicits in me a deep feeling of joy, because the harmony of so many voices truly expresses what could be called a "symphony" of the faith. The achievement of this Catechism thus reflects the collegial nature of the Episcopate; it testifies to the Church's catholicity.

As I mentioned, it was my desire to read and understand the *Catechism* that inspired this spiritual-reading program. Because the program is organized around the pillars of the *Catechism*, we can ruminate on a paragraph or two of the *Catechism* each day and supplement that material with the wisdom of the Fathers of the Church and other great spiritual writers of the last two thousand years. And by reading the *Catechism*—even little by little—we can completely digest, in a concise form, the systematically

---

[59] Archbishop Fulton J. Sheen, *The World's First Love* (Garden City, NY: Doubleday, 1956), p 45.

organized teachings of the Catholic Church. That is no minor thing. As Catholics, it is incumbent upon us to understand the teaching of the Church. Our learning does not end when we are confirmed. We must be lifelong learners if we have any desire to pass our Faith along to the next generation of Catholics. The question *why* is one we must be able to answer if we are to influence those around us. Frank Sheed explains in his *Theology for Beginners*:

> The most obvious fact of our day is that we are surrounded by millions who are starved of food that Christ Our Lord wanted them to have — they are getting too small a ration of truth, and of the Eucharist there is no ration at all. We regret their starvation, of course, but we do not lose any sleep over it, which raises the question of whether we really appreciate the food we ourselves get from the Church. We should not take it so calmly if their starvation were bodily, for we do know the value of the bread that perishes.[60]

If we fail to comprehend the basic tenets of our Faith, how can we possibly share them with our neighbor, whom we are called to love completely? What kind of love allows another to starve?

According to the United States Conference of Catholic Bishops in their *Pastoral Plan for Adult Faith Formation in the United States*, "The gift of the *Catechism of the Catholic Church* is an indispensable resource in our time for helping adults become stronger in their relationship with God and grow in their knowledge of the Faith" (no. 31). We must be able to articulate our Faith before we can answer Saint Peter's call: "Always be prepared to make a defense to any one who calls you to account for the hope that is in you" (1 Pet. 3:15). That is our call: to read the *Catechism* for ourselves and for the sake of our brethren.

Frank Sheed offers a final comment on our obligation to understand and share our Faith:

---

[60] Sheed, *Theology for Beginners*, 6.

But it is not only for their sake. For our own sake too, for it is not good for us, or our children, to be the sane minority in a society that is losing contact with God.[61]

READING READINESS

If you don't own a copy of the *Catechism of the Catholic Church*, it would be worthwhile to invest in one. It is also available online. If you do have a copy, read Pope John Paul II's apostolic constitution *Fidei Depositum*, which serves as an introduction to the *Catechism*. Then take some time to flip through the *Catechism*, reviewing the four pillars of the Faith. If you haven't read the *Catechism* by section before, glance at its format; notice how the paragraphs are organized, including the brief summary paragraphs at the end of each section. In the reading program provided in part 3 of this book, you'll notice that often you will read these summary paragraphs in one sitting, while in the normal course of assignments, you will only read one or two paragraphs per day.

A Little Aside on *Sola Scriptura*

As a former Protestant, I had always known that the Bible was important. I can't say that I ever read much of it, as I wasn't particularly active in my faith when I was young; but I did attend

---

[61] Ibid.

vacation Bible school once or twice. I pretty much looked forward to hanging out with friends and doing crafts for a week, but I am eternally grateful for the focus and time spent on John 3:16. My attendance and attention span were pretty weak, but I would have had to be catatonic not to learn that verse.

In those days, the term *sola Scriptura* (Scripture alone) wasn't used on elementary-school day-campers, but I do remember that the Bible was supposed to be something like the be-all and end-all of what little religion I had back then. I first learned the term *sola Scriptura* many years later while reading Scott and Kimberly Hahn's *Rome Sweet Home*. From Scott Hahn I learned that the Bible alone was not the key to understanding our call as Christians. Rather, Christ endowed the *apostles* with His message and directed *them* to spread the gospel to the ends of the earth (see Acts 1:8). At that time, there was not even a Gospel in print, and Christ never directed the apostles to record one. When Saint Paul started writing his letters around AD 50, nearly two decades after the death of Christ, there were no printing presses, and the inspired documents were not widely distributed. Most scholars agree that Mark's was the first Gospel written, around the year 70, nearly forty years after the Resurrection. At that time, many texts not included in the final canon were being distributed. Eventually, the sacred books were distinguished from them by the authority of the early bishops, in communion with the pope, at the Councils of Hippo (393) and Carthage (397).

Sometimes we think the Bible just dropped out of the sky like manna from heaven. But those who don't think about where it actually came from do themselves a disservice. A great book on the origin of the Bible is *Where We Got the Bible* by Henry Graham, a former Presbyterian minister from Scotland who researched the authority of the Catholic Church and ultimately converted, becoming a Catholic priest. Also see the booklet *Scripture Alone? 21 Reasons to Reject Sola Scriptura*, by Joel Peters.

Chapter 9

READING THE WISDOM OF THE AGES

Have always before you some good and pious book, and
read a little in it each day with devotion, as if you were
reading letters which the saints had sent you from Heaven,
to show you the way and encourage you to follow it.

— SAINT FRANCIS DE SALES, *INTRODUCTION TO THE DEVOUT LIFE*

Throughout the history of the Catholic Church, great writing has served to encourage, illuminate, advise, lead, and teach the Faithful. Whether it's a how-to, such as Venerable Louis of Granada's *Sinner's Guide*; a magisterial document, such as Pope Paul VI's *Humanae Vitae*; an autobiography, such as Saint Thérèse of Lisieux's *Story of a Soul*; or even an excellent novel, such as Evelyn Waugh's *Brideshead Revisited*, a great Catholic book can provide much enlightenment.

Saint Thérèse eloquently describes the impact of high quality spiritual books on her life:

My spiritual life up to now had been nourished by the "fine flour" of *The Imitation* and it was the only book which did me any good, because I had not yet discovered the hidden treasures of the Gospels. Much to everybody's amusement, I always used to have it with me, and my aunt would often open it at random and make me say by heart the first chapter she came to.

At fourteen my thirst for knowledge had become so great that God thought it was time to season the "fine flour" with the honey and oil of Fr. Arminjon's conferences on The End of This World and the Mysteries of the World to Come. As I read, I experienced that joy which the world cannot give, something of what God has prepared for those who love Him.[62]

We could read all day every day for the rest of our lives and not exhaust all the wonderful works that are available for our instruction and edification. Yet the number of choices can leave us overwhelmed. How do we choose?

First, consider a topic on which you'd like to focus. I have organized this program around the pillars of the Faith. Are you interested in learning more about any particular pillar in general: what we believe, the liturgy, the sacraments, how to live our life in Christ, or prayer? Or, within a pillar you can choose a particular focus. For example, within the section of the Catechism that teaches about liturgy and the sacraments, you could focus on the sacrament of Marriage. There are many great books on that topic, including Three to Get Married by Archbishop Fulton J. Sheen, Covenanted Happiness by Cormac Burke, Marriage: The Mystery of Faithful Love by Dietrich von Hildebrand, Love and Responsibility by Karol Wojtyła, and many others. We could easily spend an entire year deepening our knowledge and understanding of this one sacrament.

Choosing Good Books

Sure, you say. I'd like to collect some great titles under any particular topic, but how can I tell a good book from one that is less than desirable? After all, we are not looking for cafeteria-style reading material. We are looking for good spiritual food with a lot of meat. Well, you needn't look further than the appendices to find some great resources.

---

[62] The Story of a Soul, chap. 5.

You can also find recommended reading lists online and in other books — check out the EWTN Catalogue or the Catholic Answers website. Father John Hardon's excellent *Catholic Lifetime Reading Plan* lists books by 104 authors, ranking the top works of each. This book may be out of print, but used copies are readily available.

But what if you don't get a book from a source you trust? What if your sister-in-law hands you something she thought was great, but you aren't quite sure whether it will lead you astray?

The most important consideration when choosing a book to read is whether its contents align with the teaching of the Magisterium of the Catholic Church — that is, the teaching office of the Church, which consists of the bishops in union with the pope. A *nihil obstat, imprimatur*, or *imprimi potest*, which can be found on a book's copyright page, indicates that the book does not profess anything that conflicts with Catholic teaching. Here is the meaning of each:

+ *Nihil obstat*: The stamp of "nihil obstat" means that "nothing stands in the way" of a book's being printed. The nihil obstat is issued by a diocese's censor, to whom the book is submitted by the author. The censor is appointed by the local bishop or by an episcopal conference to examine a book's claims regarding faith and morals to determine whether that content is in alignment with the Church's Magisterium.

+ *Imprimatur*: Once an author receives a nihil obstat, he will send his book to his bishop for further examination. If the bishop finds nothing in conflict with Church teaching, he will give the book his imprimatur, meaning "Let it be printed."

+ *Imprimi potest*: Books written by members of religious orders receive an additional stamp. Before being submitted to a censor, these books are sent to the author's religious superior. If the superior finds nothing that should keep the book from being printed, he will give it a stamp of "Imprimi potest," which means "It can be printed."

A book may carry this additional caveat: "The 'Nihil Obstat' and 'Imprimatur' are official declarations that a book or pamphlet is free of doctrinal or moral error. No implication is contained therein that those who have granted the Nihil Obstat and the Imprimatur agree with the content, opinions, or statements expressed."[63] In other words, these declarations do not guarantee that everything in a text is true and they are not an official endorsement of a work by the Church. They assert only that the work does not posit false Catholic teaching.[64]

Not all good books on theology contain a nihil obstat or an imprimatur, nor are they required to have one. Years ago, I heard Frank Sheed's *Theology and Sanity* cited often on Catholic Answers, so I decided to pick up a copy. I was shocked to find no sign of a nihil obstat or an imprimatur; no verification whatsoever that it was a free from doctrinal error. Yet I had read somewhere that any "good" Catholic book would contain an imprimatur, so I called Catholic Answers and asked about it. Jimmy Aiken and host Patrick Coffin took the call. They both assured me that, yes, *Theology and Sanity* is an excellent book, and no, I needn't be concerned that it might lead me astray. So apparently not all good books contain these stamps.

In recent years, the timeline for having a censor and a bishop review a book has become increasingly long, as parish resources have been depleted, while the publication of books has risen exponentially. Many

---

[63] "'Imprimi Potest,' 'Nihil Obstat,' and 'Imprimature,'" Fish Eaters, http://www.fisheaters.com/imprimatur.html.

[64] In case you desire to look into the matter further, *The Code of Canon Law* addresses the publication of books for Catholic use, under "Catholic education," in the section "Instruments of Social Communication and Books in Particular" (canons 822-832). For our purposes, however, it is good to know that books of Sacred Scripture are required to have the approval of the Apostolic See or the conference of bishops with respect to content and translation before they can be published (can. 825 §1).

Also, prayer books for public or private use, as well as catechetical books and other books intended to instruct the faithful at the elementary, middle, or high school levels must obtain approval by the proper ecclesial authority (can. 826 §3; can. 827 §§1-2).

authors will go ahead and publish without these seals rather than delay publication inordinately.

And last but not least, we cannot even presume the dependability of a specific author simply because he has written something valuable in the past. For example, while Thomas Merton is widely hailed for his autobiography, *The Seven Storey Mountain*, his later works drifted from the teaching of the Church and are not recommended reading for Catholics.

So what to do?

I suppose all these caveats leave us right back where we started: obtain suggestions for great reading only from reputable sources.

Church Documents

In addition to books, there are other great works that can help us to live out Faith more fully, such as encyclicals and other Church documents. Works like *Humanae Vitae* are life changing and should not be overlooked. I was greatly edified by reading Saint John Paul II's encyclical *Laborem Exercens* (Through work), which taught me how work unites us to God, as well as the spiritual value God places on work and its place in our sanctification. My favorite encyclical has to be John Paul II's *Familiaris Consortio*. This poignant letter on the role of the Christian family in the modern world moved me to tears with its loving juxtaposition of God's plan for the family with the world we live in today.

Documents written by popes or collegially through the bishops (like the *Catechism*) are meant to guide us on our journey to eternal life with God in heaven, and so they should definitely be included in our spiritual reading.

READING READINESS

Prayerfully consider in which areas our Lord most wants you to grow. Then look through the list of books included in "The Program" in part 3 of this book. Have you read any of them? Have you been wanting to read any of them or wanting to read them again? Look over the books listed in the five-year program, which begins on page 123. You'll notice each of these books appears on at least one of the lists in the appendices. Begin to familiarize yourself with these lists and to discern whether you feel called to a one-, three-, or five-year program.

Chapter 10

STRUCTURING YOUR READING TIME

Need we be astonished at the fidelity with which the Saints have put
their maxims into practice? I defy any one to find even one of them
who did not employ his time to the best advantage. Are not holiness
and the proper employment of time intimately related, then?

REVEREND P. LEJEUNE, *COUNSELS OF
PERFECTION FOR CHRISTIAN MOTHERS*

We've talked about how to approach spiritual reading from a mental
perspective—reading for knowledge of the heart as well as for the head.
But there are practical, hands-on considerations for reading as well.

Schedule Time to Read

I've found that reading in the morning is more productive than reading
in the evening. There are several reasons for this:

In the morning, my mind is less distracted by events of the day, or
things that must be done tomorrow. First thing in the morning, before
showers and business, my mind is fresh and at ease.

Other than e-mail and Facebook, which I can control, there are very
few distractions, provided I wake early enough to avoid the chaos of the
morning rush in our house each day.

By the time I've finished my reading, I have already braced my heart and soul against concerns of this world and placed them squarely on the one thing that matters: the salvation of my soul, and the souls of my family. Reading in the morning helps me to face the challenges of this world with a different attitude, one that is less concerned about the immediate threat and more concerned with eternity.

I can meditate throughout the day on what I've read. Whether during prayer time or while I'm making dinner, words come to mind and I find myself thinking about the message God intends me to store in my heart, as well as how I can apply it to my life that day. This is not true when I read at night. Although I may go to sleep fresh with ideas, I've found they tend to evaporate with my dreams, completely lost as the alarm rings and I'm off to shower, feed kids, organize schedules, and begin my daily chores.

Morning prayer and meditation comes highly recommended from the greatest authorities. According to Saint Francis de Sales:

> Holy Scripture, the example of the Saints and our natural reason, all commend the morning as the best and most profitable part of the day. Our Blessed Lord Himself is called the Rising Sun and His Mother the Morning Star. I recommend you, therefore, go to rest early at night so that you may be awake and rise early in the morning, which is the pleasantest and the least cumbered time of the day; the very birds call us to awaken to the praise of God; and early rising is profitable both for health and holiness.[65]

All that said, if you absolutely cannot read in the morning, please do not use that as an excuse not to read. I know it can be tough to find time in the morning. For many years, no matter how early or quietly I woke, at least one of my children woke with me. My youngest child is now five years old, and I have finally found that I can beat the rush, provided I get going by around 6:00. (If you are me a few years ago, you can do only

---

[65] Saint Francis de Sales, *Introduction to the Devout Life* 3, 23.

what you can do. And know that there will be time for early-morning reading again.)

Father Larry Richards, founder of The Reason for Our Hope Foundation, often says, "Bible before breakfast; Bible before bed." Wise advice if you find yourself short on time in the morning. Either split up your reading, so that you can both open and close your eyes to a day with our Lord in your thoughts, or just commit to reading at night.

Despite the challenges I mentioned above, there are things you can do to allow for meditation on evening reading the following day. If you keep a spiritual-reading journal (discussion on that coming up), jot down a few notes as you read in the evening. Pay special attention to inspiration that you would like to ponder, or steps you plan to take to amend your life. When you wake in the morning, take a few moments to recap last night's high points from your journal. This will get the juices flowing and allow you throughout the day to make better use of what you've read. Regardless of how you do it, please remember that it is *absolutely, hands down, without a doubt* better to read at night than not to read at all.

Choose a Peaceful Place

Find a place in your home that will allow for quiet, prayerful reading. Prayerful reading cannot be found at my usual perch. From a favorite seat at our kitchen counter, I do just about everything. From there I can see the television, reach any necessary snacks and drinks without too much trouble, spread out with plenty of counter space and manage kids in every direction because I can pretty much see the entire first floor. This is where I pay our bills, plan our weekly meals and make our grocery lists, edit posts, help kids with school work, and make plans with my husband. For all the reasons mentioned above, it is *not* where I do my spiritual reading. Instead, I've found that a chair in my bedroom is the best place to read. It is quiet and away from all the bustle in the house. Other than during my spiritual-reading time, I don't think that chair even gets used. This provides an added benefit, because I can keep my reading schedule, book, and spiritual-reading journal there with little concern that anyone will move them, write on them, manipulate them, or separate them (I cannot say the same about items I leave in the kitchen).

For you, reading may be most productive in your office, your living room, your back porch, or even your kitchen. Choose a spot that is comfortable, but sans distractions. Otherwise, you'll find the distractions will too easily steal your focus. Next thing you know, your spiritual reading will take a backseat to checking e-mail and mediating squabbles between kids.

Another consideration when deciding where to do your reading is aesthetics. Just as we are inspired by the beautiful stained-glass windows, statues, and artwork we find in a church, we can also be inspired by the environment in which we read. Once you choose a location, consider placing something inspirational there to remind you of why you are there. It doesn't matter how small your space is. Whether with artwork, a statue, or even an inspirational quote from a saint (whether embossed in gold or neatly written on a Post-it note), you can make your space a personal respite from the world, a space that guides your heart and mind to heaven throughout your prayer and reading time.

One final suggestion—a prayerful atmosphere can always be enhanced with a candle. Candles remind us of holiness. They represent for us the Light of the World. They are also a reminder of our Baptism, when we received the Source of all light, who guides us on our spiritual journey. Likewise, they are a reminder of Easter, when we light the Paschal candle, symbolizing the Eternal Light, the Light of our salvation, the guiding light that shines amid the darkness of the world. Light a candle, and you will be amazed at the change of atmosphere. (On a practical level, a candle is not a substitute for adequate lighting by which to read. For the purposes of spiritual reading, a candle is for atmosphere, not utility.)

Invoke the Holy Spirit

The Holy Spirit has the means to transform our souls completely, to enable them to be open to, receive, and act upon the wisdom of God. We are poor and blind—we need the Holy Spirit to guide us from above. So as you prepare to read each day, begin with a prayer asking the Holy Spirit to enlighten you, to open your heart and your mind to the message God wants you to hear.

This is the prayer I've often used to prepare my heart to hear God's voice:

> Come, Holy Spirit,
> Fill the hearts of the faithful, and enkindle in them the
>   fire of Your love.
> Send forth Your Spirit and they shall be created, and You
>   shall renew the face of the earth.
> God, who has taught the hearts of the faithful by the
> light of the Holy Spirit, grant us in the same spirit to
> be truly wise, and ever to rejoice in His consolation.
> Through Jesus Christ, our Lord. Amen.

Whether you use this prayer or speak directly from your heart with your own invocation, or both, what matters is that you place yourself in God's presence and begin your time by invoking the Holy Spirit, asking Him to guide you as you read.

Keep a Spiritual Reading Journal

So much has been made of journaling in recent years that many of us have begun to dispense with the idea as yet one more way for a "me, me" culture to express itself. Sadly, the advent of the *blog* has made journaling a very public endeavor. Those who bare their souls for all to see are often considered either a little too full of themselves or in need of a little too much attention, to say the least. Many of the faithful have dispensed with the idea of journaling because journals have come to be seen as the activity of the ego driven.

But perhaps you should take another look. Journaling has been around a lot longer than this season of self-expression! Many of the saints and other notable Catholics throughout history kept journals. Thank goodness for us, some have even been preserved and made public, so that we might learn from the experiences of those who have gone before us. Two of my absolute favorites are *The Secret Diary of Elisabeth Leseur* and *The Journal of a Soul* by Saint John XXIII.

Elisabeth Leseur and Pope John XXIII used their journals as a way to hold themselves accountable in their journey through this world. They set goals, made promises, offered prayers, and even made to-do lists.

Here are some reasons to keep a spiritual journal:

+ *A recording of prayers.* The most important purpose for keeping a spiritual journal is to record our personal conversation with our Lord. Rereading what we've written about those intimate moments with our Greatest Love can be very comforting. As we look back at our journal through the years, we can see our struggles, our successes, our sin, and our love. By keeping a record of our conversation, we can see how we've grown through the years. We can evaluate where God has been working in our lives and where we continue to struggle, and we can recognize our misplaced priorities, our stumbles along the road to sanctity, and our perseverance along the way.

+ *A record of answers to our prayer.* Keeping a spiritual journal can have an amazing effect on our faith, as we watch God at work in our lives from day to day, and year to year.

+ *Accountability.* Keeping a journal helps us follow through on our promises. Early in his journal, Pope John XXIII made daily, weekly, monthly, and annual commitments. Throughout his life, he reread those pledges to make sure he was following them. If he wasn't, he would make adjustments in his schedule and try again. As you read through his journal, you can both see and feel the gradual transformation of this man in Christ. The book offers much hope to those of us who continue to fall day after day.

Keeping a journal is a very personal experience. This experience is about recording your most secret thoughts, prayers, and resolutions.

Technically, there is no one way to do it. But there are a few things to consider when getting started:

+ *Consistency is not important.* Some days you might not write at all. On other days, you may find yourself pouring your heart out to God through the written word. On some days you may make resolutions for the coming weeks or months, in an effort to effect the changes suggested by your reading. On other days, you may choose to check on past entries in order to gauge your progress.

+ *Make your journal a love letter.* It is not a critical practice, but I always begin every entry with "Dear Lord" to remind myself that I am in prayer and that this is not a diary or a conversation with myself; rather, it is a conversation with God, who longs for me to pour out my deepest thoughts, greatest struggles, and most heartfelt thanksgiving for all His blessings in my life.

+ *Keep your journal available as you read.* While you are reading, make note of any points you'd like to remember or explore further. Journal any thoughts or prayers stimulated by your reading each day. Ask yourself questions so that you can apply what you are reading to your everyday life. You may record those questions, along with resolutions as you progress. You may write in complete sentences or just jot down notes, as long as you will be able to understand them later upon review. I often find myself using a shorthand that only I understand. For example, when reading a passage, if I really like a quote or concept, I will highlight it. Then in my journal, under the appropriate date, I will note the book, page number and paragraph. Then I might write a note about why that particular point or passage was important to me. How simple or complicated your entries are is up to you. Just make sure you use your journal as a tool in your spiritual journey. You'll be grateful for it.

+ *What you write is unique to you.* The journals of Saint John XXIII and Elisabeth Leseur are each amazing in their own right, but very different from each other. John XXIII kept his journal from the time he was a seminarian through his papacy—from 1895 until shortly before his death in 1962! Elisabeth's journal spans only about fifteen years. Both record activities, resolutions, thoughts, prayers, and meditations, but each has a very personal feel. These two individuals were beautiful but unique souls, and both qualities are reflected on every page of each journal. Your journal should reflect your own personality and as such will illustrate a spiritual journey that is unique to you.

✦ *Allow yourself to develop a routine over time.* Gradually, you'll find yourself writing before, during, or after your reading. You may write between readings. Regardless, you will find that you develop a habit of recording your thoughts and prayers in a way that works best for you, and you may find that your process rarely varies from day to day. That's okay. What matters is that it works for you. Routine is a wonderful thing. It helps us to keep our minds on the readings as opposed to pens, paper, and rules of writing.

Keep in mind that whatever you write in your journal is not meant for posterity. You may say whatever you'd like because this is your spiritual life. Your journal is about you and your relationship with Christ; it is not meant for other eyes. Be honest. Be real. This is not about poetic language or profound thoughts. Just be you. God knows who you are, so don't waste time and energy trying to hide yourself from Him or trying to create a "you" that you wouldn't mind sharing with others. Just keep your journal in a place where others won't read it. Sometimes private things are best kept right out in the open. I keep my journal under my spiritual books, and no one ever thinks to go through the pile!

Cherish Your Reading Time

More than anything else, enjoy this time. Bask in it. Whenever you read, wherever you read, however you read, make this entire experience about improving your relationship with your Savior. Quiet yourself. Call Him to mind. And spend this time *with Him* by cherishing His word, uncovering the Deposit of Faith He left for your sanctification, and discovering the wisdom that has been passed down through the ages. Time spent here will vastly improve every moment of your day spent elsewhere, whether that time is spent at work, at home with family, or even at Mass. Time spent in prayerful reading will remind you of who you are called to be and help you to become that person.

READING READINESS

Find a place to call your own. In other words, is there a place in your home where you can comfortably spend time in prayerful reading without interruption? Granted, if your home is anything like mine, the interruptions will come, but try to choose a location that will provide the greatest opportunity for silence and uninterrupted prayer. Personalize the space in a way that draws your mind and heart to heaven. If it helps to light a candle, then find one to preserve for your reading time. (Keep a lighter handy as well.)

Select a journal, appropriate a pen, and even find a highlighter to keep in your spiritual-reading location. These will serve you well from day to day as you make resolutions or take notes on your reading; additionally, you may find quotes or passages that you'd like to highlight for review.

Spend some practice time in your space today for quiet meditation. Sit peacefully and close your eyes, just resting in God's presence. This is the mindset we desire when we approach spiritual reading. Calm. Quiet. It is a time to separate ourselves from the world outside. Practice this before reading each day, asking God to speak to you through the words you've chosen at His behest. Finally, ask yourself: Is the place you've found conducive to this calm and prayerful spirit? Does it help raise your heart and mind to heaven? If not, now is the time to make appropriate adjustments.

PART III

PILLARS OF JOY: A COMPLETE SPIRITUAL-READING PROGRAM

Chapter 11

THE TIME FACTOR

When I created this program, I planned to repeat it every five years for the rest of my life. That is still my plan. But I must be honest: I did not complete it in five years. Periodically I set it down to pursue other reading for various purposes before coming back to the program to continue where I left off. For example, sometimes when the reading for our book club at SpiritualDirection.com was heavy and life was busy, I set my other reading aside for a week or two and focused on the spiritual reading for our online book club. But that's the great thing about this program. Because I had a plan and a checklist, I knew right where I had left off and was able to get back into my schedule with no problems.

Flexibility is exactly the point of this program. It was never intended to be a black-and-white, live-or-die regimen but rather a lifelong guide to keep us on the right track. Although I recommend the complete five-year program, remember that this is *your* faith journey, and it can certainly be completed in one year, three years, five years, or ten — whatever works best for your schedule. If you hit an overly busy time in your life, you can certainly choose to read only Scripture for a week, or only Scripture and the *Catechism*, coming back at a more peaceful time to follow up with the spiritual reading for that interval. Although it is best to read Sacred Scripture every day, it is better to make things work for you to ensure that you keep going.

Remember that you are not running a marathon. If you can spare only ten to fifteen minutes in the morning, you may choose to split the readings into two days or between morning and evening. For example, read Scripture and the *Catechism* one day, and your other spiritual work the next. This option will still allow the benefits of syntopical reading. But your topics would be covered in tandem weekly rather than daily.

The key is to remain faithful to that special one-on-one time with our Lord. By scheduling a little spiritual reading each day, you will be amazed at what you can accomplish over time.

A Note on Moving Forward

Whether you use the ready-made program here in part 3 or customize the program to fit your needs, I'm confident that if you commit to one year, you will be hesitant to stop after twelve months of faithful, prayer-filled spiritual reading. Your prayer life will be much so more rewarding, your Faith so much more a part of your everyday life, and your soul so much more at peace, that I would not be surprised if you progressed from a one-year to a three- or five-year program. I hope you began your spiritual-reading program back in the introduction by setting aside thirty minutes per day, five days per week to read this book. If so, then at this point it shouldn't be too difficult to continue holding that time sacred each day for an ongoing spiritual-reading program. If you are ready to commit to a program, I will consider our time together to have been a great success.

Let's take a brief look at the program details now. Some general notes:

At the time of this printing, all of these books are available through Amazon.com. You might also find them at stores and websites that sell Catholic books, at used bookstores, and in church libraries. I was able to find several through my public-library system.

Catechism references are usually listed by paragraph numbers. Please also read any introductory text at the beginning of new section.

Forewords and prefaces are assigned only if written by the author or if included in all known editions of the books.

·———• Five-Year Program •———·

Five years will take you through each pillar of Faith as laid out in the *Catechism of the Catholic Church*, with a full program of Sacred Scripture and a complete reading of the *Catechism*. The spiritual books selected for each year correspond with the section of the *Catechism* scheduled for that year.

If you choose this program—and I recommend that you do—just begin at the beginning. Your schedule is completely laid out for all five years. Blank lines have been added for each day so that you can complete the program again and again, adding books to the schedule in coming years. Or, if you find there is a book on the schedule that you've read and are not interested in rereading, you can use those lines to write in a substitution. Following is the layout for the five-year program:

Year 1

Sacred Scripture: Gospels, Acts of the Apostles, Letters of Paul, Gospels
Catechism: The Profession of Faith (first half)
Spiritual Reading:

> *Rome Sweet Home* by Scott and Kimberly Hahn (4 weeks)
> *A Map of Life* by Frank Sheed (3 weeks)
> *Mary the Second Eve* by John Henry Newman (1 week)
> *Scripture Alone* by Joel Peters (1 week)
> *50 Questions on the Natural Law* by Charles Rice (8 weeks)
> *Theology for Beginners* by Frank Sheed (5 weeks)
> *The Spirit of Catholicism* by Karl Adam and Justin McCann (8 weeks)
> *The Spirit and Forms of Protestantism* by Louis Bouyer (8 weeks)
> *The Great Heresies* by Hilaire Belloc (4 weeks)
> *Practical Theology* by Peter Kreeft (10 weeks)

Year 2

Sacred Scripture: Old Testament—Genesis through 1 Chronicles

Catechism: The Profession of Faith (second half)

Spiritual Reading:

Theology and Sanity by Frank Sheed (15 weeks)

Christianity for Modern Pagans by Peter Kreeft (12 weeks)

The End of the Modern World by Romano Guardini (6 weeks)

How the Reformation Happened by Hilaire Belloc (6 weeks)

Triumph: The Power and the Glory of the Catholic Church by H. W. Crocker III (12 weeks)

Year 3

Sacred Scripture: Old Testament—1 Chronicles through Song of Solomon

Catechism: The Celebration of the Christian Mystery

Spiritual Reading:

This Tremendous Lover by Eugene Boylan (7 weeks)

The Diary of a Country Priest by Georges Bernanos (5 weeks)

The Sinner's Guide by Venerable Louis of Grenada (8 weeks)

The Lord by Romano Guardini (18 weeks)

Covenanted Happiness by Cormac Burke (3 weeks)

The Betrothed by Alessandro Manzoni (11 weeks)

Year 4

Sacred Scripture: Old Testament—Wisdom through 2 Maccabees

Catechism: Life in Christ

Spiritual Reading:

Something Beautiful for God by Malcolm Muggeridge (2 weeks)

The Hidden Power of Kindness by Father Lawrence G. Lovasik (4 weeks)

The Story of a Soul by Saint Thérèse of Lisieux (4 weeks)

Spiritual Combat by Lorenzo Scupoli (4 weeks)

Journal of a Soul by Saint Pope John XXIII (8 weeks)

Trustful Surrender to Divine Providence by Father Jean Baptiste Saint-Jure (2 weeks)

The Way of Perfection by Saint Teresa of Ávila (4 weeks)

The 12 Steps to Holiness and Salvation by Saint Alphonsus Liguori (4 weeks)

The Privilege of Being a Woman by Alice von Hildebrand (2 weeks)

The Imitation of Christ by Thomas à Kempis (4 weeks)

Witness to Hope by George Weigel (14 weeks)

Year 5

Sacred Scripture: The entire New Testament

Catechism: Prayer

Spiritual Reading:

Meditations from a Simple Path by Mother Teresa (1 week)

In Silence with God by Benedict Baur (4 weeks)

Interior Freedom by Jacques Philippe (3 weeks)

Conversation with Christ by Peter Thomas Rohrbach (4 weeks)

True Devotion to the Holy Spirit by Luis M. Martinez (6 weeks)

Furrow by Saint Josemaría Escrivá (3 weeks)

Interior Castle by Saint Teresa of Ávila (4 weeks)

Difficulties in Mental Prayer by Eugene Boylan (4 weeks)

Introduction to the Devout Life by Saint Francis de Sales (10 weeks)

True Devotion to Mary by Saint Louis de Montfort (3 weeks)

The Soul of the Apostolate by Dom Jean-Baptiste Chautard (7 weeks)

Little Talks with God by Saint Catherine of Siena (3 weeks)

⸱•⸺ One-Year Program ⸺•⸱

If you are excited about the idea of a program but are a bit daunted by a five-year commitment and want find out whether this program is something you can commit to forever, begin with Year 5. If you complete Year 5 and decide that organized spiritual reading is a must for your life and you enjoy having a program that holds you accountable and keeps you on a focused track, then you will be able to flip right back to Year 1 at the end of the year and begin anew, without losing any ground on the program.

Year 5 covers the following:

Sacred Scripture: The entire New Testament

Catechism: Prayer

Spiritual Reading:

> *Meditations from a Simple Path* by Mother Teresa (1 week)
>
> *In Silence with God* by Benedict Baur (4 weeks)
>
> *Interior Freedom* by Jacques Philippe (3 weeks)
>
> *Conversation with Christ* by Peter Thomas Rohrbach (4 weeks)
>
> *True Devotion to the Holy Spirit* by Luis M. Martinez (6 weeks)
>
> *Furrow* by Saint Josemaría Escrivá (3 weeks)
>
> *Interior Castle* by Saint Teresa of Ávila (4 weeks)
>
> *Difficulties in Mental Prayer* by Eugene Boylan (4 weeks)
>
> *Introduction to the Devout Life* by Saint Francis de Sales (10 weeks)
>
> *True Devotion to Mary* by Saint Louis de Montfort (3 weeks)
>
> *The Soul of the Apostolate* by Dom Jean-Baptiste Chautard (7 weeks)
>
> *Little Talks with God* by Saint Catherine of Siena (3 weeks)

·—— Three-Year Program ——·

If you have not read the New Testament, I do not recommend the three-year program, because I agree with Frank Sheed and many others who recommend that the Gospels should be read first, followed by the letters of Paul.

The three-year plan covers the entire Old Testament in only a chapter or two per day. As the New Testament is a fulfillment of the Old, you may find that you gain fresh insight into the New Testament when you pick it up again.

As with the one-year plan, this program will allow you to read some of the best spiritual classics in an integral fashion. Yet with more time, it allows a greater array of subject matter. Over the course of three years, you will read sections in the *Catechism* as well as several spiritual books on theology, the sacraments, and the life of Christ.
Sacred Scripture: The entire Old Testament
Catechism: The Profession of Faith, the Celebration of the Christian Mystery, and Life in Christ

For Year 1, you will read Years 1 and 2 of the *Catechism* assignments in the five-year program. Begin at Year 1 and read two assignments per day; so, instead of reading two paragraphs per day, you will read about four, which is still very manageable. This will allow you to complete the section on the Profession of Faith in one year.

For Years 2 and 3, follow the *Catechism* checklists for Years 3 and 4, which cover the Celebration of the Christian Mystery and Life in Christ.

Spiritual reading: I should forewarn you that Year 1 provides a gradual introduction to theology and history. In Year 2, the books are a little more demanding. That makes this three-year option a great choice if you've been doing some spiritual reading—maybe you've read several books covered in Year 1 and are ready to dig a bit deeper.

Begin in Year 2 and follow assignments as written:

Year 2: The Profession of Faith—Part 2

Theology and Sanity by Frank Sheed (15 weeks)

Christianity for Modern Pagans by Peter Kreeft (12 weeks)

The End of the Modern World by Romano Guardini (7 weeks)

How the Reformation Happened by Hilaire Belloc (6 weeks)

Triumph: The Power and the Glory of the Catholic Church by H. W. Crocker III (12 weeks)

Year 3: The Celebration of the Christian Mystery

This Tremendous Lover by M. Eugene Boylan (7 weeks)

The Diary of a Country Priest by Georges Bernanos (5 weeks)

The Sinner's Guide by Venerable Louis of Grenada (8 weeks)

The Lord by Romano Guardini (18 weeks)

Covenanted Happiness by Corma Burke (3 weeks)

The Betrothed by Alessandro Manzoni (11 weeks)

Year 4: Life in Christ

Something Beautiful for God by Malcolm Muggeridge (2 weeks)

The Hidden Power of Kindness by Father Lawrence G. Lovasik (4 weeks)

The Story of a Soul by Saint Thérèse of Lisieux (4 weeks)

Spiritual Combat by Lorenzo Scupoli (4 weeks)

Journal of a Soul by Saint Pope John XXIII (8 weeks)

Trustful Surrender to Divine Providence by Father Jean Baptiste Saint-Jure (2 weeks)

The Way of Perfection by Saint Teresa of Ávila (4 weeks)

The 12 Steps to Holiness and Salvation by Saint Alphonsus Liguori (4 weeks)

The Privilege of Being a Woman by Alice von Hildebrand (2 weeks)

The Imitation of Christ by Thomas à Kempis (4 weeks)

Witness to Hope by George Weigel (14 weeks)

CONCLUSION

I challenge you to set aside that *other* self-help book you are reading. Whether it's about success in business or success in the home, there is a better one to be found in the great libraries of the Church. Through spiritual reading you will be a better spouse, a better parent, a better friend, colleague, or acquaintance.

For the next thirty days, renew your focus as a child of God. Set in motion those habits that are most worthy of your journey to heaven. That doesn't mean you can't read those other books again. But for thirty days, prayerfully explore your Faith through the written word. Begin your reading program today. If you find that time also allows for other books and resources, add them back in. But do not abandon your spiritual-reading time. Give it thirty days. Make it part of your daily routine. Keep a journal. Note the difference that time with our Lord makes on any given day. The more you record the benefits, the less the challenges will matter.

I hope that, beginning today, you will make spiritual reading an integral and organized part of your life, growing day by day in relationship with our Lord, for as Venerable Louis of Granada reminds us,

> So great is the light and fruit of spiritual reading that we know from experience many persons who have changed their entire lives by this means. When asked the root and cause of such a change, they responded that after reading such and such a book they resolved to amend their lives ...

So sublime are the mysteries that the Christian religion proposes to man and so powerful for moving hearts that I would not be surprised if they effected a great change in anyone who attentively considers them.[66]

As you embark on this spiritual and intellectual journey, may you find yourself at the very feet of Christ, choosing the "good portion," as Mary did (Luke 10:39-42). And as you rest at His feet, may your soul be filled with the great wisdom offered in the works you read. For the rest of your days, may the Holy Spirit use spiritual reading as a tool to mold you so that, like Saint Paul, you can say, "It is no longer I who live, but Christ who lives in me" (Gal. 2:20).

May the Holy Spirit accompany you on your journey, and may your worries lessen as your faith is strengthened along the way. As your heart is filled with His love and mercy, I pray that the light of Christ will shine forth from you for all to see. For that Light is your salvation, and the world's only hope.

---

[66] Venerable Louis of Granada, *Summa of the Christian Life*, vol. 1 (Rockford, IL: TAN Books, 1979), pp. 7-8.

— YEAR 1 —

READING LIST

Sacred Scripture: Gospels, Acts of the Apostles, Letters of Paul, Gospels
Catechism of the Catholic Church: Profession of Faith (first half)

Spiritual Reading:
+ *Rome Sweet Home* by Scott and Kimberly Hahn (4 weeks)
+ *Map of Life* by Frank Sheed (3 weeks)
+ *Mary the Second Eve* by John Henry Newman (1 week)
+ *Scripture Alone* by Joel Peters (1 week)
+ *50 Questions on the Natural Law* by Charles Rice (8 weeks)
+ *Theology for Beginners* by Frank Sheed (5 weeks)
+ *The Spirit of Catholicism* by Karl Adam and Justin McCann (8 weeks)
+ *The Spirit and Forms of Protestantism* by Louis Bouyer (8 weeks)
+ *The Great Heresies* by Hilaire Belloc (4 weeks)
+ *Practical Theology* by Peter Kreeft (10 weeks)

I remember that among the feelings with which my heart
was overflowing the most powerful of all was a great love for
the Church, for the cause of Christ, for the Pope, and a sense
of total dedication to the service of Jesus and of the Church,
and of an intention, indeed a sacred oath, of allegiance to
the Chair of St. Peter and of unwearying work for souls.

— SAINT JOHN XXIII, *JOURNAL OF A SOUL*

Year 1, Week 1

Day 1
- ☐ Matthew 1
- ☐ CCC, *Fidei Depositum* (FD), to no. 1
- ☐ *Rome Sweet Home* (RSH), preface and introduction
- ☐ _____
- ☐ _____

Day 2
- ☐ Matthew 2
- ☐ CCC, FD, no. 1
- ☐ RSH, chap. 1 (Scott)
- ☐ _____
- ☐ _____

Day 3
- ☐ Matthew 3
- ☐ CCC, FD, no. 2
- ☐ RSH, chap. 1 (Kimberly); chap. 2 (Scott)
- ☐ _____
- ☐ _____

Day 4
- ☐ Matthew 4
- ☐ CCC, FD, no. 3
- ☐ RSH, chap. 2 (Kimberly)
- ☐ _____
- ☐ _____

Day 5
- ☐ Matthew 5
- ☐ CCC 1-2
- ☐ RSH, chap. 3 (Scott)
- ☐ _____
- ☐ _____

Year 1, Week 2

Day 1
- ☐ Matthew 6
- ☐ CCC 3
- ☐ RSH, chap. 3 (Kimberly)
- ☐ _____
- ☐ _____

Day 2
- ☐ Matthew 7
- ☐ CCC 4-5
- ☐ RSH, chap. 4 (Scott)
- ☐ _____
- ☐ _____

Day 3
- ☐ Matthew 8
- ☐ CCC 6-7
- ☐ RSH, chap. 4 (Kimberly); chap. 5 (Scott) (half of section)
- ☐ _____
- ☐ _____

Day 4
- ☐ Matthew 9
- ☐ CCC 8-9
- ☐ RSH, chap. 5 (Scott) (finish section)
- ☐ _____
- ☐ _____

Day 5
- ☐ Matthew 10
- ☐ CCC 10
- ☐ RSH, chap. 5 (Kimberly)
- ☐ _____
- ☐ _____

Seek not to understand that you may believe, but
believe that you may understand.

— SAINT AUGUSTINE, TRACTATE 29, 6

Year 1, Week 3

Day 1
- ☐ Matthew 11
- ☐ CCC 11-12
- ☐ RSH, chap. 6 (Scott)
- ☐ _____
- ☐ _____

Day 2
- ☐ Matthew 12
- ☐ CCC 13-14
- ☐ RSH, chap. 6 (Kimberly)
- ☐ _____
- ☐ _____

Day 3
- ☐ Matthew 13
- ☐ CCC 15-17
- ☐ RSH, chap. 7 (Scott)
- ☐ _____
- ☐ _____

Day 4
- ☐ Matthew 14
- ☐ CCC 18-19
- ☐ RSH, chap. 7 (Kimberly)
- ☐ _____
- ☐ _____

Day 5
- ☐ Matthew 15
- ☐ CCC 20-22
- ☐ RSH, chap. 8 (Scott) (half of section)
- ☐ _____
- ☐ _____

Year 1, Week 4

Day 1
- ☐ Matthew 16
- ☐ CCC 23-24
- ☐ RSH, chap. 8 (Scott) (finish section)
- ☐ _____
- ☐ _____

Day 2
- ☐ Matthew 17
- ☐ CCC 25
- ☐ RSH, chap. 8 (Kimberly) (half of section)
- ☐ _____
- ☐ _____

Day 3
- ☐ Matthew 18
- ☐ CCC 26
- ☐ RSH, chap. 8 (Kimberly) (finish section)
- ☐ _____
- ☐ _____

Day 4
- ☐ Matthew 19
- ☐ CCC 27-28
- ☐ RSH, chap. 9 (Scott)
- ☐ _____
- ☐ _____

Day 5
- ☐ Matthew 20
- ☐ CCC 29-30
- ☐ RSH, chap. 9 (Kimberly); conclusion
- ☐ _____
- ☐ _____

Remember, O Lord, your Church. Deliver it from
every evil and perfect it in your love.

— DIDACHE

Year 1, Week 5

Day 1
- ☐ Matthew 21
- ☐ CCC 31-32
- ☐ *Map of Life* (MOL), introduction (only two pages)
- ☐ _____
- ☐ _____

Day 2
- ☐ Matthew 22
- ☐ CCC 33-34
- ☐ MOL, chap. 1
- ☐ _____
- ☐ _____

Day 3
- ☐ Matthew 23
- ☐ CCC 35-36
- ☐ MOL, chap. 2
- ☐ _____
- ☐ _____

Day 4
- ☐ Matthew 24
- ☐ CCC 37-38
- ☐ MOL, chap. 3
- ☐ _____
- ☐ _____

Day 5
- ☐ Matthew 25
- ☐ CCC 39-41
- ☐ MOL, chap. 4
- ☐ _____
- ☐ _____

Year 1, Week 6

Day 1
- ☐ Matthew 26
- ☐ CCC 42-43
- ☐ MOL, chap. 5
- ☐ _____
- ☐ _____

Day 2
- ☐ Matthew 27
- ☐ CCC 44-46
- ☐ MOL, chap. 6
- ☐ _____
- ☐ _____

Day 3
- ☐ Matthew 28
- ☐ CCC 47-49
- ☐ MOL, chap. 7
- ☐ _____
- ☐ _____

Day 4
- ☐ Mark 1
- ☐ CCC 50
- ☐ MOL, chap. 8
- ☐ _____
- ☐ _____

Day 5
- ☐ Mark 2
- ☐ CCC 51-52
- ☐ MOL, chap. 9
- ☐ _____
- ☐ _____

> He that is within the sanctuary is pure; but he that is outside the sanctuary is not pure. In other words, anyone who acts without the bishop and the presbytery and the deacons does not have a clean conscience.
>
> —ST. IGNATIUS OF ANTIOCH, *LETTER TO THE TRALLIANS*, CA. AD 110

Year 1, Week 7

Day 1
- ☐ Mark 3
- ☐ CCC 53
- ☐ MOL, chaps. 10 and 11 (through "Prayer")
- ☐ _____
- ☐ _____

Day 2
- ☐ Mark 4
- ☐ CCC 54-55
- ☐ MOL, chap. 11 ("Mass" through end)
- ☐ _____
- ☐ _____

Day 3
- ☐ Mark 5
- ☐ CCC 56-57
- ☐ MOL, chap. 12
- ☐ _____
- ☐ _____

Day 4
- ☐ Mark 6
- ☐ CCC 58
- ☐ MOL, chap. 13
- ☐ _____
- ☐ _____

Day 5
- ☐ Mark 7
- ☐ CCC 59-61
- ☐ MOL, chap. 14
- ☐ _____
- ☐ _____

Year 1, Week 8

Day 1
- ☐ Mark 8
- ☐ CCC 62-63
- ☐ *Mary, The Second Eve* (MSE), introduction, "The Second Eve"
- ☐ _____
- ☐ _____

Day 2
- ☐ Mark 9
- ☐ CCC 64
- ☐ MSE, "The Immaculate Conception"; "Exaltation"
- ☐ _____
- ☐ _____

Day 3
- ☐ Mark 10
- ☐ CCC 65
- ☐ MSE, "Theotocos"
- ☐ _____
- ☐ _____

Day 4
- ☐ Mark 11
- ☐ CCC 66-67
- ☐ MSE, "The Assumption"
- ☐ _____
- ☐ _____

Day 5
- ☐ Mark 12
- ☐ CCC 68-70
- ☐ MSE, "Intercessory Power"; "Devotion"
- ☐ _____
- ☐ _____

> The Lord opened the understanding of my unbelieving
> heart, so that I should recall my sins.
>
> — SAINT PATRICK, *CONFESSION*

Year 1, Week 9

Day 1
- ☐ Mark 13
- ☐ CCC 71-73
- ☐ *Scripture Alone* (SA), "What Is Sola Scriptura?", Reasons 1-2
- ☐ _____
- ☐ _____

Day 2
- ☐ Mark 14
- ☐ CCC 74-75
- ☐ SA, Reasons 3-6
- ☐ _____
- ☐ _____

Day 3
- ☐ Mark 15
- ☐ CCC 76
- ☐ SA, Reasons 7-12
- ☐ _____
- ☐ _____

Day 4
- ☐ Mark 16
- ☐ CCC 77-78
- ☐ SA, Reasons 13-18
- ☐ _____
- ☐ _____

Day 5
- ☐ Luke 1
- ☐ CCC 79
- ☐ SA, Reasons 19-Summary
- ☐ _____
- ☐ _____

Year 1, Week 10

Day 1
- ☐ Luke 2
- ☐ CCC 80-82
- ☐ *50 Questions on the Natural Law* (QNL), Qs. 1-2
- ☐ _____
- ☐ _____

Day 2
- ☐ Luke 3
- ☐ CCC 83
- ☐ QNL, Qs. 3-4
- ☐ _____
- ☐ _____

Day 3
- ☐ Luke 4
- ☐ CCC 84
- ☐ QNL, Q. 5
- ☐ _____
- ☐ _____

Day 4
- ☐ Luke 5
- ☐ CCC 85-87
- ☐ QNL, Q. 6
- ☐ _____
- ☐ _____

Day 5
- ☐ Luke 6
- ☐ CCC 88-90
- ☐ QNL, Q. 7-8
- ☐ _____
- ☐ _____

> Our Apostles ... appointed those who have already been mentioned, and afterward, added the further provision that, if they should die, other approved men should succeed to their ministry.
>
> — ST. CLEMENT OF ROME, *LETTER TO THE CORINTHIANS*, CA. AD 80

Year 1, Week 11

Day 1
☐ Luke 7
☐ CCC 91-93
☐ QNL, Q. 9
☐ _____
☐ _____

Day 2
☐ Luke 8
☐ CCC 94-95
☐ QNL, Qs. 10-11
☐ _____
☐ _____

Day 3
☐ Luke 9
☐ CCC 96-100
☐ QNL, Q. 12
☐ _____
☐ _____

Day 4
☐ Luke 10
☐ CCC 101-102
☐ QNL, Qs. 13-14
☐ _____
☐ _____

Day 5
☐ Luke 11
☐ CCC 103-104
☐ QNL, Qs. 15-16
☐ _____
☐ _____

Year 1, Week 12

Day 1
☐ Luke 12
☐ CCC 105-106
☐ QNL, Q. 17
☐ _____
☐ _____

Day 2
☐ Luke 13
☐ CCC 107-108
☐ QNL, Q. 18
☐ _____
☐ _____

Day 3
☐ Luke 14
☐ CCC 109-110
☐ QNL, Q. 19
☐ _____
☐ _____

Day 4
☐ Luke 15
☐ CCC 111-112
☐ QNL, Qs. 20-21
☐ _____
☐ _____

Day 5
☐ Luke 16
☐ CCC 113-114
☐ QNL, Q. 22
☐ _____
☐ _____

Christ made [Peter] the head and primate of His Church, as a rock standing in His own place, not as though Peter were immortal and so could hold office forever, but many would successively follow him into that office, and these not all of equal merit.

—SAINT THOMAS MORE, *RESPONSIO AD LUTHERUM*

Year 1, Week 13

Day 1
- ☐ Luke 17
- ☐ CCC 115-117
- ☐ QNL, Q. 23
- ☐ _____
- ☐ _____

Day 2
- ☐ Luke 18
- ☐ CCC 118-119
- ☐ QNL, Qs. 24-25
- ☐ _____
- ☐ _____

Day 3
- ☐ Luke 19
- ☐ CCC 120
- ☐ QNL, Qs. 26-27
- ☐ _____
- ☐ _____

Day 4
- ☐ Luke 20
- ☐ CCC 121-123
- ☐ QNL, Q. 28
- ☐ _____
- ☐ _____

Day 5
- ☐ Luke 21
- ☐ CCC 124-125
- ☐ QNL, Q. 29
- ☐ _____
- ☐ _____

Year 1, Week 14

Day 1
- ☐ Luke 22
- ☐ CCC 126-127
- ☐ QNL, Q. 30
- ☐ _____
- ☐ _____

Day 2
- ☐ Luke 23
- ☐ CCC 128-130
- ☐ QNL, Q. 31
- ☐ _____
- ☐ _____

Day 3
- ☐ Luke 24
- ☐ CCC 131-133
- ☐ QNL, Q. 32
- ☐ _____
- ☐ _____

Day 4
- ☐ John 1
- ☐ CCC 134-137
- ☐ QNL, Qs. 33-34
- ☐ _____
- ☐ _____

Day 5
- ☐ John 2
- ☐ CCC 138-141
- ☐ QNL, Q. 35
- ☐ _____
- ☐ _____

Obedience is the greatest sacrifice that God exacts of man and the greatest gift that man can give to God, because in this he gives himself.

—VENERABLE LOUIS OF GRANADA, *SUMMA OF THE CHRISTIAN LIFE*

Year 1, Week 15

Day 1
- ☐ John 3
- ☐ CCC 142-143
- ☐ QNL, Q. 36
- ☐ _____
- ☐ _____

Day 2
- ☐ John 4
- ☐ CCC 144
- ☐ QNL, Q. 37
- ☐ _____
- ☐ _____

Day 3
- ☐ John 5
- ☐ CCC 145-147
- ☐ QNL, Q. 38
- ☐ _____
- ☐ _____

Day 4
- ☐ John 6
- ☐ CCC 148-149
- ☐ QNL, Q. 39
- ☐ _____
- ☐ _____

Day 5
- ☐ John 7
- ☐ CCC 150-151
- ☐ QNL, Q. 40
- ☐ _____
- ☐ _____

Year 1, Week 16

Day 1
- ☐ John 8
- ☐ CCC 152
- ☐ QNL, Q. 41
- ☐ _____
- ☐ _____

Day 2
- ☐ John 9
- ☐ CCC 153
- ☐ QNL, Q. 42
- ☐ _____
- ☐ _____

Day 3
- ☐ John 10
- ☐ CCC 154-155
- ☐ QNL, Q. 43
- ☐ _____
- ☐ _____

Day 4
- ☐ John 11
- ☐ CCC 156-157
- ☐ QNL, Q. 44
- ☐ _____
- ☐ _____

Day 5
- ☐ John 12
- ☐ CCC 158-159
- ☐ QNL, Q. 45
- ☐ _____
- ☐ _____

When we obey lawful superiors we are more sure of doing the will of God than if Jesus Christ Himself would appear and speak to us.

—SAINT ALPHONSUS LIGUORI, *THE 12 STEPS TO HOLINESS AND SALVATION*

Year 1, Week 17

Day 1
- ☐ John 13
- ☐ CCC 160-161
- ☐ QNL, Q. 46
- ☐ _____
- ☐ _____

Day 2
- ☐ John 14
- ☐ CCC 162-163
- ☐ QNL, Q. 47
- ☐ _____
- ☐ _____

Day 3
- ☐ John 15
- ☐ CCC 164-165
- ☐ QNL, Q. 48
- ☐ _____
- ☐ _____

Day 4
- ☐ John 16
- ☐ CCC 166-167
- ☐ QNL, Q. 49
- ☐ _____
- ☐ _____

Day 5
- ☐ John 17
- ☐ CCC 168-169
- ☐ QNL, Q. 50
- ☐ _____
- ☐ _____

Year 1, Week 18

Day 1
- ☐ John 18
- ☐ CCC 170-171
- ☐ _Theology for Beginners_ (TFB), chap. 1
- ☐ _____
- ☐ _____

Day 2
- ☐ John 19
- ☐ CCC 172-173
- ☐ TFB, chap. 2
- ☐ _____
- ☐ _____

Day 3
- ☐ John 20
- ☐ CCC 174-175
- ☐ TFB, chap. 3
- ☐ _____
- ☐ _____

Day 4
- ☐ John 21
- ☐ CCC 176-180
- ☐ TFB, chap. 4
- ☐ _____
- ☐ _____

Day 5
- ☐ Acts 1
- ☐ CCC 181-184
- ☐ TFB, chap. 5
- ☐ _____
- ☐ _____

Authoritarianism is based on force, and therefore is physical, but authority is founded on reverence and love, and therefore is moral.

—ARCHBISHOP FULTON SHEEN, _LIFE IS WORTH LIVING_

Year 1, Week 19

Day 1
- ☐ Acts 2-3
- ☐ CCC, The Credo
- ☐ TFB, chap. 6
- ☐ _____
- ☐ _____

Day 2
- ☐ Acts 4
- ☐ CCC 185-187
- ☐ TFB, chap. 7
- ☐ _____
- ☐ _____

Day 3
- ☐ Acts 5-6
- ☐ CCC 188
- ☐ TFB, chap. 8
- ☐ _____
- ☐ _____

Day 4
- ☐ Acts 7
- ☐ CCC 189-191
- ☐ TFB, chap. 9
- ☐ _____
- ☐ _____

Day 5
- ☐ Acts 8-9
- ☐ CCC 192-193
- ☐ TFB, chap. 10
- ☐ _____
- ☐ _____

Year 1, Week 20

Day 1
- ☐ Acts 10
- ☐ CCC 194-195
- ☐ TFB, chap. 11 (half)
- ☐ _____
- ☐ _____

Day 2
- ☐ Acts 11-12
- ☐ CCC 196-197
- ☐ TFB, chap. 11 (finish chapter)
- ☐ _____
- ☐ _____

Day 3
- ☐ Acts 13
- ☐ CCC 198
- ☐ TFB, chap. 12
- ☐ _____
- ☐ _____

Day 4
- ☐ Acts 14-15
- ☐ CCC 199
- ☐ TFB, chap. 13 (half)
- ☐ _____
- ☐ _____

Day 5
- ☐ Acts 16
- ☐ CCC 200-201
- ☐ TFB, chap. 13 (finish chapter)
- ☐ _____
- ☐ _____

Those, indeed, who belong to God and to Jesus Christ—they are with the bishop. And those who repent and come to the unity of the Church—they too shall be of God, and will be living according to Jesus Christ.

—ST. IGNATIUS OF ANTIOCH, *LETTER TO THE ROMANS*, CA. AD 110

Year 1, Week 21

Day 1
☐ Acts 17-18
☐ CCC 202
☐ TFB, chap. 14
☐ _____
☐ _____

Day 2
☐ Acts 19
☐ CCC 203-204
☐ TFB, chap. 15
☐ _____
☐ _____

Day 3
☐ Acts 20-21
☐ CCC 205
☐ TFB, chap. 16
☐ _____
☐ _____

Day 4
☐ Acts 22
☐ CCC 206-207
☐ TFB, chap. 17 (half)
☐ _____
☐ _____

Day 5
☐ Acts 23-24
☐ CCC 208-209
☐ TFB, chap. 17 (finish chapter)
☐ _____
☐ _____

Year 1, Week 22

Day 1
☐ Acts 25
☐ CCC 210-211
☐ TFB, chap. 18
☐ _____
☐ _____

Day 2
☐ Acts 26-27
☐ CCC 212-213
☐ TFB, chap. 19 (half)
☐ _____
☐ _____

Day 3
☐ Acts 28
☐ CCC 214
☐ TFB, chap. 19 (finish chapter)
☐ _____
☐ _____

Day 4
☐ Romans 1-2
☐ CCC 215-217
☐ TFB, chap. 20
☐ _____
☐ _____

Day 5
☐ Romans 3
☐ CCC 218-221
☐ TFB, epilogue
☐ _____
☐ _____

> I am glad that you love processions, and all the external practices
> of our Holy Mother the Church, so as to render God the worship
> due to him ... and that you really put yourself into them!
>
> — ST. JOSEMARÍA ESCRIVÁ, *FURROW*

Year 1, Week 23

Day 1
- ☐ Romans 4-5
- ☐ CCC 222-224
- ☐ *The Spirit of Catholicism* (SOC), chap. 1 (half)
- ☐ _____
- ☐ _____

Day 2
- ☐ Romans 6
- ☐ CCC 225-227
- ☐ SOC, chap. 1 (finish chapter)
- ☐ _____
- ☐ _____

Day 3
- ☐ Romans 7-8
- ☐ CCC 228-231
- ☐ SOC, chap. 2 (one-third)
- ☐ _____
- ☐ _____

Day 4
- ☐ Romans 9
- ☐ CCC 232-233
- ☐ SOC, chap. 2 (one-third)
- ☐ _____
- ☐ _____

Day 5
- ☐ Romans 10-11
- ☐ CCC 234-235
- ☐ SOC, chap. 2 (finish chapter)
- ☐ _____
- ☐ _____

Year 1, Week 24

Day 1
- ☐ Romans 12
- ☐ CCC 236-237
- ☐ SOC, chap. 3 (one-third)
- ☐ _____
- ☐ _____

Day 2
- ☐ Romans 13-14
- ☐ CCC 238-239
- ☐ SOC, chap. 3 (one-third)
- ☐ _____
- ☐ _____

Day 3
- ☐ Romans 15
- ☐ CCC 240-242
- ☐ SOC, chap. 3 (finish chapter)
- ☐ _____
- ☐ _____

Day 4
- ☐ Romans 16
- ☐ CCC 243-244
- ☐ SOC, chap. 4 (one-third)
- ☐ _____
- ☐ _____

Day 5
- ☐ 1 Corinthians 1
- ☐ CCC 245-246
- ☐ SOC, chap. 4 (one-third)
- ☐ _____
- ☐ _____

Year 1, Week 25

Day 1
- ☐ 1 Corinthians 2-3
- ☐ CCC 247-248
- ☐ SOC, chap. 4 (finish chapter)
- ☐ _____
- ☐ _____

Day 2
- ☐ 1 Corinthians 4
- ☐ CCC 249-250
- ☐ SOC, chap. 5 (one-fourth)
- ☐ _____
- ☐ _____

Day 3
- ☐ 1 Corinthians 5-6
- ☐ CCC 251-252
- ☐ SOC, chap. 5 (one-fourth)
- ☐ _____
- ☐ _____

Day 4
- ☐ 1 Corinthians 7
- ☐ CCC 253-254
- ☐ SOC, chap. 5 (one-fourth)
- ☐ _____
- ☐ _____

Day 5
- ☐ 1 Corinthians 8-9
- ☐ CCC 255-256
- ☐ SOC, chap. 5 (finish chapter)
- ☐ _____
- ☐ _____

Year 1, Week 26

Day 1
- ☐ 1 Corinthians 10
- ☐ CCC 257-258
- ☐ SOC, chap. 6 (half)
- ☐ _____
- ☐ _____

Day 2
- ☐ 1 Corinthians 11-12
- ☐ CCC 259-260
- ☐ SOC, chap. 6 (finish chapter)
- ☐ _____
- ☐ _____

Day 3
- ☐ 1 Corinthians 13
- ☐ CCC 261-264
- ☐ SOC, chap. 7 (one-third)
- ☐ _____
- ☐ _____

Day 4
- ☐ 1 Corinthians 14-15
- ☐ CCC 265-267
- ☐ SOC, chap. 7 (one-third)
- ☐ _____
- ☐ _____

Day 5
- ☐ 1 Corinthians 16
- ☐ CCC 268-269
- ☐ SOC, chap. 7 (finish chapter)
- ☐ _____
- ☐ _____

It will always be my principle, in all spheres of religious
knowledge and in all theological or biblical questions, to find
out first of all the traditional teaching of the Church, and on this
basis to judge the findings of contemporary scholarship.

— SAINT JOHN XXIII, *JOURNAL OF A SOUL*

Year 1, Week 27

Day 1
- ☐ 2 Corinthians 1-2
- ☐ CCC 270-271
- ☐ SOC, chap. 8 (one-fifth)
- ☐ _____
- ☐ _____

Day 2
- ☐ 2 Corinthians 3
- ☐ CCC 272
- ☐ SOC, chap. 8 (one-fifth)
- ☐ _____
- ☐ _____

Day 3
- ☐ 2 Corinthians 4-5
- ☐ CCC 273-274
- ☐ SOC, chap. 8 (one-fifth)
- ☐ _____
- ☐ _____

Day 4
- ☐ 2 Corinthians 6
- ☐ CCC 275-278
- ☐ SOC, chap. 8 (one-fifth)
- ☐ _____
- ☐ _____

Day 5
- ☐ 2 Corinthians 7
- ☐ CCC 279-281
- ☐ SOC, chap. 8 (finish chapter)
- ☐ _____
- ☐ _____

Year 1, Week 28

Day 1
- ☐ 2 Corinthians 8-9
- ☐ CCC 282-283
- ☐ SOC, chap. 9 (one-fourth)
- ☐ _____
- ☐ _____

Day 2
- ☐ 2 Corinthians 10
- ☐ CCC 284-285
- ☐ SOC, chap. 9 (one-fourth)
- ☐ _____
- ☐ _____

Day 3
- ☐ 2 Corinthians 11-12
- ☐ CCC 286-287
- ☐ SOC, chap. 9 (one-fourth)
- ☐ _____
- ☐ _____

Day 4
- ☐ 2 Corinthians 13
- ☐ CCC 288-289
- ☐ SOC, chap. 9 (finish chapter)
- ☐ _____
- ☐ _____

Day 5
- ☐ Galatians 1
- ☐ CCC 290-291
- ☐ SOC, chap. 10 (half)
- ☐ _____
- ☐ _____

> How great should each one's love for the Church be! As
> a good child prays for the mother it loves, so should every
> Christian soul pray for the Church, its Mother.
>
> — *DIARY OF SAINT MARIA FAUSTINA KOWALSKA*

Year 1, Week 29

Day 1
- ☐ Galatians 2-3
- ☐ CCC 292
- ☐ SOC, chap. 10 (finish chapter)
- ☐ _____
- ☐ _____

Day 2
- ☐ Galatians 4
- ☐ CCC 293
- ☐ SOC, chap. 11 (one-third)
- ☐ _____
- ☐ _____

Day 3
- ☐ Galatians 5-6
- ☐ CCC 294
- ☐ SOC, chap. 11 (one-third)
- ☐ _____
- ☐ _____

Day 4
- ☐ Ephesians 1-2
- ☐ CCC 295
- ☐ SOC, chap. 11 (finish chapter)
- ☐ _____
- ☐ _____

Day 5
- ☐ Ephesians 3-4
- ☐ CCC 296-297
- ☐ SOC, chap. 12 (half)
- ☐ _____
- ☐ _____

Year 1, Week 30

Day 1
- ☐ Ephesians 5-6
- ☐ CCC 298-299
- ☐ SOC, chap. 12 (finish chapter)
- ☐ _____
- ☐ _____

Day 2
- ☐ Philippians 1-2
- ☐ CCC 300-301
- ☐ SOC, chap. 13 (one-fourth)
- ☐ _____
- ☐ _____

Day 3
- ☐ Philippians 3
- ☐ CCC 302-303
- ☐ SOC, chap. 13 (one-fourth)
- ☐ _____
- ☐ _____

Day 4
- ☐ Philippians 4
- ☐ CCC 304-305
- ☐ SOC, chap. 13 (one-fourth)
- ☐ _____
- ☐ _____

Day 5
- ☐ Colossians 1-2
- ☐ CCC 306-307
- ☐ SOC, chap. 13 (finish chapter)
- ☐ _____
- ☐ _____

When, therefore, we have such proofs, it is not necessary to seek among others the truth which is easily obtained from the Church. For the Apostles, like a rich man in a bank, deposited with her most copiously everything which pertains to the truth; and everyone whosoever wishes draws from her the drink of life.

—SAINT IRENAEUS, *AGAINST HERESIES*, CA. AD 180

Year 1, Week 31

Day 1
- ☐ Colossians 3-4
- ☐ CCC 308
- ☐ *The Spirit and Forms of Protestantism* (SFP), chap. 1 (one-third)
- ☐ _____
- ☐ _____

Day 2
- ☐ 1 Thessalonians 1
- ☐ CCC 309-310
- ☐ SFP, chap. 1 (one-third)
- ☐ _____
- ☐ _____

Day 3
- ☐ 1 Thessalonians 2-3
- ☐ CCC 311-312
- ☐ SFP, chap. 1 (finish chapter)
- ☐ _____
- ☐ _____

Day 4
- ☐ 1 Thessalonians 4-5
- ☐ CCC 313-314
- ☐ SFP, chap. 2 (one-sixth)
- ☐ _____
- ☐ _____

Day 5
- ☐ 2 Thessalonians 1-2
- ☐ CCC 315-319
- ☐ SFP, chap. 2 (one-sixth)
- ☐ _____
- ☐ _____

Year 1, Week 32

Day 1
- ☐ 2 Thessalonians 3
- ☐ CCC 320-324
- ☐ SFP, chap. 2 (one-sixth)
- ☐ _____
- ☐ _____

Day 2
- ☐ 1 Timothy 1-2
- ☐ CCC 325-326
- ☐ SFP, chap. 2 (one-sixth)
- ☐ _____
- ☐ _____

Day 3
- ☐ 1 Timothy 3-4
- ☐ CCC 327-328
- ☐ SFP, chap. 2 (one-sixth)
- ☐ _____
- ☐ _____

Day 4
- ☐ 1 Timothy 5-6
- ☐ CCC 329-330
- ☐ SFP, chap. 2 (finish chapter)
- ☐ _____
- ☐ _____

Day 5
- ☐ 2 Timothy 1-2
- ☐ CCC 331-332
- ☐ SFP, chap. 3 (half)
- ☐ _____
- ☐ _____

The Church comes into being from the Eucharist. She receives her unity and her mission from the Eucharist. She is derived from the Last Supper, that is to say, from Christ's death and Resurrection, which he anticipated in the gift of his body and blood.

— POPE BENEDICT XVI, *JESUS OF NAZARETH*

Year 1, Week 33

Day 1
- ☐ 2 Timothy 3-4
- ☐ CCC 333
- ☐ SFP, chap. 3 (finish chapter)
- ☐ _____
- ☐ _____

Day 2
- ☐ Titus 1-3
- ☐ CCC 334-336
- ☐ SFP, chap. 4 (one-fifth)
- ☐ _____
- ☐ _____

Day 3
- ☐ Philemon
- ☐ CCC 337-338
- ☐ SFP, chap. 4 (one-fifth)
- ☐ _____
- ☐ _____

Day 4
- ☐ Hebrews 1-2
- ☐ CCC 339-340
- ☐ SFP, chap. 4 (one-fifth)
- ☐ _____
- ☐ _____

Day 5
- ☐ Hebrews 3-4
- ☐ CCC 341-343
- ☐ SFP, chap. 4 (one-fifth)
- ☐ _____
- ☐ _____

Year 1, Week 34

Day 1
- ☐ Hebrews 5-6
- ☐ CCC 344-346
- ☐ SFP, chap. 4 (finish chapter)
- ☐ _____
- ☐ _____

Day 2
- ☐ Hebrews 7
- ☐ CCC 347-349
- ☐ SFP, chap. 5 (one-third)
- ☐ _____
- ☐ _____

Day 3
- ☐ Hebrews 8-9
- ☐ CCC 350-354
- ☐ SFP, chap. 5 (one-third)
- ☐ _____
- ☐ _____

Day 4
- ☐ Hebrews 10
- ☐ CCC 355-356
- ☐ SFP, chap. 5 (finish chapter)
- ☐ _____
- ☐ _____

Day 5
- ☐ Hebrews 11-12
- ☐ CCC 357-358
- ☐ SFP, chap. 6 (one-third)
- ☐ _____
- ☐ _____

For every good man is bounden between truth and falsehood, the Catholic Church and heretics, between God and the devil, to be partial, and plainly to declare himself to be full and whole upon the one side and clear against the other.

— SAINT THOMAS MORE, *APOLOGY*

Year 1, Week 35

Day 1
- ☐ Hebrews 13
- ☐ CCC 359-361
- ☐ SFP, chap. 6 (one-third)
- ☐ _____
- ☐ _____

Day 2
- ☐ Matthew 1
- ☐ CCC 362-363
- ☐ SFP, chap. 6 (finish chapter)
- ☐ _____
- ☐ _____

Day 3
- ☐ Matthew 2
- ☐ CCC 364-365
- ☐ SFP, chap. 7 (one-fifth)
- ☐ _____
- ☐ _____

Day 4
- ☐ Matthew 3
- ☐ CCC 366-368
- ☐ SFP, chap. 7 (one-fifth)
- ☐ _____
- ☐ _____

Day 5
- ☐ Matthew 4
- ☐ CCC 369-370
- ☐ SFP, chap 7 (one-fifth)
- ☐ _____
- ☐ _____

Year 1, Week 36

Day 1
- ☐ Matthew 5
- ☐ CCC 371-372
- ☐ SFP, chap. 7 (one-fifth)
- ☐ _____
- ☐ _____

Day 2
- ☐ Matthew 6
- ☐ CCC 373
- ☐ SFP, chap. 7 (finish chapter)
- ☐ _____
- ☐ _____

Day 3
- ☐ Matthew 7
- ☐ CCC 374-376
- ☐ SFP, chap. 8 (half)
- ☐ _____
- ☐ _____

Day 4
- ☐ Matthew 8
- ☐ CCC 377-379
- ☐ SFP, chap. 8 (finish chapter)
- ☐ _____
- ☐ _____

Day 5
- ☐ Matthew 9
- ☐ CCC 380-384
- ☐ SFP, chap. 9 (one-third)
- ☐ _____
- ☐ _____

> You then, my son, be strong in the grace that is in Christ
> Jesus, and what you have heard from me before many witnesses
> entrust to faithful men who will be able to teach others also.
>
> — 2 TIMOTHY 2:1–2

Year 1, Week 37

Day 1
- ☐ Matthew 10
- ☐ CCC 385
- ☐ SFP, chap. 9 (one-third)
- ☐ _____
- ☐ _____

Day 2
- ☐ Matthew 11
- ☐ CCC 386-387
- ☐ SFP, chap. 9 (finish chapter)
- ☐ _____
- ☐ _____

Day 3
- ☐ Matthew 12
- ☐ CCC 388-389
- ☐ SFP, chap. 10 (one-fifth)
- ☐ _____
- ☐ _____

Day 4
- ☐ Matthew 13
- ☐ CCC 390
- ☐ SFP, chap. 10 (one-fifth)
- ☐ _____
- ☐ _____

Day 5
- ☐ Matthew 14
- ☐ CCC 391-393
- ☐ SFP, chap. 10 (one-fifth)
- ☐ _____
- ☐ _____

Year 1, Week 38

Day 1
- ☐ Matthew 15
- ☐ CCC 394-395
- ☐ SFP, chap. 10 (one-fifth)
- ☐ _____
- ☐ _____

Day 2
- ☐ Matthew 16
- ☐ CCC 396
- ☐ SFP, chap. 10 (finish chapter)
- ☐ _____
- ☐ _____

Day 3
- ☐ Matthew 17
- ☐ CCC 397-399
- ☐ SFP, chap. 11 (half)
- ☐ _____
- ☐ _____

Day 4
- ☐ Matthew 18
- ☐ CCC 400-401
- ☐ SFP, chap. 11 (finish chapter)
- ☐ _____
- ☐ _____

Day 5
- ☐ Matthew 19
- ☐ CCC 402-404
- ☐ SFP, Appendix
- ☐ _____
- ☐ _____

> If we had a living Head upon the earth, such as once our Savior was with His disciples, teaching and directing us in all things, the visible Church might so far be dispensed with. But, since we have not, a form of doctrine, a system of laws, a bond of subordination connecting in one, is the next best mode of securing the stability of sacred Truth.
>
> — SAINT JOHN HENRY NEWMAN, *PAROCHIAL AND PLAIN SERMONS*

Year 1, Week 39

Day 1
- ☐ Matthew 20
- ☐ CCC 405-406
- ☐ *The Great Heresies* (TGH), chap. 1
- ☐ _____
- ☐ _____

Day 2
- ☐ Matthew 21
- ☐ CCC 407
- ☐ TGH, chap. 2
- ☐ _____
- ☐ _____

Day 3
- ☐ Matthew 22
- ☐ CCC 408-409
- ☐ TGH, chap. 3 (one-third)
- ☐ _____
- ☐ _____

Day 4
- ☐ Matthew 23
- ☐ CCC 410
- ☐ TGH, chap. 3 (one-third)
- ☐ _____
- ☐ _____

Day 5
- ☐ Matthew 24
- ☐ CCC 411-412
- ☐ TGH, chap. 3 (finish chapter)
- ☐ _____
- ☐ _____

Year 1, Week 40

Day 1
- ☐ Matthew 25
- ☐ CCC 413-416
- ☐ TGH, chap. 4 (one-fifth)
- ☐ _____
- ☐ _____

Day 2
- ☐ Matthew 26
- ☐ CCC 417-421
- ☐ TGH, chap. 4 (one-fifth)
- ☐ _____
- ☐ _____

Day 3
- ☐ Matthew 27
- ☐ CCC 422-425
- ☐ TGH, chap. 4 (one-fifth)
- ☐ _____
- ☐ _____

Day 4
- ☐ Matthew 28
- ☐ CCC 426-427
- ☐ TGH, chap. 4 (one-fifth)
- ☐ _____
- ☐ _____

Day 5
- ☐ Mark 1
- ☐ CCC 428-429
- ☐ TGH, chap. 4 (finish chapter)
- ☐ _____
- ☐ _____

What the Church celebrates in the Mass is not the Last Supper;
no, it is what the Lord instituted in the course of the Last Supper and
entrusted to the Church: the memorial of his sacrificial death.

—JOSEF ANDREAS JUNGMANN, *MESSE IN GOTTESVOLK*

Year 1, Week 41

Day 1
- ☐ Mark 2
- ☐ CCC 430-431
- ☐ TGH, chap. 5 (half)
- ☐ _____
- ☐ _____

Day 2
- ☐ Mark 3
- ☐ CCC 432-433
- ☐ TGH, chap. 5 (finish chapter)
- ☐ _____
- ☐ _____

Day 3
- ☐ Mark 4
- ☐ CCC 434-435
- ☐ TGH, chap. 6 (one-fifth)
- ☐ _____
- ☐ _____

Day 4
- ☐ Mark 5
- ☐ CCC 436-437
- ☐ TGH, chap. 6 (one-fifth)
- ☐ _____
- ☐ _____

Day 5
- ☐ Mark 6
- ☐ CCC 438-439
- ☐ TGH, chap. 6 (one-fifth)
- ☐ _____
- ☐ _____

Year 1, Week 42

Day 1
- ☐ Mark 7
- ☐ CCC 440
- ☐ TGH, chap. 6 (one-fifth)
- ☐ _____
- ☐ _____

Day 2
- ☐ Mark 8
- ☐ CCC 441-442
- ☐ TGH, chap. 6 (finish chapter)
- ☐ _____
- ☐ _____

Day 3
- ☐ Mark 9
- ☐ CCC 443-445
- ☐ TGH, chap. 7 (one-third)
- ☐ _____
- ☐ _____

Day 4
- ☐ Mark 10
- ☐ CCC 446-448
- ☐ TGH, chap. 7 (one-third)
- ☐ _____
- ☐ _____

Day 5
- ☐ Mark 11
- ☐ CCC 449-451
- ☐ TGH, chap. 7 (finish chapter)
- ☐ _____
- ☐ _____

On the heart, therefore, in the Church of Christ, there
remains inscribed the true gospel of Christ which was
written there before the books of all the evangelists.

— THOMAS MORE, *COMPLETE WORKS*

Year 1, Week 43

Day 1
- ☐ Mark 12
- ☐ CCC 452-455
- ☐ *Practical Theology* (PT), introduction, Ways 1-5
- ☐ _____
- ☐ _____

Day 2
- ☐ Mark 13
- ☐ CCC 456-457
- ☐ PT, Ways 6-11
- ☐ _____
- ☐ _____

Day 3
- ☐ Mark 14
- ☐ CCC 458-460
- ☐ PT, Ways 12-17
- ☐ _____
- ☐ _____

Day 4
- ☐ Mark 15
- ☐ CCC 461
- ☐ PT, Ways 18-24
- ☐ _____
- ☐ _____

Day 5
- ☐ Mark 16
- ☐ CCC 462-463
- ☐ PT, Ways 25-32
- ☐ _____
- ☐ _____

Year 1, Week 44

Day 1
- ☐ Luke 1
- ☐ CCC 464
- ☐ PT, Ways 33-39
- ☐ _____
- ☐ _____

Day 2
- ☐ Luke 2
- ☐ CCC 465
- ☐ PT, Ways 40-47
- ☐ _____
- ☐ _____

Day 3
- ☐ Luke 3
- ☐ CCC 466
- ☐ PT, Ways 48-54
- ☐ _____
- ☐ _____

Day 4
- ☐ Luke 4
- ☐ CCC 467
- ☐ PT, Ways 55-61
- ☐ _____
- ☐ _____

Day 5
- ☐ Luke 5
- ☐ CCC 468
- ☐ PT, Ways 62-68
- ☐ _____
- ☐ _____

> Through Christ's body, the Church became one, she became herself, and at the same time, through his death, she was opened up to the breadth of the world and its history.
>
> — POPE BENEDICT XVI, *JESUS OF NAZARETH*

Year 1, Week 45

Day 1
- ☐ Luke 6
- ☐ CCC 469
- ☐ PT, Ways 69-75
- ☐ _____
- ☐ _____

Day 2
- ☐ Luke 7
- ☐ CCC 470
- ☐ PT, Ways 76-82
- ☐ _____
- ☐ _____

Day 3
- ☐ Luke 8
- ☐ CCC 471-472
- ☐ PT, Ways 83-89
- ☐ _____
- ☐ _____

Day 4
- ☐ Luke 9
- ☐ CCC 473-474
- ☐ PT, Ways 90-96
- ☐ _____
- ☐ _____

Day 5
- ☐ Luke 10
- ☐ CCC 475
- ☐ PT, Ways 97-103
- ☐ _____
- ☐ _____

Year 1, Week 46

Day 1
- ☐ Luke 11
- ☐ CCC 476-477
- ☐ PT, Ways 104-111
- ☐ _____
- ☐ _____

Day 2
- ☐ Luke 12
- ☐ CCC 478
- ☐ PT, Ways 112-119
- ☐ _____
- ☐ _____

Day 3
- ☐ Luke 13
- ☐ CCC 479-483
- ☐ PT, Ways 120-127
- ☐ _____
- ☐ _____

Day 4
- ☐ Luke 14
- ☐ CCC 484
- ☐ PT, Ways 128-135
- ☐ _____
- ☐ _____

Day 5
- ☐ Luke 15
- ☐ CCC 485
- ☐ PT, Ways 136-142
- ☐ _____
- ☐ _____

The Church … believes these things just as if she had but one soul
and one and the same heart; and harmoniously she proclaims them and
teaches them and hands them down, as if she possessed but one mouth.

— SAINT IRENAEUS, *AGAINST HERESIES*, CA. AD 180

Year 1, Week 47

Day 1
- ☐ Luke 16
- ☐ CCC 486
- ☐ PT, Ways 143-150
- ☐ _____
- ☐ _____

Day 2
- ☐ Luke 17
- ☐ CCC 487-488
- ☐ PT, Ways 151-158
- ☐ _____
- ☐ _____

Day 3
- ☐ Luke 18
- ☐ CCC 489
- ☐ PT, Ways 159-166
- ☐ _____
- ☐ _____

Day 4
- ☐ Luke 19
- ☐ CCC 490-491
- ☐ PT, Ways 167-174
- ☐ _____
- ☐ _____

Day 5
- ☐ Luke 20
- ☐ CCC 492-493
- ☐ PT, Ways 175-180
- ☐ _____
- ☐ _____

Year 1, Week 48

Day 1
- ☐ Luke 21
- ☐ CCC 494
- ☐ PT, Ways 181-188
- ☐ _____
- ☐ _____

Day 2
- ☐ Luke 22
- ☐ CCC 495
- ☐ PT, Ways 189-195
- ☐ _____
- ☐ _____

Day 3
- ☐ Luke 23
- ☐ CCC 496
- ☐ PT, Ways 196-202
- ☐ _____
- ☐ _____

Day 4
- ☐ Luke 24
- ☐ CCC 497
- ☐ PT, Ways 203-210
- ☐ _____
- ☐ _____

Day 5
- ☐ John 1
- ☐ CCC 498
- ☐ PT, Ways 211-218
- ☐ _____
- ☐ _____

If [the Evangelists] had not been lovers of truth, but, as Celsus says, inventors of fictions, they would not have written of Peter as having made a denial, nor of the disciples of Jesus as having been scandalized.

— ORIGEN, *AGAINST CELSUS*, POST AD 248

Year 1, Week 49

Day 1
☐ John 2
☐ CCC 499
☐ PT, Ways 219-226
☐ _____
☐ _____

Day 2
☐ John 3
☐ CCC 500-501
☐ PT, Ways 227-234
☐ _____
☐ _____

Day 3
☐ John 4
☐ CCC 502-503
☐ PT, Ways 235-242
☐ _____
☐ _____

Day 4
☐ John 5
☐ CCC 504-505
☐ PT, Ways 243-249
☐ _____
☐ _____

Day 5
☐ John 6
☐ CCC 506-507
☐ PT, Ways 250-256
☐ _____
☐ _____

Year 1, Week 50

Day 1
☐ John 7
☐ CCC 508-509
☐ PT, Ways 257-263
☐ _____
☐ _____

Day 2
☐ John 8
☐ CCC 510-511
☐ PT, Ways 264-271
☐ _____
☐ _____

Day 3
☐ John 9
☐ CCC 512-513
☐ PT, Ways 272-279
☐ _____
☐ _____

Day 4
☐ John 10
☐ CCC 514-515
☐ PT, Ways 280-285
☐ _____
☐ _____

Day 5
☐ John 11
☐ CCC 516
☐ PT, Ways 286-292
☐ _____
☐ _____

I believe though I do not comprehend, and I hold
by faith what I cannot grasp with the mind.

— SAINT BERNARD, SERMON 76

Year 1, Week 51

Day 1
- ☐ John 12
- ☐ CCC 517
- ☐ PT, Ways 293-299
- ☐ _____
- ☐ _____

Day 2
- ☐ John 13
- ☐ CCC 518
- ☐ PT, Ways 300-305
- ☐ _____
- ☐ _____

Day 3
- ☐ John 14
- ☐ CCC 519
- ☐ PT, Ways 306-311
- ☐ _____
- ☐ _____

Day 4
- ☐ John 15
- ☐ CCC 520
- ☐ PT, Ways 312-318
- ☐ _____
- ☐ _____

Day 5
- ☐ John 16
- ☐ CCC 521
- ☐ PT, Ways 319-325
- ☐ _____
- ☐ _____

Year 1, Week 52

Day 1
- ☐ John 17
- ☐ CCC 522
- ☐ PT, Ways 326-331
- ☐ _____
- ☐ _____

Day 2
- ☐ John 18
- ☐ CCC 523
- ☐ PT, Ways 332-338
- ☐ _____
- ☐ _____

Day 3
- ☐ John 19
- ☐ CCC 524
- ☐ PT, Ways 339-345
- ☐ _____
- ☐ _____

Day 4
- ☐ John 20
- ☐ CCC 525
- ☐ PT, Ways 346-352
- ☐ _____
- ☐ _____

Day 5
- ☐ John 21
- ☐ CCC 526
- ☐ PT, Way 353-postscript
- ☐ _____
- ☐ _____

The Bride of Christ cannot be defiled. She is inviolate and chaste. She knows but one home, and with a chaste modesty she guards the sanctity of one bedchamber. It is she that keeps us for God, she that seals for the kingdom the sons whom she bore.

—St. Cyprian of Carthage, *The Unity of The Catholic Church*, AD 251/256

— Year 2 —

Elect for yourselves, therefore, bishops and deacons worthy of
the Lord, humble men and not lovers of money, truthful and
proven; for they also serve you in the ministry of the prophets
and teachers. Do not, therefore, despise them; for they are your
honorable men, together with the prophets and teachers.

— *DIDACHE*

Year 2, Week 1

Day 1
- ☐ Genesis 1
- ☐ CCC 527
- ☐ *Theology and Sanity* (TAS), chap. 1 (half)
- ☐ _____
- ☐ _____

Day 2
- ☐ Genesis 2-3
- ☐ CCC 528
- ☐ TAS, chap. 1 (finish chapter)
- ☐ _____
- ☐ _____

Day 3
- ☐ Genesis 4
- ☐ CCC 529
- ☐ TAS, chap. 2 (half)
- ☐ _____
- ☐ _____

Day 4
- ☐ Genesis 5-6
- ☐ CCC 530
- ☐ TAS, chap. 2 (finish chapter)
- ☐ _____
- ☐ _____

Day 5
- ☐ Genesis 7
- ☐ CCC 531-532
- ☐ TAS, chap. 3 (half)
- ☐ _____
- ☐ _____

Year 2, Week 2

Day 1
- ☐ Genesis 8
- ☐ CCC 533-534
- ☐ TAS, chap. 3 (finish chapter)
- ☐ _____
- ☐ _____

Day 2
- ☐ Genesis 9-10
- ☐ CCC 535
- ☐ TAS, chap. 4 (one-third)
- ☐ _____
- ☐ _____

Day 3
- ☐ Genesis 11
- ☐ CCC 536
- ☐ TAS, chap. 4 (one-third)
- ☐ _____
- ☐ _____

Day 4
- ☐ Genesis 12-13
- ☐ CCC 537
- ☐ TAS, chap. 4 (finish chapter)
- ☐ _____
- ☐ _____

Day 5
- ☐ Genesis 14
- ☐ CCC 538
- ☐ TAS, chap. 5 (half)
- ☐ _____
- ☐ _____

For where the Church is, there is the Spirit of God; and where the Spirit of God, there the Church and every grace. The Spirit, however, is Truth.

— SAINT IRENAEUS, *AGAINST HERESIES*, CA. AD 180

Year 2, Week 3

Day 1
☐ Genesis 15
☐ CCC 539
☐ TAS, chap. 5 (finish chapter)
☐ _____
☐ _____

Day 2
☐ Genesis 16-17
☐ CCC 540
☐ TAS, chap. 6 (half)
☐ _____
☐ _____

Day 3
☐ Genesis 18
☐ CCC 541-542
☐ TAS, chap. 6 (finish chapter)
☐ _____
☐ _____

Day 4
☐ Genesis 19-20
☐ CCC 543-544
☐ TAS, chap. 7 (half)
☐ _____
☐ _____

Day 5
☐ Genesis 21
☐ CCC 545-546
☐ TAS, chap. 7 (finish chapter)
☐ _____
☐ _____

Year 2, Week 4

Day 1
☐ Genesis 22-23
☐ CCC 547-548
☐ TAS, chap. 8
☐ _____
☐ _____

Day 2
☐ Genesis 24
☐ CCC 549-550
☐ TAS, chap. 9 (half)
☐ _____
☐ _____

Day 3
☐ Genesis 25-26
☐ CCC 551
☐ TAS, chap. 9 (finish chapter)
☐ _____
☐ _____

Day 4
☐ Genesis 27
☐ CCC 552
☐ TAS, chap. 10 (half)
☐ _____
☐ _____

Day 5
☐ Genesis 28-29
☐ CCC 553
☐ TAS, chap. 10 (finish chapter)
☐ _____
☐ _____

In this double outpouring of blood and water, the Fathers saw an image of the two fundamental sacraments—Eucharist and Baptism—which spring forth from the Lord's pierced side, from his heart.

—POPE BENEDICT XVI, *JESUS OF NAZARETH*

Year 2, Week 5

Day 1
- ☐ Genesis 30
- ☐ CCC 554
- ☐ TAS, chap. 11 (half)
- ☐ _____
- ☐ _____

Day 2
- ☐ Genesis 31-32
- ☐ CCC 555
- ☐ TAS, chap. 11 (finish chapter)
- ☐ _____
- ☐ _____

Day 3
- ☐ Genesis 33
- ☐ CCC 556
- ☐ TAS, chap. 12 (one-fourth)
- ☐ _____
- ☐ _____

Day 4
- ☐ Genesis 34-35
- ☐ CCC 557-558
- ☐ TAS, chap. 12 (one-fourth)
- ☐ _____
- ☐ _____

Day 5
- ☐ Genesis 36
- ☐ CCC 559-560
- ☐ TAS, chap. 12 (one-fourth)
- ☐ _____
- ☐ _____

Year 2, Week 6

Day 1
- ☐ Genesis 37
- ☐ CCC 561-563
- ☐ TAS, chap. 12 (finish chapter)
- ☐ _____
- ☐ _____

Day 2
- ☐ Genesis 38-39
- ☐ CCC 564-567
- ☐ TAS, chap. 13 (one-third)
- ☐ _____
- ☐ _____

Day 3
- ☐ Genesis 40
- ☐ CCC 568-570
- ☐ TAS, chap. 13 (one-third)
- ☐ _____
- ☐ _____

Day 4
- ☐ Genesis 41-42
- ☐ CCC 571-573
- ☐ TAS, chap. 13 (finish chapter)
- ☐ _____
- ☐ _____

Day 5
- ☐ Genesis 43
- ☐ CCC 574
- ☐ TAS, chap. 14 (one-third)
- ☐ _____
- ☐ _____

So then, brethren, stand firm and hold to the traditions which
you were taught by us, either by word of mouth or by letter.

— 2 THESSALONIANS 2:15

Year 2, Week 7

Day 1
- ☐ Genesis 44
- ☐ CCC 575
- ☐ TAS, chap. 14 (one-third)
- ☐ _____
- ☐ _____

Day 2
- ☐ Genesis 45-46
- ☐ CCC 576
- ☐ TAS, chap. 14 (finish chapter)
- ☐ _____
- ☐ _____

Day 3
- ☐ Genesis 47
- ☐ CCC 577
- ☐ TAS, chap. 15 (one-fourth)
- ☐ _____
- ☐ _____

Day 4
- ☐ Genesis 48-49
- ☐ CCC 578
- ☐ TAS, chap. 15 (one-fourth)
- ☐ _____
- ☐ _____

Day 5
- ☐ Genesis 50
- ☐ CCC 579-580
- ☐ TAS, chap. 15 (one-fourth)
- ☐ _____
- ☐ _____

Year 2, Week 8

Day 1
- ☐ Exodus 1-2
- ☐ CCC 581-582
- ☐ TAS, chap. 15 (finish chapter)
- ☐ _____
- ☐ _____

Day 2
- ☐ Exodus 3
- ☐ CCC 583-584
- ☐ TAS, chap. 16 (half)
- ☐ _____
- ☐ _____

Day 3
- ☐ Exodus 4-5
- ☐ CCC 585-586
- ☐ TAS, chap. 16 (finish chapter)
- ☐ _____
- ☐ _____

Day 4
- ☐ Exodus 6
- ☐ CCC 587-588
- ☐ TAS, chap. 17 (half)
- ☐ _____
- ☐ _____

Day 5
- ☐ Exodus 7-8
- ☐ CCC 589-590
- ☐ TAS, chap. 17 (finish chapter)
- ☐ _____
- ☐ _____

Christian soul, if you desire to walk securely, be
guided in all your actions by obedience.

—SAINT ALPHONSUS LIGUORI, *THE 12 STEPS TO HOLINESS AND SALVATION*

Year 2, Week 9

Day 1
- ☐ Exodus 9-10
- ☐ CCC 591
- ☐ TAS, chap. 18 (half)
- ☐ _____
- ☐ _____

Day 2
- ☐ Exodus 11
- ☐ CCC 592-594
- ☐ TAS, chap. 18 (finish chapter)
- ☐ _____
- ☐ _____

Day 3
- ☐ Exodus 12-13
- ☐ CCC 595
- ☐ TAS, chap. 19 (half)
- ☐ _____
- ☐ _____

Day 4
- ☐ Exodus 14
- ☐ CCC 596
- ☐ TAS, chap. 19 (finish chapter)
- ☐ _____
- ☐ _____

Day 5
- ☐ Exodus 15-16
- ☐ CCC 597
- ☐ TAS, chap. 20 (half)
- ☐ _____
- ☐ _____

Year 2, Week 10

Day 1
- ☐ Exodus 17-18
- ☐ CCC 598
- ☐ TAS, chap. 20 (finish chapter)
- ☐ _____
- ☐ _____

Day 2
- ☐ Exodus 19
- ☐ CCC 599-600
- ☐ TAS, chap. 21 (one-third)
- ☐ _____
- ☐ _____

Day 3
- ☐ Exodus 20-21
- ☐ CCC 601
- ☐ TAS, chap. 21 (one-third)
- ☐ _____
- ☐ _____

Day 4
- ☐ Exodus 22
- ☐ CCC 602
- ☐ TAS, chap. 21 (finish chapter)
- ☐ _____
- ☐ _____

Day 5
- ☐ Exodus 23-24
- ☐ CCC 603
- ☐ TAS, chap. 22 (half)
- ☐ _____
- ☐ _____

You must all follow the bishop as Jesus Christ follows the Father, and the presbytery as you would the Apostles.

— SAINT IGNATIUS OF ANTIOCH, *LETTER TO THE SMYRNAEANS*, CA. AD 110

Year 2, Week 11

Day 1
- ☐ Exodus 25-26
- ☐ CCC 604-605
- ☐ TAS, chap. 22 (finish chapter)
- ☐ _____
- ☐ _____

Day 2
- ☐ Exodus 27
- ☐ CCC 606
- ☐ TAS, chap. 23 (half)
- ☐ _____
- ☐ _____

Day 3
- ☐ Exodus 28-29
- ☐ CCC 607
- ☐ TAS, chap. 23 (finish chapter)
- ☐ _____
- ☐ _____

Day 4
- ☐ Exodus 30
- ☐ CCC 608
- ☐ TAS, chap. 24 (half)
- ☐ _____
- ☐ _____

Day 5
- ☐ Exodus 31-32
- ☐ CCC 609
- ☐ TAS, chap. 24 (finish chapter)
- ☐ _____
- ☐ _____

Year 2, Week 12

Day 1
- ☐ Exodus 33-34
- ☐ CCC 610-611
- ☐ TAS, chap. 25 (half)
- ☐ _____
- ☐ _____

Day 2
- ☐ Exodus 35
- ☐ CCC 612
- ☐ TAS, chap. 25 (finish chapter)
- ☐ _____
- ☐ _____

Day 3
- ☐ Exodus 36-37
- ☐ CCC 613-614
- ☐ TAS, chap. 26 (half)
- ☐ _____
- ☐ _____

Day 4
- ☐ Exodus 38
- ☐ CCC 615
- ☐ TAS, chap. 26 (finish chapter)
- ☐ _____
- ☐ _____

Day 5
- ☐ Exodus 39-40
- ☐ CCC 616-617
- ☐ TAS, chap. 27 (half)
- ☐ _____
- ☐ _____

For where the Church is, there is the Spirit of God; and where the Spirit of God, there the Church and every grace. The Spirit, however, is Truth.

— SAINT IRENAEUS, *AGAINST HERESIES*, CA. AD 180

Year 2, Week 13

Day 1
☐ Leviticus 1
☐ CCC 618
☐ TAS, chap. 27 (finish chapter)
☐ _____
☐ _____

Day 2
☐ Leviticus 2
☐ CCC 619-621
☐ TAS, chap. 28 (half)
☐ _____
☐ _____

Day 3
☐ Leviticus 3-4
☐ CCC 622-623
☐ TAS, chap. 28 (finish chapter)
☐ _____
☐ _____

Day 4
☐ Leviticus 5
☐ CCC 624
☐ TAS, chap. 29 (half)
☐ _____
☐ _____

Day 5
☐ Leviticus 6
☐ CCC 625-626
☐ TAS, chap. 29 (finish chapter)
☐ _____
☐ _____

Year 2, Week 14

Day 1
☐ Leviticus 7
☐ CCC 627-628
☐ TAS, chap. 30 (one-third)
☐ _____
☐ _____

Day 2
☐ Leviticus 8-9
☐ CCC 629-630
☐ TAS, chap. 30 (one-third)
☐ _____
☐ _____

Day 3
☐ Leviticus 10
☐ CCC 631
☐ TAS, Ch 30 (finish chapter)
☐ _____
☐ _____

Day 4
☐ Leviticus 11-12
☐ CCC 632-633
☐ TAS, chap. 31 (one-fourth)
☐ _____
☐ _____

Day 5
☐ Leviticus 13
☐ CCC 634-635
☐ TAS, chap. 31 (one-fourth)
☐ _____
☐ _____

Those who have been illuminated are, after
Baptism, to be anointed with celestial chrism.

— COUNCIL OF LAODICEA

Year 2, Week 15

Day 1
- ☐ Leviticus 14
- ☐ CCC 636-637
- ☐ TAS, chap. 31 (one-fourth)
- ☐ _____
- ☐ _____

Day 2
- ☐ Leviticus 15-16
- ☐ CCC 638
- ☐ TAS, chap. 31 (finish chapter)
- ☐ _____
- ☐ _____

Day 3
- ☐ Leviticus 17
- ☐ CCC 639
- ☐ TAS, chap. 32 (one-third)
- ☐ _____
- ☐ _____

Day 4
- ☐ Leviticus 18-19
- ☐ CCC 640
- ☐ TAS, chap. 32 (one-third)
- ☐ _____
- ☐ _____

Day 5
- ☐ Leviticus 20
- ☐ CCC 641-642
- ☐ TAS, chap. 32 (finish chapter)
- ☐ _____
- ☐ _____

Year 2, Week 16

Day 1
- ☐ Leviticus 21
- ☐ CCC 643
- ☐ *Christianity for Modern Pagans* (CMP), preface (half)
- ☐ _____
- ☐ _____

Day 2
- ☐ Leviticus 22-23
- ☐ CCC 644
- ☐ CMP, finish preface
- ☐ _____
- ☐ _____

Day 3
- ☐ Leviticus 24
- ☐ CCC 645-646
- ☐ CMP, chap. 1 (half)
- ☐ _____
- ☐ _____

Day 4
- ☐ Leviticus 25-26
- ☐ CCC 647
- ☐ CMP, chap. 1 (finish chapter)
- ☐ _____
- ☐ _____

Day 5
- ☐ Leviticus 27
- ☐ CCC 648
- ☐ CMP, chap. 2 (half)
- ☐ _____
- ☐ _____

> For those who do penance in accord with the kind of sin they
> have committed are not to despair of receiving God's mercy in the
> Holy Church, for the remission of their crimes, however serious.
>
> — SAINT AUGUSTINE, *ENCHIRIDION*, AD 421

Year 2, Week 17

Day 1
- ☐ Numbers 1
- ☐ CCC 649-650
- ☐ CMP, chap. 2 (finish chapter)
- ☐ _____
- ☐ _____

Day 2
- ☐ Numbers 2-3
- ☐ CCC 651-652
- ☐ CMP, chap. 3
- ☐ _____
- ☐ _____

Day 3
- ☐ Numbers 4
- ☐ CCC 653
- ☐ CMP, chap. 4 (one-fifth)
- ☐ _____
- ☐ _____

Day 4
- ☐ Numbers 5-6
- ☐ CCC 654
- ☐ CMP, chap. 4 (one-fifth)
- ☐ _____
- ☐ _____

Day 5
- ☐ Numbers 7
- ☐ CCC 655
- ☐ CMP, chap. 4 (one-fifth)
- ☐ _____
- ☐ _____

Year 2, Week 18

Day 1
- ☐ Numbers 8
- ☐ CCC 656-658
- ☐ CMP, chap. 4 (one-fifth)
- ☐ _____
- ☐ _____

Day 2
- ☐ Numbers 9-10
- ☐ CCC 659
- ☐ CMP, chap. 4 (finish chapter)
- ☐ _____
- ☐ _____

Day 3
- ☐ Numbers 11
- ☐ CCC 660-661
- ☐ CMP, chap. 5 (one-third)
- ☐ _____
- ☐ _____

Day 4
- ☐ Numbers 12-13
- ☐ CCC 662-664
- ☐ CMP, chap. 5 (one-third)
- ☐ _____
- ☐ _____

Day 5
- ☐ Numbers 14
- ☐ CCC 665-667
- ☐ CMP, chap. 5 (finish chapter)
- ☐ _____
- ☐ _____

> And I tell you, you are Peter, and on this rock I will build my church, and the powers of death shall not prevail against it. I will give you the keys of the kingdom of heaven, and whatever you bind on earth shall be bound in heaven, and whatever you loose on earth shall be loosed in heaven.
>
> — MATTHEW 16:18–19

Year 2, Week 19

Day 1
- ☐ Numbers 15-16
- ☐ CCC 668-670
- ☐ CMP, chap. 6 (half)
- ☐ _____
- ☐ _____

Day 2
- ☐ Numbers 17
- ☐ CCC 671
- ☐ CMP, chap. 6 (finish chapter)
- ☐ _____
- ☐ _____

Day 3
- ☐ Numbers 18-19
- ☐ CCC 672
- ☐ CMP, chap. 7 (half)
- ☐ _____
- ☐ _____

Day 4
- ☐ Numbers 20
- ☐ CCC 673-674
- ☐ CMP, chap. 7 (finish chapter)
- ☐ _____
- ☐ _____

Day 5
- ☐ Numbers 21-22
- ☐ CCC 675
- ☐ CMP, chap. 8 (half)
- ☐ _____
- ☐ _____

Year 2, Week 20

Day 1
- ☐ Numbers 23
- ☐ CCC 676-677
- ☐ CMP, chap. 8 (finish chapter)
- ☐ _____
- ☐ _____

Day 2
- ☐ Numbers 24-25
- ☐ CCC 678-679
- ☐ CMP, chap. 9
- ☐ _____
- ☐ _____

Day 3
- ☐ Numbers 26
- ☐ CCC 680-682
- ☐ CMP, chap. 10 (one-fourth)
- ☐ _____
- ☐ _____

Day 4
- ☐ Numbers 27-28
- ☐ CCC 683
- ☐ CMP, chap. 10 (one-fourth)
- ☐ _____
- ☐ _____

Day 5
- ☐ Numbers 29
- ☐ CCC 684
- ☐ CMP, chap. 10 (one-fourth)
- ☐ _____
- ☐ _____

I am amazed that some are utterly in doubt as to whether or not the Holy Virgin is able to be called Mother of God. For if our Lord Jesus Christ is God, how should the Holy Virgin who bore Him not be the Mother of God?

— SAINT CYRIL OF ALEXANDRIA, *LETTER TO THE MONKS OF EGYPT*, AD 423/431

Year 2, Week 21

Day 1
- ☐ Numbers 30
- ☐ CCC 685-686
- ☐ CMP, chap. 10 (finish chapter)
- ☐ _____
- ☐ _____

Day 2
- ☐ Numbers 31-32
- ☐ CCC 687
- ☐ CMP, chap. 11
- ☐ _____
- ☐ _____

Day 3
- ☐ Numbers 33
- ☐ CCC 688
- ☐ CMP, chap. 12 (one-third)
- ☐ _____
- ☐ _____

Day 4
- ☐ Numbers 34-35
- ☐ CCC 689
- ☐ CMP, chap. 12 (one-third)
- ☐ _____
- ☐ _____

Day 5
- ☐ Numbers 36
- ☐ CCC 690
- ☐ CMP, chap. 12 (finish chapter)
- ☐ _____
- ☐ _____

Year 2, Week 22

Day 1
- ☐ Deuteronomy 1
- ☐ CCC 691
- ☐ CMP, chap. 13 (one-fourth)
- ☐ _____
- ☐ _____

Day 2
- ☐ Deuteronomy 2-3
- ☐ CCC 692-693
- ☐ CMP, chap. 13 (one-fourth)
- ☐ _____
- ☐ _____

Day 3
- ☐ Deuteronomy 4
- ☐ CCC 694-695
- ☐ CMP, chap. 13 (one-fourth)
- ☐ _____
- ☐ _____

Day 4
- ☐ Deuteronomy 5-6
- ☐ CCC 696-697
- ☐ CMP, chap. 13 (finish chapter)
- ☐ _____
- ☐ _____

Day 5
- ☐ Deuteronomy 7
- ☐ CCC 698-701
- ☐ CMP, chap. 14 (one-third)
- ☐ _____
- ☐ _____

Although among the people of God there are many
priests and many pastors, it is really Peter who rules them
all, of whom, too, it is Christ who is their chief ruler.

— ST. LEO, SERMON 4

Year 2, Week 23

Day 1
- ☐ Deuteronomy 8
- ☐ CCC 702
- ☐ CMP, chap. 14 (one-third)
- ☐ _____
- ☐ _____

Day 2
- ☐ Deuteronomy 9-10
- ☐ CCC 703-704
- ☐ CMP, chap. 14 (finish chapter)
- ☐ _____
- ☐ _____

Day 3
- ☐ Deuteronomy 11
- ☐ CCC 705-706
- ☐ CMP, part 4, introduction; chap. 15 (half)
- ☐ _____
- ☐ _____

Day 4
- ☐ Deuteronomy 12-13
- ☐ CCC 707-708
- ☐ CMP, chap. 15 (finish chapter)
- ☐ _____
- ☐ _____

Day 5
- ☐ Deuteronomy 14
- ☐ CCC 709-710
- ☐ CMP, chap. 16 (half)
- ☐ _____
- ☐ _____

Year 2, Week 24

Day 1
- ☐ Deuteronomy 15
- ☐ CCC 711-712
- ☐ CMP, chap. 16 (finish chapter)
- ☐ _____
- ☐ _____

Day 2
- ☐ Deuteronomy 16
- ☐ CCC 713-714
- ☐ CMP, chap. 17 (half)
- ☐ _____
- ☐ _____

Day 3
- ☐ Deuteronomy 17-18
- ☐ CCC 715-716
- ☐ CMP, chap. 17 (finish chapter)
- ☐ _____
- ☐ _____

Day 4
- ☐ Deuteronomy 19
- ☐ CCC 717-718
- ☐ CMP, chap. 18
- ☐ _____
- ☐ _____

Day 5
- ☐ Deuteronomy 20
- ☐ CCC 719-720
- ☐ CMP, chap. 19 (one third)
- ☐ _____
- ☐ _____

Neither faith without works nor works without faith is of any avail, except, perhaps, that works may go towards the reception of faith.

— SAINT GREGORY, *HOMILIES ON EZEKIEL*, AD 593

Year 2, Week 25

Day 1
☐ Deuteronomy 21
☐ CCC 721-722
☐ CMP, chap. 19 (one-third)
☐ _____
☐ _____

Day 2
☐ Deuteronomy 22-23
☐ CCC 723-726
☐ CMP, chap. 19 (finish chapter)
☐ _____
☐ _____

Day 3
☐ Deuteronomy 24
☐ CCC 727-728
☐ CMP, chap. 20
☐ _____
☐ _____

Day 4
☐ Deuteronomy 25-26
☐ CCC 729-730
☐ CMP, chap. 21
☐ _____
☐ _____

Day 5
☐ Deuteronomy 27
☐ CCC 731-732
☐ CMP, chaps. 22-23
☐ _____
☐ _____

Year 2, Week 26

Day 1
☐ Deuteronomy 28
☐ CCC 733-736
☐ CMP, chap. 24 (half)
☐ _____
☐ _____

Day 2
☐ Deuteronomy 29-30
☐ CCC 737-738
☐ CMP, chap. 24 (finish chapter)
☐ _____
☐ _____

Day 3
☐ Deuteronomy 31
☐ CCC 739-741
☐ CMP, chap. 25 (one-third)
☐ _____
☐ _____

Day 4
☐ Deuteronomy 32-33
☐ CCC 742-747
☐ CMP, chap. 25 (one-third)
☐ _____
☐ _____

Day 5
☐ Deuteronomy 34
☐ CCC 748
☐ CMP, chap. 25 (finish chapter)
☐ _____
☐ _____

For Jesus Christ, our inseparable life, is the will of
the Father, just as the bishops, who have been appointed
throughout the world, are the will of Jesus Christ.

— ST. IGNATIUS OF ANTIOCH, *LETTER TO THE EPHESIANS*, CA. AD 110

Year 2, Week 27

Day 1
- ☐ Joshua 1-2
- ☐ CCC 749-750
- ☐ CMP, chap. 26
- ☐ _____
- ☐ _____

Day 2
- ☐ Joshua 3
- ☐ CCC 751-752
- ☐ CMP, chap. 27 (half)
- ☐ _____
- ☐ _____

Day 3
- ☐ Joshua 4-5
- ☐ CCC 753-755
- ☐ CMP, chap. 27 (finish chapter)
- ☐ _____
- ☐ _____

Day 4
- ☐ Joshua 6
- ☐ CCC 756-757
- ☐ CMP, chap. 28 (half)
- ☐ _____
- ☐ _____

Day 5
- ☐ Joshua 7-8
- ☐ CCC 758-759
- ☐ CMP, chap. 28 (finish chapter)
- ☐ _____
- ☐ _____

Year 2, Week 28

Day 1
- ☐ Joshua 9-10
- ☐ CCC 760
- ☐ *The End of the Modern World* (EMW), chap. 1, I (half)
- ☐ _____
- ☐ _____

Day 2
- ☐ Joshua 11
- ☐ CCC 761-762
- ☐ EMW, chap. 1, I (finish section)
- ☐ _____
- ☐ _____

Day 3
- ☐ Joshua 12-13
- ☐ CCC 763-764
- ☐ EMW, chap. 1, II (half)
- ☐ _____
- ☐ _____

Day 4
- ☐ Joshua 14
- ☐ CCC 765-766
- ☐ EMW, chap. 1, II (finish section)
- ☐ _____
- ☐ _____

Day 5
- ☐ Joshua 15-16
- ☐ CCC 767-768
- ☐ EMW, chap. 1, III
- ☐ _____
- ☐ _____

He cannot have God for his Father who does
not have the Church for his Mother.

— ST. CYPRIAN OF CARTHAGE, *THE UNITY OF
THE CATHOLIC CHURCH*, AD 251/256

Year 2, Week 29

Day 1
☐ Joshua 17-18
☐ CCC 769-770
☐ EMW, chap. 2, I (one-third)
☐ _____
☐ _____

Day 2
☐ Joshua 19
☐ CCC 771
☐ EMW, chap. 2, I (one-third)
☐ _____
☐ _____

Day 3
☐ Joshua 20-21
☐ CCC 772-773
☐ EMW, chap. 2, I (finish section)
☐ _____
☐ _____

Day 4
☐ Joshua 22
☐ CCC 774-775
☐ EMW, chap. 2, II
☐ _____
☐ _____

Day 5
☐ Joshua 23-24
☐ CCC 776
☐ EMW, chap. 3, I
☐ _____
☐ _____

Year 2, Week 30

Day 1
☐ Judges 1
☐ CCC 777-780
☐ EMW, chap. 3, II
☐ _____
☐ _____

Day 2
☐ Judges 2-3
☐ CCC 781
☐ EMW, chap. 3, III (one-third)
☐ _____
☐ _____

Day 3
☐ Judges 4
☐ CCC 782
☐ EMW, chap. 3, III (one-third)
☐ _____
☐ _____

Day 4
☐ Judges 5-6
☐ CCC 783-784
☐ EMW, chap. 3, III (finish section)
☐ _____
☐ _____

Day 5
☐ Judges 7
☐ CCC 785-786
☐ EMW, chap. 3, IV (one-third)
☐ _____
☐ _____

> The difference between Christians and the rest of men is neither
> in country, nor in language, nor in customs.... They pass their
> time on earth; but their citizenship is in heaven. They obey the
> established laws, and in their private lives they surpass the laws.
>
> — LETTER OF MATHETES TO DIOGNETUS, AD 125/200

Year 2, Week 31

Day 1
- [ ] Judges 8
- [ ] CCC 787-789
- [ ] EMW, chap. 3, IV (one-third)
- [ ] _____
- [ ] _____

Day 2
- [ ] Judges 9-10
- [ ] CCC 790-791
- [ ] EMW, chap. 3, IV (finish section)
- [ ] _____
- [ ] _____

Day 3
- [ ] Judges 11
- [ ] CCC 792-794
- [ ] EMW, chap. 3, V (half)
- [ ] _____
- [ ] _____

Day 4
- [ ] Judges 12-13
- [ ] CCC 795
- [ ] EMW, chap. 3, V (finish section)
- [ ] _____
- [ ] _____

Day 5
- [ ] Judges 14
- [ ] CCC 796
- [ ] EMW, chap. 4: introduction and I
- [ ] _____
- [ ] _____

Year 2, Week 32

Day 1
- [ ] Judges 15
- [ ] CCC 797
- [ ] EMW, chap. 4, II, III
- [ ] _____
- [ ] _____

Day 2
- [ ] Judges 16
- [ ] CCC 798
- [ ] EMW, chap. 5, I
- [ ] _____
- [ ] _____

Day 3
- [ ] Judges 17-18
- [ ] CCC 799-801
- [ ] EMW, chap. 5, II
- [ ] _____
- [ ] _____

Day 4
- [ ] Judges 19
- [ ] CCC 802-806
- [ ] EMW, chap. 5, III
- [ ] _____
- [ ] _____

Day 5
- [ ] Judges 20
- [ ] CCC 807-810
- [ ] EMW, chap. 6, I
- [ ] _____
- [ ] _____

I presume that you are not ignorant of the fact that the living Church is the body of Christ. The Scripture says, "God made man male and female." The male is Christ, and the female is the Church. Moreover, the Books and the Apostles declare that the Church belongs not to the present, but has existed from the beginning.

— "SECOND LETTER" OF CLEMENT OF ROME
TO THE CORINTHIANS, CA. AD 150

Year 2, Week 33

Day 1
- ☐ Judges 21
- ☐ CCC 811-812
- ☐ EMW, chap. 6, II (half)
- ☐ _____
- ☐ _____

Day 2
- ☐ Ruth 1
- ☐ CCC 813
- ☐ EMW, chap. 6, II (finish section)
- ☐ _____
- ☐ _____

Day 3
- ☐ Ruth 2
- ☐ CCC 814-815
- ☐ EMW, chap. 7, I
- ☐ _____
- ☐ _____

Day 4
- ☐ Ruth 3
- ☐ CCC 816
- ☐ EMW, chap. 7, II
- ☐ _____
- ☐ _____

Day 5
- ☐ Ruth 4
- ☐ CCC 817-819
- ☐ EMW, chap. 7, III (half)
- ☐ _____
- ☐ _____

Year 2, Week 34

Day 1
- ☐ 1 Samuel 1-2
- ☐ CCC 820-821
- ☐ EMW, chap. 7, III (finish section)
- ☐ _____
- ☐ _____

Day 2
- ☐ 1 Samuel 3
- ☐ CCC 822
- ☐ EMW, chap. 7, IV (half)
- ☐ _____
- ☐ _____

Day 3
- ☐ 1 Samuel 4-5
- ☐ CCC 823-825
- ☐ EMW, chap. 7, IV (finish section)
- ☐ _____
- ☐ _____

Day 4
- ☐ 1 Samuel 6
- ☐ CCC 826
- ☐ EMW, chap. 8, I
- ☐ _____
- ☐ _____

Day 5
- ☐ 1 Samuel 7-8
- ☐ CCC 827
- ☐ EMW, chap. 8, II
- ☐ _____
- ☐ _____

It is necessary to obey those who are the presbyters in the Church, those who, as we have shown, have succession from the Apostles; those who have received, with the succession of the episcopate, the sure charism of truth according to the good pleasure of the Father.

— SAINT IRENAEUS, *AGAINST HERESIES*, CA. AD 180

Year 2, Week 35

Day 1
- ☐ 1 Samuel 9
- ☐ CCC 828-829
- ☐ *How the Reformation Happened* (HRH), chap. 1 (one-seventh)
- ☐ _____
- ☐ _____

Day 2
- ☐ 1 Samuel 10-11
- ☐ CCC 830-831
- ☐ HRH, chap. 1 (one-seventh)
- ☐ _____
- ☐ _____

Day 3
- ☐ 1 Samuel 12
- ☐ CCC 832-833
- ☐ HRH, chap. 1 (one-seventh)
- ☐ _____
- ☐ _____

Day 4
- ☐ 1 Samuel 13-14
- ☐ CCC 834-835
- ☐ HRH, chap. 1 (one-seventh)
- ☐ _____
- ☐ _____

Day 5
- ☐ 1 Samuel 15
- ☐ CCC 836-838
- ☐ HRH, chap. 1 (one-seventh)
- ☐ _____
- ☐ _____

Year 2, Week 36

Day 1
- ☐ 1 Samuel 16-17
- ☐ CCC 839-840
- ☐ HRH, chap. 1 (one-seventh)
- ☐ _____
- ☐ _____

Day 2
- ☐ 1 Samuel 18
- ☐ CCC 841-843
- ☐ HRH, chap. 1 (finish chapter)
- ☐ _____
- ☐ _____

Day 3
- ☐ 1 Samuel 19-20
- ☐ CCC 844-845
- ☐ HRH, chap. 2 (one-third)
- ☐ _____
- ☐ _____

Day 4
- ☐ 1 Samuel 21
- ☐ CCC 846-848
- ☐ HRH, chap. 2 (one-third)
- ☐ _____
- ☐ _____

Day 5
- ☐ 1 Samuel 22-23
- ☐ CCC 849-850
- ☐ HRH, chap. 2 (finish chapter)
- ☐ _____
- ☐ _____

> Wherever it shall be clear that the truth of the Christian discipline and faith are present, there also will be found the truth of the Scriptures and of their explanation, and of all the Christian traditions.
>
> —TERTULLIAN, *THE DEMURRER AGAINST THE HERETICS*, CA. AD 200

Year 2, Week 37

Day 1
- ☐ 1 Samuel 24-25
- ☐ CCC 851-853
- ☐ HRH, chap. 3 (one-third)
- ☐ _____
- ☐ _____

Day 2
- ☐ 1 Samuel 26
- ☐ CCC 854-856
- ☐ HRH, chap. 3 (one-third)
- ☐ _____
- ☐ _____

Day 3
- ☐ 1 Samuel 27-28
- ☐ CCC 857
- ☐ HRH, chap. 3 (finish chapter)
- ☐ _____
- ☐ _____

Day 4
- ☐ 1 Samuel 29
- ☐ CCC 858-860
- ☐ HRH, chap. 4 (half)
- ☐ _____
- ☐ _____

Day 5
- ☐ 1 Samuel 30-31
- ☐ CCC 861-862
- ☐ HRH, chap. 4 (finish chapter)
- ☐ _____
- ☐ _____

Year 2, Week 38

Day 1
- ☐ 2 Samuel 1
- ☐ CCC 863-865
- ☐ HRH, chap. 5 (half)
- ☐ _____
- ☐ _____

Day 2
- ☐ 2 Samuel 2
- ☐ CCC 866-870
- ☐ HRH, chap. 5 (finish chapter)
- ☐ _____
- ☐ _____

Day 3
- ☐ 2 Samuel 3-4
- ☐ CCC 871-872
- ☐ HRH, chap. 6 (one-sixth)
- ☐ _____
- ☐ _____

Day 4
- ☐ 2 Samuel 5
- ☐ CCC 873
- ☐ HRH, chap. 6 (one-sixth)
- ☐ _____
- ☐ _____

Day 5
- ☐ 2 Samuel 6
- ☐ CCC 874-875
- ☐ HRH, chap. 6 (one-sixth)
- ☐ _____
- ☐ _____

When a presbyter is ordained, the bishop shall impose his hand upon his head, while the presbyters touch the one to be ordained; and the bishop shall speak after the fashion of those things said above, where we prescribed what was to be said in the ordination of a bishop.

— ST. HIPPOLYTUS OF ROME, *THE APOSTOLIC TRADITION*, CA. AD 215

Year 2, Week 39

Day 1
- ☐ 2 Samuel 7
- ☐ CCC 876-877
- ☐ HRH, chap. 6 (one-sixth)
- ☐ _____
- ☐ _____

Day 2
- ☐ 2 Samuel 8
- ☐ CCC 878-879
- ☐ HRH, chap. 6 (one-sixth)
- ☐ _____
- ☐ _____

Day 3
- ☐ 2 Samuel 9-10
- ☐ CCC 880-882
- ☐ HRH, chap. 6 (finish chapter)
- ☐ _____
- ☐ _____

Day 4
- ☐ 2 Samuel 11
- ☐ CCC 883-885
- ☐ HRH, chap. 7 (half)
- ☐ _____
- ☐ _____

Day 5
- ☐ 2 Samuel 12
- ☐ CCC 886-887
- ☐ HRH, chap. 7 (finish chapter)
- ☐ _____
- ☐ _____

Year 2, Week 40

Day 1
- ☐ 2 Samuel 13
- ☐ CCC 888-890
- ☐ HRH, chap. 8 (one-third)
- ☐ _____
- ☐ _____

Day 2
- ☐ 2 Samuel 14
- ☐ CCC 891-892
- ☐ HRH, chap. 8 (one-third)
- ☐ _____
- ☐ _____

Day 3
- ☐ 2 Samuel 15-16
- ☐ CCC 893-894
- ☐ HRH, chap. 8 (finish chapter)
- ☐ _____
- ☐ _____

Day 4
- ☐ 2 Samuel 17
- ☐ CCC 895-896
- ☐ HRH, chap. 9 (half)
- ☐ _____
- ☐ _____

Day 5
- ☐ 2 Samuel 18
- ☐ CCC 897-898
- ☐ HRH, chap. 9 (finish chapter)
- ☐ _____
- ☐ _____

It was the Spirit who kept preaching these words: "Do nothing without the bishop, keep your body as the temple of God, love unity, flee from divisions, be imitators of Jesus Christ, as He was imitator of the Father.

— ST. IGNATIUS OF ANTIOCH, *LETTER TO THE PHILADELPHIANS*, CA. AD 110

Year 2, Week 41

Day 1
- ☐ 2 Samuel 19
- ☐ CCC 899-900
- ☐ *Triumph: The Power and the Glory of the Catholic Church* (TPG), prologue
- ☐ _____
- ☐ _____

Day 2
- ☐ 2 Samuel 20
- ☐ CCC 901-903
- ☐ TPG, chap. 1, to "Paul, the Missionary Saint"
- ☐ _____
- ☐ _____

Day 3
- ☐ 2 Samuel 21-22
- ☐ CCC 904-905
- ☐ TPG, chap. 1, "Paul, the Missionary Saint" to end of chapter
- ☐ _____
- ☐ _____

Day 4
- ☐ 2 Samuel 23
- ☐ CCC 906-907
- ☐ TPG, chap. 2, to "How ... Christianity"
- ☐ _____
- ☐ _____

Day 5
- ☐ 2 Samuel 24
- ☐ CCC 908-910
- ☐ TPG, chap. 2, "How ... Christianity" to end of chapter
- ☐ _____
- ☐ _____

Year 2, Week 42

Day 1
- ☐ 1 Kings 1
- ☐ CCC 911-913
- ☐ TPG, chap. 3, to "The Visible Church"
- ☐ _____
- ☐ _____

Day 2
- ☐ 1 Kings 2-3
- ☐ CCC 914-916
- ☐ TPG, chap. 3, "The Visible Church" to end of chapter
- ☐ _____
- ☐ _____

Day 3
- ☐ 1 Kings 4
- ☐ CCC 917-919
- ☐ TPG, chap. 4, to "The Nicene Council"
- ☐ _____
- ☐ _____

Day 4
- ☐ 1 Kings 5-6
- ☐ CCC 920-921
- ☐ TPG, chap. 4, "The Nicene Council" to end of chapter
- ☐ _____
- ☐ _____

Day 5
- ☐ 1 Kings 7
- ☐ CCC 922-924
- ☐ TPG, chap. 5, to "Theodosius ... Imperium"
- ☐ _____
- ☐ _____

Year 2, Week 43

Day 1
- ☐ 1 Kings 8-9
- ☐ CCC 925-927
- ☐ TPG, chap. 5, "Theodosius … Imperium" to end of chapter
- ☐ _____
- ☐ _____

Day 2
- ☐ 1 Kings 10
- ☐ CCC 928-929
- ☐ TPG, chap. 6, to "The Cinders … Faith"
- ☐ _____
- ☐ _____

Day 3
- ☐ 1 Kings 11-12
- ☐ CCC 930
- ☐ TPG, chap. 6, "The Cinders … Faith" to "The Barbarian … Patrick"
- ☐ _____
- ☐ _____

Day 4
- ☐ 1 Kings 13
- ☐ CCC 931-932
- ☐ TPG, chap. 6, "The Barbarian … Patrick" to end of chapter
- ☐ _____
- ☐ _____

Day 5
- ☐ 1 Kings 14-15
- ☐ CCC 933
- ☐ TPG, chap. 7, to "Smashing the Icons"
- ☐ _____
- ☐ _____

Year 2, Week 44

Day 1
- ☐ 1 Kings 16
- ☐ CCC 934-937
- ☐ TPG, chap. 7, "Smashing the Icons" to end of chapter
- ☐ _____
- ☐ _____

Day 2
- ☐ 1 Kings 17-18
- ☐ CCC 938-941
- ☐ TPG, chap. 8, to "The … Papacy"
- ☐ _____
- ☐ _____

Day 3
- ☐ 1 Kings 19
- ☐ CCC 942-945
- ☐ TPG, chap. 8, "The … Papacy" to end of chapter
- ☐ _____
- ☐ _____

Day 4
- ☐ 1 Kings 20-21
- ☐ CCC 946-948
- ☐ TPG, chap. 9, to "The Monks … Battle"
- ☐ _____
- ☐ _____

Day 5
- ☐ 1 Kings 22
- ☐ CCC 949-953
- ☐ TPG, chap. 9 "The Monks … Battle" to "The Crusade …"
- ☐ _____
- ☐ _____

The Church received from the Apostles the tradition of giving Baptism even to infants. For the Apostles … knew that there is in everyone the innate stains of sin, which must be washed away through water and the Spirit.

— ORIGEN, *COMMENTARIES ON ROMANS*, POST AD 244

Year 2, Week 45

Day 1
- ☐ 2 Kings 1
- ☐ CCC 954-955
- ☐ TPG, chap. 9, "The Crusade ..." to end of chapter
- ☐ _____
- ☐ _____

Day 2
- ☐ 2 Kings 2
- ☐ CCC 956-957
- ☐ TPG, chap. 10, to "The Heart of Assisi"
- ☐ _____
- ☐ _____

Day 3
- ☐ 2 Kings 3-4
- ☐ CCC 958-959
- ☐ TPG, chap. 10, "The Heart of Assisi" to end of chapter
- ☐ _____
- ☐ _____

Day 4
- ☐ 2 Kings 5
- ☐ CCC 960-962
- ☐ TPG, chap. 11, to "Laying ... Law"
- ☐ _____
- ☐ _____

Day 5
- ☐ 2 Kings 6
- ☐ CCC 963-964
- ☐ TPG, chap. 11, "Laying ... Law" to "Tilting ... France"
- ☐ _____
- ☐ _____

Year 2, Week 46

Day 1
- ☐ 2 Kings 7
- ☐ CCC 965-966
- ☐ TPG, chap. 11, "Tilting ... France" to end of chapter
- ☐ _____
- ☐ _____

Day 2
- ☐ 2 Kings 8-9
- ☐ CCC 967-970
- ☐ TPG, chap. 12, to "The French Papacy"
- ☐ _____
- ☐ _____

Day 3
- ☐ 2 Kings 10
- ☐ CCC 971-972
- ☐ TPG, chap. 12, "The French Papacy" to "Albion's Seed"
- ☐ _____
- ☐ _____

Day 4
- ☐ 2 Kings 11-12
- ☐ CCC 973-975
- ☐ TPG, chap. 12, "Albion's Seed" to end of chapter
- ☐ _____
- ☐ _____

Day 5
- ☐ 2 Kings 13
- ☐ CCC 976-977
- ☐ TPG, chap. 13, to "The Borgias ... Popes"
- ☐ _____
- ☐ _____

After the martyrdom of Paul and Peter, Linus was the first
appointed to the episcopacy of the Church at Rome.

— EUSEBIUS PAMPHILUS, *HISTORY OF THE CHURCH*

Year 2, Week 47

Day 1
- ☐ 2 Kings 14
- ☐ CCC 978-980
- ☐ TPG, chap. 13, "The Borgias ... Popes" to "Viva Iberia"
- ☐ _____
- ☐ _____

Day 2
- ☐ 2 Kings 15
- ☐ CCC 981-983
- ☐ TPG, chap. 13, "Viva Iberia" to end of chapter
- ☐ _____
- ☐ _____

Day 3
- ☐ 2 Kings 16-17
- ☐ CCC 984-987
- ☐ TPG, chap. 14, to "Martin Luther"
- ☐ _____
- ☐ _____

Day 4
- ☐ 2 Kings 18
- ☐ CCC 988-989
- ☐ TPG, chap. 14, "Martin Luther" (half)
- ☐ _____
- ☐ _____

Day 5
- ☐ 2 Kings 19
- ☐ CCC 990-991
- ☐ TPG, chap. 14, "Martin Luther" (finish section)
- ☐ _____
- ☐ _____

Year 2, Week 48

Day 1
- ☐ 2 Kings 20
- ☐ CCC 992-994
- ☐ TPG, chap. 14, "Calvin ... State"
- ☐ _____
- ☐ _____

Day 2
- ☐ 2 Kings 21
- ☐ CCC 995-996
- ☐ TPG, chap. 15 through "The King's Good Servant" (half of section)
- ☐ _____
- ☐ _____

Day 3
- ☐ 2 Kings 22-23
- ☐ CCC 997-1001
- ☐ TPG, chap. 15, "The King's Good Servant" (finish section)
- ☐ _____
- ☐ _____

Day 4
- ☐ 2 Kings 24
- ☐ CCC 1002
- ☐ TPG, chap. 15, "The Honorable Company" to end of chapter
- ☐ _____
- ☐ _____

Day 5
- ☐ 2 Kings 25
- ☐ CCC 1003-1004
- ☐ TPG, chap. 16 through "The War in France" (half)
- ☐ _____
- ☐ _____

Year 2, Week 49

Day 1
- ☐ 1 Chronicles 1
- ☐ CCC 1005-1006
- ☐ TPG, chap. 16, "The War in France" (finish section)
- ☐ _____
- ☐ _____

Day 2
- ☐ 1 Chronicles 2-3
- ☐ CCC 1007-1009
- ☐ TPG, chap. 16, "The War in Germany"
- ☐ _____
- ☐ _____

Day 3
- ☐ 1 Chronicles 4
- ☐ CCC 1010-1011
- ☐ TPG, chap. 16, "An English Coda"
- ☐ _____
- ☐ _____

Day 4
- ☐ 1 Chronicles 5-6
- ☐ CCC 1012-1014
- ☐ TPG, chap. 17, to "The Sun King"
- ☐ _____
- ☐ _____

Day 5
- ☐ 1 Chronicles 7
- ☐ CCC 1015-1019
- ☐ TPG, chap. 17, "The Sun King"
- ☐ _____
- ☐ _____

Year 2, Week 50

Day 1
- ☐ 1 Chronicles 8-9
- ☐ CCC 1020
- ☐ TPG, chap. 17, "The War ... Succession" to end of chapter
- ☐ _____
- ☐ _____

Day 2
- ☐ 1 Chronicles 10
- ☐ CCC 1021-1022
- ☐ TPG, chap. 18, to "The Suppression ..."
- ☐ _____
- ☐ _____

Day 3
- ☐ 1 Chronicles 11-12
- ☐ CCC 1023-1025
- ☐ TPG, chap. 18, "The Suppression ..."
- ☐ _____
- ☐ _____

Day 4
- ☐ 1 Chronicles 13
- ☐ CCC 1026-1029
- ☐ TPG, chap. 18, "Reason's Bloody Terror"
- ☐ _____
- ☐ _____

Day 5
- ☐ 1 Chronicles 14-15
- ☐ CCC 1030-1032
- ☐ TPG, chap. 19, to "Kulturkampf" (half)
- ☐ _____
- ☐ _____

Look at the great foundation of the Church, that most solid of rocks, upon whom Christ built the Church! And what does the Lord say to him? "O you of little faith," He says, "why did you doubt?"

— ORIGEN, *HOMILIES ON EXODUS*, POST AD 244

Year 2, Week 51

Day 1
- ☐ 1 Chronicles 16
- ☐ CCC 1033-1035
- ☐ TPG, chap. 19, to "Kulturkampf" (finish section)
- ☐ _____
- ☐ _____

Day 2
- ☐ 1 Chronicles 17-18
- ☐ CCC 1036-1037
- ☐ TPG, chap. 19, "Kulturkampf"
- ☐ _____
- ☐ _____

Day 3
- ☐ 1 Chronicles 19
- ☐ CCC 1038-1039
- ☐ TPG, chap. 19, "The English ... Revival"
- ☐ _____
- ☐ _____

Day 4
- ☐ 1 Chronicles 20-21
- ☐ CCC 1040-1041
- ☐ TPG, chap. 20, to "The Age ... Dictators"
- ☐ _____
- ☐ _____

Day 5
- ☐ 1 Chronicles 22
- ☐ CCC 1042-1044
- ☐ TPG, chap. 20, "The Age ... Dictators"
- ☐ _____
- ☐ _____

Year 2, Week 52

Day 1
- ☐ 1 Chronicles 23
- ☐ CCC 1045-1047
- ☐ TPG, chap. 20, "The Crucifixion ... Spain"
- ☐ _____
- ☐ _____

Day 2
- ☐ 1 Chronicles 24-25
- ☐ CCC 1048-1050
- ☐ TPG, chap. 21, to "Restoration"
- ☐ _____
- ☐ _____

Day 3
- ☐ 1 Chronicles 26
- ☐ CCC 1051-1055
- ☐ TPG, chap. 21, "Restoration"
- ☐ _____
- ☐ _____

Day 4
- ☐ 1 Chronicles 27-28
- ☐ CCC 1056-1060
- ☐ TPG, chap. 21, "Vatican II ... Vitae"
- ☐ _____
- ☐ _____

Day 5
- ☐ 1 Chronicles 29
- ☐ CCC 1061-1065
- ☐ TPG, chap. 21, "The Era ..."; epilogue
- ☐ _____
- ☐ _____

—— Year 3 ——

Reading List

Sacred Scripture: Old Testament: 1 Chronicles through Song of Solomon

Catechism of the Catholic Church: The Celebration of the Christian Mystery

Spiritual Reading:

   This Tremendous Lover by M. Eugene Boylan (7 weeks)

   The Diary of a Country Priest by Georges Bernanos (5 weeks)

   The Sinner's Guide by Venerable Louis of Grenada (8 weeks)

   The Lord by Romano Guardini (18 weeks)

   Covenanted Happiness by Corma Burke (3 weeks)

   The Betrothed by Alessandro Manzoni (11 weeks)

My most important duty will be to pay my daily visit to the
Blessed Sacrament, with the greatest fervor. I owe everything
to the Blessed Sacrament and to the Sacred Heart of Jesus: so
I will have a most loving devotion to the Blessed Sacrament.

— SAINT JOHN XXIII, *JOURNAL OF A SOUL*

Year 3, Week 1

Day 1
- ☐ 2 Chronicles 1
- ☐ CCC 1066-1068
- ☐ *This Tremendous Love* (TTL), preface; introduction
- ☐ _____
- ☐ _____

Day 2
- ☐ 2 Chronicles 2-3
- ☐ CCC 1069-1070
- ☐ TTL, chap. 1; chap. 2 (half)
- ☐ _____
- ☐ _____

Day 3
- ☐ 2 Chronicles 4
- ☐ CCC 1071-1073
- ☐ TTL, chap. 2 (finish chapter)
- ☐ _____
- ☐ _____

Day 4
- ☐ 2 Chronicles 5-6
- ☐ CCC 1074-1075
- ☐ TTL, chap. 3
- ☐ _____
- ☐ _____

Day 5
- ☐ 2 Chronicles 7
- ☐ CCC 1076
- ☐ TTL, chap. 4
- ☐ _____
- ☐ _____

Year 3, Week 2

Day 1
- ☐ 2 Chronicles 8
- ☐ CCC 1077-1080
- ☐ TTL, chap. 5
- ☐ _____
- ☐ _____

Day 2
- ☐ 2 Chronicles 9-10
- ☐ CCC 1081-1083
- ☐ TTL, chap. 6
- ☐ _____
- ☐ _____

Day 3
- ☐ 2 Chronicles 11
- ☐ CCC 1084-1085
- ☐ TTL, chap. 7 (half)
- ☐ _____
- ☐ _____

Day 4
- ☐ 2 Chronicles 12-13
- ☐ CCC 1086-1087
- ☐ TTL, chap. 7 (finish chapter)
- ☐ _____
- ☐ _____

Day 5
- ☐ 2 Chronicles 14
- ☐ CCC 1088-1089
- ☐ TTL, chap. 8 (half)
- ☐ _____
- ☐ _____

Confess your offenses in the Church, and do not go up to your prayer with an evil conscience. This is the way of life.

— *DIDACHE*

Year 3, Week 3

Day 1
- ☐ 2 Chronicles 15-16
- ☐ CCC 1090-1092
- ☐ TTL, chap. 8 (finish chapter)
- ☐ _____
- ☐ _____

Day 2
- ☐ 2 Chronicles 17
- ☐ CCC 1093-1095
- ☐ TTL, chap. 9 (half)
- ☐ _____
- ☐ _____

Day 3
- ☐ 2 Chronicles 18-19
- ☐ CCC 1096-1098
- ☐ TTL, chap. 9 (finish chapter)
- ☐ _____
- ☐ _____

Day 4
- ☐ 2 Chronicles 20
- ☐ CCC 1099-1101
- ☐ TPG, chap. 10
- ☐ _____
- ☐ _____

Day 5
- ☐ 2 Chronicles 21-22
- ☐ CCC 1102-1103
- ☐ TPG, chap. 11 (half)
- ☐ _____
- ☐ _____

Year 3, Week 4

Day 1
- ☐ 2 Chronicles 23
- ☐ CCC 1104-1107
- ☐ TTL, chap. 11 (finish chapter)
- ☐ _____
- ☐ _____

Day 2
- ☐ 2 Chronicles 24-25
- ☐ CCC 1108-1109
- ☐ TTL, chap. 12
- ☐ _____
- ☐ _____

Day 3
- ☐ 2 Chronicles 26
- ☐ CCC 1110-1112
- ☐ TTL, chap. 13
- ☐ _____
- ☐ _____

Day 4
- ☐ 2 Chronicles 27-28
- ☐ CCC 1113-1116
- ☐ TTL, chap. 14
- ☐ _____
- ☐ _____

Day 5
- ☐ 2 Chronicles 29
- ☐ CCC 1117-1119
- ☐ TTL, chap. 15 (half)
- ☐ _____
- ☐ _____

> I have no taste for corruptible food nor for the pleasures of this life. I desire the Bread of God, which is the Flesh of Jesus Christ, who was of the seed of David; and for drink I desire His Blood, which is love incorruptible.
>
> —ST. IGNATIUS OF ANTIOCH, *LETTER TO THE ROMANS*, CA. AD 110

Year 3, Week 5

Day 1
- ☐ 2 Chronicles 30
- ☐ CCC 1120-1121
- ☐ TTL, chap. 15 (finish chapter)
- ☐ _____
- ☐ _____

Day 2
- ☐ 2 Chronicles 31-32
- ☐ CCC 1122-1124
- ☐ TTL, chap. 16 (half)
- ☐ _____
- ☐ _____

Day 3
- ☐ 2 Chronicles 33
- ☐ CCC 1125-1126
- ☐ TTL, chap. 16 (finish chapter)
- ☐ _____
- ☐ _____

Day 4
- ☐ 2 Chronicles 34-35
- ☐ CCC 1127-1129
- ☐ TTL, chap. 17 (half)
- ☐ _____
- ☐ _____

Day 5
- ☐ 2 Chronicles 36
- ☐ CCC 1130
- ☐ TTL, chap. 17 (finish chapter)
- ☐ _____
- ☐ _____

Year 3, Week 6

Day 1
- ☐ Ezra 1
- ☐ CCC 1131-1134
- ☐ TTL, chap. 18 (half)
- ☐ _____
- ☐ _____

Day 2
- ☐ Ezra 2
- ☐ CCC 1135
- ☐ TTL, chap. 18 (finish chapter)
- ☐ _____
- ☐ _____

Day 3
- ☐ Ezra 3
- ☐ CCC 1136-1139
- ☐ TTL, chap. 19
- ☐ _____
- ☐ _____

Day 4
- ☐ Ezra 4
- ☐ CCC 1140-1141
- ☐ TTL, chap. 20 (half)
- ☐ _____
- ☐ _____

Day 5
- ☐ Ezra 5
- ☐ CCC 1142-1144
- ☐ TTL, chap. 20 (finish chapter)
- ☐ _____
- ☐ _____

This is the Bread that strengthens the heart of a man, sustains
the traveler, raises the fallen, strengthens the weak, arms the
strong, gladdens the sorrowful, arouses the lukewarm, awakens the
slothful, cures the sick, and is the common remedy for all needs.

—VENERABLE LOUIS OF GRANADA, *SUMMA OF THE CHRISTIAN LIFE*

Year 3, Week 7

Day 1
- ☐ Ezra 6
- ☐ CCC 1145-1148
- ☐ TTL, chap. 21 (half)
- ☐ _____
- ☐ _____

Day 2
- ☐ Ezra 7
- ☐ CCC 1149-1152
- ☐ TTL, chap. 21 (finish chapter)
- ☐ _____
- ☐ _____

Day 3
- ☐ Ezra 8
- ☐ CCC 1153-1155
- ☐ TTL, chap. 22
- ☐ _____
- ☐ _____

Day 4
- ☐ Ezra 9
- ☐ CCC 1156
- ☐ TTL, chap. 23
- ☐ _____
- ☐ _____

Day 5
- ☐ Ezra 10
- ☐ CCC 1157-1158
- ☐ TTL, chap. 24
- ☐ _____
- ☐ _____

Year 3, Week 8

Day 1
- ☐ Nehemiah 1
- ☐ CCC 1159-1160
- ☐ *The Diary of a Country Priest* (DCP), chap. 1 (half)
- ☐ _____
- ☐ _____

Day 2
- ☐ Nehemiah 2-3
- ☐ CCC 1161-1162
- ☐ DCP, chap. 1 (finish chapter)
- ☐ _____
- ☐ _____

Day 3
- ☐ Nehemiah 4
- ☐ CCC 1163-1165
- ☐ DCP, chap. 2 (one-third)
- ☐ _____
- ☐ _____

Day 4
- ☐ Nehemiah 5-6
- ☐ CCC 1166-1167
- ☐ DCP, chap. 2 (one-third)
- ☐ _____
- ☐ _____

Day 5
- ☐ Nehemiah 7
- ☐ CCC 1168-1169
- ☐ DCP, chap. 2 (finish chapter)
- ☐ _____
- ☐ _____

Speak to my sisters that they love the Lord, and be content with their husbands in body and soul. In like manner, exhort my brothers in the name of Jesus Christ to love their wives as the Lord loved the Church.

— ST. IGNATIUS OF ANTIOCH, *LETTER TO POLYCARP*, CA. AD 110

Year 3, Week 9

Day 1
- ☐ Nehemiah 8
- ☐ CCC 1170-1171
- ☐ DCP, chap. 3 (one-third)
- ☐ _____
- ☐ _____

Day 2
- ☐ Nehemiah 9
- ☐ CCC 1172-1173
- ☐ DCP, chap. 3 (one-third)
- ☐ _____
- ☐ _____

Day 3
- ☐ Nehemiah 10-11
- ☐ CCC 1174-1175
- ☐ DCP, chap. 3 (finish chapter)
- ☐ _____
- ☐ _____

Day 4
- ☐ Nehemiah 12
- ☐ CCC 1176-1178
- ☐ DCP, chap. 4 (one-fourth)
- ☐ _____
- ☐ _____

Day 5
- ☐ Nehemiah 13
- ☐ CCC 1179-1180
- ☐ DCP, chap. 4 (one-fourth)
- ☐ _____
- ☐ _____

Year 3, Week 10

Day 1
- ☐ Tobit 1
- ☐ CCC 1181-1182
- ☐ DCP, chap. 4 (one-fourth)
- ☐ _____
- ☐ _____

Day 2
- ☐ Tobit 2-3
- ☐ CCC 1183-1184
- ☐ DCP, chap. 4 (finish chapter)
- ☐ _____
- ☐ _____

Day 3
- ☐ Tobit 4
- ☐ CCC 1185-1186
- ☐ DCP, chap. 5 (one-fourth)
- ☐ _____
- ☐ _____

Day 4
- ☐ Tobit 5-6
- ☐ CCC 1187-1189
- ☐ DCP, chap. 5 (one-fourth)
- ☐ _____
- ☐ _____

Day 5
- ☐ Tobit 7
- ☐ CCC 1190-1192
- ☐ DCP, chap. 5 (one-fourth)
- ☐ _____
- ☐ _____

The people who are dragging their shame into a confessional box ... have courage to face their own shame. It is the cowards who are running off to pillboxes, and to a thousand and one other escapes, who have not the courage to face that which has within themselves the possibility of great dignity.

—ARCHBISHOP FULTON SHEEN, *ON BEING HUMAN*

Year 3, Week 11

Day 1
☐ Tobit 8
☐ CCC 1193-1195
☐ DCP, chap. 5 (finish chapter)
☐ _____
☐ _____

Day 2
☐ Tobit 9-10
☐ CCC 1196-1199
☐ DCP, chap. 6 (one-third)
☐ _____
☐ _____

Day 3
☐ Tobit 11
☐ CCC 1200-1201
☐ DCP, chap. 6 (one-third)
☐ _____
☐ _____

Day 4
☐ Tobit 12-13
☐ CCC 1202-1203
☐ DCP, chap. 6 (finish chapter)
☐ _____
☐ _____

Day 5
☐ Tobit 14
☐ CCC 1204-1206
☐ DCP, chap. 7 (one-third)
☐ _____
☐ _____

Year 3, Week 12

Day 1
☐ Judith 1-2
☐ CCC 1207-1209
☐ DCP, chap. 7 (one-third)
☐ _____
☐ _____

Day 2
☐ Judith 3
☐ CCC 1210-1211
☐ DCP, chap. 7 (finish chapter)
☐ _____
☐ _____

Day 3
☐ Judith 4-5
☐ CCC 1212
☐ DCP, chap. 8 (one-third)
☐ _____
☐ _____

Day 4
☐ Judith 6
☐ CCC 1213
☐ DCP, chap. 8 (one-third)
☐ _____
☐ _____

Day 5
☐ Judith 7-8
☐ CCC 1214-1216
☐ DCP, chap. 8 (finish chapter)
☐ _____
☐ _____

No Christian married couple can want to block the
well-springs of life. For their love is based on the Love
of Christ, which entails dedication and sacrifice.

— SAINT JOSEMARÍA ESCRIVÁ, *FURROW*

Year 3, Week 13

Day 1
- ☐ Judith 9-10
- ☐ CCC 1217-1218
- ☐ *The Sinner's Guide* (SG), chap. 1
- ☐ _____
- ☐ _____

Day 2
- ☐ Judith 11
- ☐ CCC 1219-1220
- ☐ SG, chap. 2
- ☐ _____
- ☐ _____

Day 3
- ☐ Judith 12-13
- ☐ CCC 1221-1222
- ☐ SG, chap. 3
- ☐ _____
- ☐ _____

Day 4
- ☐ Judith 14
- ☐ CCC 1223-1225
- ☐ SG, chap. 4
- ☐ _____
- ☐ _____

Day 5
- ☐ Judith 15-16
- ☐ CCC 1226-1228
- ☐ DCP, chap. 5
- ☐ _____
- ☐ _____

Year 3, Week 14

Day 1
- ☐ Esther 1
- ☐ CCC 1229-1230
- ☐ SG, chaps. 6-7
- ☐ _____
- ☐ _____

Day 2
- ☐ Esther 2
- ☐ CCC 1231-1233
- ☐ SG, chap. 8
- ☐ _____
- ☐ _____

Day 3
- ☐ Esther 3
- ☐ CCC 1234-1235
- ☐ SG, chap. 9
- ☐ _____
- ☐ _____

Day 4
- ☐ Esther 4
- ☐ CCC 1236-1237
- ☐ DCP, chap. 10
- ☐ _____
- ☐ _____

Day 5
- ☐ Esther 5
- ☐ CCC 1238-1240
- ☐ SG, chap. 11
- ☐ _____
- ☐ _____

They abstain from the Eucharist and from prayer, because they do not confess that the Eucharist is the Flesh of our Savior Jesus Christ, Flesh which suffered for our sins and which the Father, in His goodness, raised up again. They who deny the gift of God are perishing in their disputes.

— ST. IGNATIUS OF ANTIOCH, *LETTER TO THE SMYRNAEANS*, CA. AD 110

Year 3, Week 15

Day 1
- ☐ Esther 6
- ☐ CCC 1241-1243
- ☐ SG, chap. 12
- ☐ _____
- ☐ _____

Day 2
- ☐ Esther 7
- ☐ CCC 1244-1245
- ☐ SG, chaps. 13-14
- ☐ _____
- ☐ _____

Day 3
- ☐ Esther 8-9
- ☐ CCC 1246-1249
- ☐ SG, chaps. 15-16
- ☐ _____
- ☐ _____

Day 4
- ☐ Esther 10
- ☐ CCC 1250-1252
- ☐ SG, chap. 17
- ☐ _____
- ☐ _____

Day 5
- ☐ Esther 11
- ☐ CCC 1253-1255
- ☐ SG, chap. 18
- ☐ _____
- ☐ _____

Year 3, Week 16

Day 1
- ☐ Job 1
- ☐ CCC 1256
- ☐ SG, chaps. 19-20
- ☐ _____
- ☐ _____

Day 2
- ☐ Job 2-3
- ☐ CCC 1257-1258
- ☐ SG, chaps. 21-22
- ☐ _____
- ☐ _____

Day 3
- ☐ Job 4
- ☐ CCC 1259-1261
- ☐ SG, chap. 23
- ☐ _____
- ☐ _____

Day 4
- ☐ Job 5-6
- ☐ CCC 1262-1264
- ☐ SG, chap. 24
- ☐ _____
- ☐ _____

Day 5
- ☐ Job 7
- ☐ CCC 1265-1266
- ☐ SG, chap. 25
- ☐ _____
- ☐ _____

> O how great and honorable is the ministry of priests to whom
> it is given to consecrate with sacred words the Lord of majesty, to
> bless Him with their lips, to hold Him in their hands, to receive
> Him with their mouths, and to administer Him to others.
>
> —THOMAS À KEMPIS, *THE IMITATION OF CHRIST*

Year 3, Week 17

Day 1
- ☐ Job 8
- ☐ CCC 1267-1268
- ☐ SG, chap. 26
- ☐ _____
- ☐ _____

Day 2
- ☐ Job 9-10
- ☐ CCC 1269-1270
- ☐ SG, chap. 27
- ☐ _____
- ☐ _____

Day 3
- ☐ Job 11
- ☐ CCC 1271
- ☐ SG, chap. 28 (half)
- ☐ _____
- ☐ _____

Day 4
- ☐ Job 12-13
- ☐ CCC 1272-1274
- ☐ SG, chap. 28 (finish chapter)
- ☐ _____
- ☐ _____

Day 5
- ☐ Job 14
- ☐ CCC 1275-1280
- ☐ SG, chap. 29
- ☐ _____
- ☐ _____

Year 3, Week 18

Day 1
- ☐ Job 15
- ☐ CCC 1281-1284
- ☐ SG, chap. 30
- ☐ _____
- ☐ _____

Day 2
- ☐ Job 16-17
- ☐ CCC 1285
- ☐ SG, chap. 31
- ☐ _____
- ☐ _____

Day 3
- ☐ Job 18
- ☐ CCC 1286-1287
- ☐ SG, chap. 32
- ☐ _____
- ☐ _____

Day 4
- ☐ Job 19-20
- ☐ CCC 1288-1289
- ☐ DCP, chaps. 33-34
- ☐ _____
- ☐ _____

Day 5
- ☐ Job 21
- ☐ CCC 1290-1292
- ☐ SG, chaps. 35-36
- ☐ _____
- ☐ _____

In this way He says that we descend into the water full
of sins and foulness, and we come up bearing fruit in our
heart, having fear and hope in Jesus in the spirit.

— LETTER OF BARNABAS, CA. AD 70/79 OR 117/132

Year 3, Week 19

Day 1
- ☐ Job 22
- ☐ CCC 1293-1294
- ☐ SG, chaps. 37-38
- ☐ _____
- ☐ _____

Day 2
- ☐ Job 23-24
- ☐ CCC 1295-1296
- ☐ SG, chap. 39
- ☐ _____
- ☐ _____

Day 3
- ☐ Job 25
- ☐ CCC 1297-1298
- ☐ SG, chap. 40 (half)
- ☐ _____
- ☐ _____

Day 4
- ☐ Job 26-27
- ☐ CCC 1299
- ☐ SG, chap. 40 (finish chapter)
- ☐ _____
- ☐ _____

Day 5
- ☐ Job 28
- ☐ CCC 1300-1301
- ☐ SG, chap. 41
- ☐ _____
- ☐ _____

Year 3, Week 20

Day 1
- ☐ Job 29
- ☐ CCC 1302-1303
- ☐ SG, chap. 42 (half)
- ☐ _____
- ☐ _____

Day 2
- ☐ Job 30-31
- ☐ CCC 1304-1305
- ☐ SG, chap. 42 (finish chapter)
- ☐ _____
- ☐ _____

Day 3
- ☐ Job 32
- ☐ CCC 1306-1307
- ☐ SG, chaps. 43-44
- ☐ _____
- ☐ _____

Day 4
- ☐ Job 33-34
- ☐ CCC 1308-1309
- ☐ SG, chaps. 45-46
- ☐ _____
- ☐ _____

Day 5
- ☐ Job 35
- ☐ CCC 1310-1311
- ☐ SG, chaps. 47-48
- ☐ _____
- ☐ _____

When will you get rid of that feeling of vain self-esteem? You
will then go to confession happy to show yourself as you are
to "that man," who, being anointed, is another Christ—Christ
himself—and gives you absolution, God's forgiveness.

— ST. JOSEMARÍA ESCRIVÁ, *FURROW*

Year 3, Week 21

Day 1
- ☐ Job 36
- ☐ CCC 1312
- ☐ *The Lord* (TL), part 1, chap. 1
- ☐ _____
- ☐ _____

Day 2
- ☐ Job 37-38
- ☐ CCC 1313-1314
- ☐ TL, part 1, chap. 2
- ☐ _____
- ☐ _____

Day 3
- ☐ Job 39
- ☐ CCC 1315-1317
- ☐ TL, part 1, chap. 3
- ☐ _____
- ☐ _____

Day 4
- ☐ Job 40-41
- ☐ CCC 1318-1321
- ☐ TL, part 1, chap. 4
- ☐ _____
- ☐ _____

Day 5
- ☐ Job 42
- ☐ CCC 1322-1323
- ☐ TL, part 1, chap. 5
- ☐ _____
- ☐ _____

Year 3, Week 22

Day 1
- ☐ Psalm 1
- ☐ CCC 1324-1325
- ☐ TL, part 1, chap. 6
- ☐ _____
- ☐ _____

Day 2
- ☐ Psalm 2-3
- ☐ CCC 1326-1327
- ☐ TL, part 1, chap. 7
- ☐ _____
- ☐ _____

Day 3
- ☐ Psalm 4
- ☐ CCC 1328-1329
- ☐ TL, part 1, chap. 8
- ☐ _____
- ☐ _____

Day 4
- ☐ Psalm 5-6
- ☐ CCC 1330
- ☐ TL, part 1, chap. 9
- ☐ _____
- ☐ _____

Day 5
- ☐ Psalm 7
- ☐ CCC 1331-1332
- ☐ TL, part 1, chap. 10
- ☐ _____
- ☐ _____

On the Lord's Day gather together, break bread and give thanks, after confessing your transgressions so that your sacrifice may be pure.

— *DIDACHE*

Year 3, Week 23

Day 1
- ☐ Psalm 8
- ☐ CCC 1333
- ☐ TL, part 1, chap. 11 (half)
- ☐ _____
- ☐ _____

Day 2
- ☐ Psalm 9
- ☐ CCC 1334
- ☐ TL, part 1, chap. 11 (finish chapter)
- ☐ _____
- ☐ _____

Day 3
- ☐ Psalm 10-11
- ☐ CCC 1335
- ☐ TL, part 1, chap. 12
- ☐ _____
- ☐ _____

Day 4
- ☐ Psalm 12
- ☐ CCC 1336
- ☐ TL, part 2, chap. 1
- ☐ _____
- ☐ _____

Day 5
- ☐ Psalm 13
- ☐ CCC 1337
- ☐ TL, part 2, chap. 2
- ☐ _____
- ☐ _____

Year 3, Week 24

Day 1
- ☐ Psalm 14
- ☐ CCC 1338
- ☐ TL, part 2, chap. 3
- ☐ _____
- ☐ _____

Day 2
- ☐ Psalm 15-16
- ☐ CCC 1339
- ☐ TL, part 2, chap. 4
- ☐ _____
- ☐ _____

Day 3
- ☐ Psalm 17
- ☐ CCC 1340
- ☐ TL, part 2, chap. 5
- ☐ _____
- ☐ _____

Day 4
- ☐ Psalm 18
- ☐ CCC 1341-1342
- ☐ TL, part 2, chap. 6
- ☐ _____
- ☐ _____

Day 5
- ☐ Psalm 19-20
- ☐ CCC 1343-1344
- ☐ TL, part 2, chap. 7
- ☐ _____
- ☐ _____

Write for the benefit of religious souls that it delights
Me to come to their hearts in Holy Communion.

—JESUS TO SAINT FAUSTINA, *DIARY OF SAINT MARIA FAUSTINA KOWALSKA*

Year 3, Week 25

Day 1
☐ Psalm 21
☐ CCC 1345
☐ TL, part 2, chap. 8
☐ _____
☐ _____

Day 2
☐ Psalm 22
☐ CCC 1346-1347
☐ TL, part 2, chap. 9
☐ _____
☐ _____

Day 3
☐ Psalm 23-24
☐ CCC 1348
☐ TL, part 2, chap. 10
☐ _____
☐ _____

Day 4
☐ Psalm 25
☐ CCC 1349
☐ TL, part 2, chap. 11
☐ _____
☐ _____

Day 5
☐ Psalm 26
☐ CCC 1350
☐ TL, part 2, chap. 12
☐ _____
☐ _____

Year 3, Week 26

Day 1
☐ Psalm 27
☐ CCC 1351
☐ TL, part 3, chap. 1
☐ _____
☐ _____

Day 2
☐ Psalm 28-29
☐ CCC 1352
☐ TL, part 3, chap. 2
☐ _____
☐ _____

Day 3
☐ Psalm 30
☐ CCC 1353
☐ TL, part 3, chap. 3
☐ _____
☐ _____

Day 4
☐ Psalm 31-32
☐ CCC 1354-1355
☐ TL, part 3, chap. 4
☐ _____
☐ _____

Day 5
☐ Psalm 33
☐ CCC 1356-1358
☐ TL, part 3, chap. 5
☐ _____
☐ _____

We call this food Eucharist; and no one else is permitted to partake of it, except one who believes our teaching to be true and who has been washed in the washing which is for the remission of sins for regeneration, and is thereby living as Christ has enjoined.

— Saint Justin Martyr, *First Apology*, ca. AD 148–155

Year 3, Week 27

Day 1
- ☐ Psalm 34
- ☐ CCC 1359-1361
- ☐ TL, part 3, chap. 6
- ☐ _____
- ☐ _____

Day 2
- ☐ Psalm 35
- ☐ CCC 1362-1363
- ☐ TL, part 3, chap. 7
- ☐ _____
- ☐ _____

Day 3
- ☐ Psalm 36-37
- ☐ CCC 1364-1365
- ☐ TL, part 3, chap. 8
- ☐ _____
- ☐ _____

Day 4
- ☐ Psalm 38
- ☐ CCC 1366-1367
- ☐ TL, part 3, chap. 9
- ☐ _____
- ☐ _____

Day 5
- ☐ Psalm 39
- ☐ CCC 1368-1369
- ☐ TL, part 3, chap. 10 (half)
- ☐ _____
- ☐ _____

Year 3, Week 28

Day 1
- ☐ Psalm 40
- ☐ CCC 1370
- ☐ TL, part 3, chap. 10 (finish chapter)
- ☐ _____
- ☐ _____

Day 2
- ☐ Psalm 41-42
- ☐ CCC 1371
- ☐ TL, part 4, chap. 1
- ☐ _____
- ☐ _____

Day 3
- ☐ Psalm 43
- ☐ CCC 1372
- ☐ TL, part 4, chap. 2
- ☐ _____
- ☐ _____

Day 4
- ☐ Psalm 44-45
- ☐ CCC 1373-1374
- ☐ TL, part 4, chap. 3
- ☐ _____
- ☐ _____

Day 5
- ☐ Psalm 46
- ☐ CCC 1375-1376
- ☐ TL, part 4, chap. 4
- ☐ _____
- ☐ _____

Are you unwilling to be anointed with the oil of God? It is on this account that we are called Christians: because we are anointed with the oil of God.

— ST. THEOPHILUS OF ANTIOCH, TO AUTOLYCUS, CA. AD 181

Year 3, Week 29

Day 1
- ☐ Psalm 47
- ☐ CCC 1377-1378
- ☐ TL, part 4, chap. 5
- ☐ _____
- ☐ _____

Day 2
- ☐ Psalm 48
- ☐ CCC 1379-1380
- ☐ TL, part 4, chap. 6
- ☐ _____
- ☐ _____

Day 3
- ☐ Psalm 49-50
- ☐ CCC 1381
- ☐ TL, part 4, chap. 7
- ☐ _____
- ☐ _____

Day 4
- ☐ Psalm 51
- ☐ CCC 1382-1383
- ☐ TL, part 4, chap. 8
- ☐ _____
- ☐ _____

Day 5
- ☐ Psalm 52
- ☐ CCC 1384-1385
- ☐ TL, part 4, chap. 9
- ☐ _____
- ☐ _____

Year 3, Week 30

Day 1
- ☐ Psalm 53
- ☐ CCC 1386-1387
- ☐ TL, part 4, chap. 10
- ☐ _____
- ☐ _____

Day 2
- ☐ Psalm 54-55
- ☐ CCC 1388-1390
- ☐ TL, part 4, chap. 11
- ☐ _____
- ☐ _____

Day 3
- ☐ Psalm 56
- ☐ CCC 1391-1392
- ☐ TL, part 4, chap. 12
- ☐ _____
- ☐ _____

Day 4
- ☐ Psalm 57-58
- ☐ CCC 1393-1394
- ☐ TL, part 4, chap. 13
- ☐ _____
- ☐ _____

Day 5
- ☐ Psalm 59
- ☐ CCC 1395-1396
- ☐ TL, part 4, chap. 14
- ☐ _____
- ☐ _____

Christian marriage, like the other sacraments, "whose purpose it is to sanctify people, to build up the body of Christ, and finally, to give worship to God," is in itself a liturgical action glorifying God in Jesus Christ and in the Church.

— SAINT JOHN PAUL II, *FAMILIARIS CONSORTIO* 56

Year 3, Week 31

Day 1
- ☐ Psalm 60
- ☐ CCC 1397-1398
- ☐ TL, part 5, chap. 1
- ☐ _____
- ☐ _____

Day 2
- ☐ Psalm 61
- ☐ CCC 1399-1401
- ☐ TL, part 5, chap. 2
- ☐ _____
- ☐ _____

Day 3
- ☐ Psalm 62-63
- ☐ CCC 1402-1403
- ☐ TL, part 5, chap. 3
- ☐ _____
- ☐ _____

Day 4
- ☐ Psalm 64
- ☐ CCC 1404-1405
- ☐ TL, part 5, chap. 4
- ☐ _____
- ☐ _____

Day 5
- ☐ Psalm 65
- ☐ CCC 1406-1409
- ☐ TL, part 5, chap. 5
- ☐ _____
- ☐ _____

Year 3, Week 32

Day 1
- ☐ Psalm 66
- ☐ CCC 1410-1412
- ☐ TL, part 5, chap. 6
- ☐ _____
- ☐ _____

Day 2
- ☐ Psalm 67-68
- ☐ CCC 1413-1416
- ☐ TL, part 5, chap. 7
- ☐ _____
- ☐ _____

Day 3
- ☐ Psalm 69
- ☐ CCC 1417-1419
- ☐ TL, part 5, chap. 8
- ☐ _____
- ☐ _____

Day 4
- ☐ Psalm 70-71
- ☐ CCC 1420-1421
- ☐ TL, part 5, chap. 9
- ☐ _____
- ☐ _____

Day 5
- ☐ Psalm 72
- ☐ CCC 1422-1424
- ☐ TL, part 5, chap. 10
- ☐ _____
- ☐ _____

I aspire to holy orders; therefore I ought to
be like an angel in the sight of God.

— SAINT JOHN XXIII, *JOURNAL OF A SOUL*

Year 3, Week 33

Day 1
- ☐ Psalm 73
- ☐ CCC 1425-1426
- ☐ TL, part 5, chap. 11
- ☐ _____
- ☐ _____

Day 2
- ☐ Psalm 74
- ☐ CCC 1427-1429
- ☐ TL, part 5, chap. 12
- ☐ _____
- ☐ _____

Day 3
- ☐ Psalm 75-76
- ☐ CCC 1430-1431
- ☐ TL, part 5, chap. 13 (half)
- ☐ _____
- ☐ _____

Day 4
- ☐ Psalm 77
- ☐ CCC 1432-1433
- ☐ TL, part 5, chap. 13 (finish chapter)
- ☐ _____
- ☐ _____

Day 5
- ☐ Psalm 78
- ☐ CCC 1434-1435
- ☐ TL, part 5, chap. 14
- ☐ _____
- ☐ _____

Year 3, Week 34

Day 1
- ☐ Psalm 79
- ☐ CCC 1436-1437
- ☐ TL, part 6, chap. 1
- ☐ _____
- ☐ _____

Day 2
- ☐ Psalm 80-81
- ☐ CCC 1438-1439
- ☐ TL, part 6, chap. 2
- ☐ _____
- ☐ _____

Day 3
- ☐ Psalm 82
- ☐ CCC 1440
- ☐ TL, part 6, chap. 3
- ☐ _____
- ☐ _____

Day 4
- ☐ Psalm 83-84
- ☐ CCC 1441-1442
- ☐ TL, part 6, chap. 4
- ☐ _____
- ☐ _____

Day 5
- ☐ Psalm 85
- ☐ CCC 1443-1445
- ☐ TL, part 6, chap. 5
- ☐ _____
- ☐ _____

Christ made Himself the Bread of Life. He wanted to give Himself to us in a very special way, in a simple, tangible way, because it is hard for human beings to love a God whom they cannot see.

— SAINT TERESA OF CALCUTTA, *NO GREATER LOVE*

Year 3, Week 35

Day 1
- ☐ Psalm 86
- ☐ CCC 1446
- ☐ TL, part 6, chap. 6
- ☐ _____
- ☐ _____

Day 2
- ☐ Psalm 87
- ☐ CCC 1447
- ☐ TL, part 6, chap. 7
- ☐ _____
- ☐ _____

Day 3
- ☐ Psalm 88-89
- ☐ CCC 1448-1449
- ☐ TL, part 6, chap. 8
- ☐ _____
- ☐ _____

Day 4
- ☐ Psalm 90
- ☐ CCC 1450-1452
- ☐ TL, part 6, chap. 9
- ☐ _____
- ☐ _____

Day 5
- ☐ Psalm 91
- ☐ CCC 1453-1454
- ☐ TL, part 6, chap. 10
- ☐ _____
- ☐ _____

Year 3, Week 36

Day 1
- ☐ Psalm 92
- ☐ CCC 1455-1456
- ☐ TL, part 6, chap. 11
- ☐ _____
- ☐ _____

Day 2
- ☐ Psalm 93-94
- ☐ CCC 1457-1458
- ☐ TL, part 6, chap. 12
- ☐ _____
- ☐ _____

Day 3
- ☐ Psalm 95
- ☐ CCC 1459-1460
- ☐ TL, part 7, chap. 1
- ☐ _____
- ☐ _____

Day 4
- ☐ Psalm 96-97
- ☐ CCC 1461-1462
- ☐ TL, part 7, chap. 2
- ☐ _____
- ☐ _____

Day 5
- ☐ Psalm 98
- ☐ CCC 1463-1464
- ☐ TL, part 7, chap. 3
- ☐ _____
- ☐ _____

> For this reason, every day you give yourself to man, representing
> yourself in the sacrament of the altar, in the body of your holy
> church. Why have you done this? Your mercy. Oh, divine mercy!
>
> — SAINT CATHERINE OF SIENA, *LITTLE TALKS WITH GOD*

Year 3, Week 37

Day 1
☐ Psalm 99
☐ CCC 1465-1467
☐ TL, part 7, chap. 4
☐ _____
☐ _____

Day 2
☐ Psalm 100
☐ CCC 1468-1469
☐ TL, part 7, chap. 5
☐ _____
☐ _____

Day 3
☐ Psalm 101-102
☐ CCC 1470
☐ TL, part 7, chap. 6
☐ _____
☐ _____

Day 4
☐ Psalm 103
☐ CCC 1471
☐ TL, part 7, chap. 7
☐ _____
☐ _____

Day 5
☐ Psalm 104
☐ CCC 1472-1473
☐ TL, part 7, chap. 8
☐ _____
☐ _____

Year 3, Week 38

Day 1
☐ Psalm 105
☐ CCC 1474-1475
☐ TL, part 7, chap. 9
☐ _____
☐ _____

Day 2
☐ Psalm 106-107
☐ CCC 1476-1477
☐ TL, part 7, chap. 10
☐ _____
☐ _____

Day 3
☐ Psalm 108
☐ CCC 1478-1479
☐ TL, part 7, chap. 11
☐ _____
☐ _____

Day 4
☐ Psalm 109-110
☐ CCC 1480-1481
☐ TL, part 7, chap. 12
☐ _____
☐ _____

Day 5
☐ Psalm 111
☐ CCC 1482-1484
☐ TL, Conclusion
☐ _____
☐ _____

> When you approach the confessional, know this, that I Myself am waiting there for you. I am only hidden by the priest, but I Myself act in your soul.
>
> —JESUS TO SAINT FAUSTINA, *DIARY OF SAINT MARIA FAUSTINA KOWALSKA*

Year 3, Week 39

Day 1
- ☐ Psalm 112
- ☐ CCC 1485-1491
- ☐ *Covenanted Happiness* (CH), introduction; chap. 1
- ☐ _____
- ☐ _____

Day 2
- ☐ Psalm 113
- ☐ CCC 1492-1498
- ☐ CH, chap. 2
- ☐ _____
- ☐ _____

Day 3
- ☐ Psalm 114-115
- ☐ CCC 1499
- ☐ CH, chap. 3
- ☐ _____
- ☐ _____

Day 4
- ☐ Psalm 116
- ☐ CCC 1500-1501
- ☐ CH, chap. 4
- ☐ _____
- ☐ _____

Day 5
- ☐ Psalm 117
- ☐ CCC 1502
- ☐ CH, chap. 5
- ☐ _____
- ☐ _____

Note: CH requires a little more daily reading. Please don't give up—take your time and persevere!

Year 3, Week 40

Day 1
- ☐ Psalm 118
- ☐ CCC 1503
- ☐ CH, chap. 6
- ☐ _____
- ☐ _____

Day 2
- ☐ Psalm 119-120
- ☐ CCC 1504-1505
- ☐ CH, chap. 7
- ☐ _____
- ☐ _____

Day 3
- ☐ Psalm 121
- ☐ CCC 1506-1507
- ☐ CH, chap. 8
- ☐ _____
- ☐ _____

Day 4
- ☐ Psalm 122-123
- ☐ CCC 1508-1510
- ☐ CH, chap. 9
- ☐ _____
- ☐ _____

Day 5
- ☐ Psalm 124
- ☐ CCC 1511-1513
- ☐ CH, chap. 10
- ☐ _____
- ☐ _____

Year 3, Week 41

Day 1
- ☐ Psalm 125
- ☐ CCC 1514-1515
- ☐ CH, chap. 11
- ☐ _____
- ☐ _____

Day 2
- ☐ Psalm 126
- ☐ CCC 1516
- ☐ CH, chap. 12
- ☐ _____
- ☐ _____

Day 3
- ☐ Psalm 127-128
- ☐ CCC 1517-1519
- ☐ CH, chap. 13
- ☐ _____
- ☐ _____

Day 4
- ☐ Psalm 129
- ☐ CCC 1520-1521
- ☐ CH, appendix: Abortion (half)
- ☐ _____
- ☐ _____

Day 5
- ☐ Psalm 130
- ☐ CCC 1522-1523
- ☐ CH, appendix: Abortion (finish appendix)
- ☐ _____
- ☐ _____

Year 3, Week 42

Day 1
- ☐ Psalm 131
- ☐ CCC 1524-1525
- ☐ _The Betrothed_ (TB), chap. 1 (half)
- ☐ _____
- ☐ _____

Day 2
- ☐ Psalm 132-133
- ☐ CCC 1526-1529
- ☐ TB, chap. 1 (finish chapter)
- ☐ _____
- ☐ _____

Day 3
- ☐ Psalm 134
- ☐ CCC 1530-1532
- ☐ TB, chap. 2
- ☐ _____
- ☐ _____

Day 4
- ☐ Psalm 135-136
- ☐ CCC 1533-1535
- ☐ TB, chap. 3 (half)
- ☐ _____
- ☐ _____

Day 5
- ☐ Psalm 137
- ☐ CCC 1536
- ☐ TB, chap. 3 (finish chapter)
- ☐ _____
- ☐ _____

Confession is nothing but humility in action.

— _SAINT TERESA OF CALCUTTA_, NO GREATER LOVE

Year 3, Week 43

Day 1
- ☐ Psalm 138
- ☐ CCC 1537-1538
- ☐ TB, chap. 4 (half)
- ☐ _____
- ☐ _____

Day 2
- ☐ Psalm 139
- ☐ CCC 1539-1540
- ☐ TB, chap. 4 (finish chapter)
- ☐ _____
- ☐ _____

Day 3
- ☐ Psalm 140-141
- ☐ CCC 1541-1543
- ☐ TB, chap. 5
- ☐ _____
- ☐ _____

Day 4
- ☐ Psalm 142
- ☐ CCC 1544-1545
- ☐ TB, chap. 6
- ☐ _____
- ☐ _____

Day 5
- ☐ Psalm 143
- ☐ CCC 1546-1547
- ☐ TB, chap. 7 (half)
- ☐ _____
- ☐ _____

Year 3, Week 44

Day 1
- ☐ Psalm 144
- ☐ CCC 1548-1549
- ☐ TB, chap. 7 (finish chapter)
- ☐ _____
- ☐ _____

Day 2
- ☐ Psalm 145-146
- ☐ CCC 1550-1551
- ☐ TB, chap. 8 (half)
- ☐ _____
- ☐ _____

Day 3
- ☐ Psalm 147
- ☐ CCC 1552-1553
- ☐ TB, chap. 8 (finish chapter)
- ☐ _____
- ☐ _____

Day 4
- ☐ Psalm 148-149
- ☐ CCC 1554
- ☐ TB, chap. 9 (half)
- ☐ _____
- ☐ _____

Day 5
- ☐ Psalm 150
- ☐ CCC 1555-1556
- ☐ TB, chap. 9 (finish chapter)
- ☐ _____
- ☐ _____

In baptism too there is forgiveness of all sins; what is the difference whether priests claim this power is given them to be exercised in Penance or at the font? The mystery is the same in both.

—SAINT AMBROSE OF MILAN, *PENANCE*, AD 387/390

Year 3, Week 45

Day 1
- ☐ Proverbs 1
- ☐ CCC 1557-1558
- ☐ TB, chap. 10 (half)
- ☐ _____
- ☐ _____

Day 2
- ☐ Proverbs 2
- ☐ CCC 1559-1561
- ☐ TB, chap. 10 (finish chapter)
- ☐ _____
- ☐ _____

Day 3
- ☐ Proverbs 3-4
- ☐ CCC 1562-1565
- ☐ TB, chap. 11 (half)
- ☐ _____
- ☐ _____

Day 4
- ☐ Proverbs 5
- ☐ CCC 1566-1568
- ☐ TB, chap. 11 (finish chapter)
- ☐ _____
- ☐ _____

Day 5
- ☐ Proverbs 6
- ☐ CCC 1569-1571
- ☐ TB, chap. 12
- ☐ _____
- ☐ _____

Year 3, Week 46

Day 1
- ☐ Proverbs 7
- ☐ CCC 1572-1574
- ☐ TB, chap. 13
- ☐ _____
- ☐ _____

Day 2
- ☐ Proverbs 8
- ☐ CCC 1575-1576
- ☐ TB, chap. 14
- ☐ _____
- ☐ _____

Day 3
- ☐ Proverbs 9-10
- ☐ CCC 1577-1580
- ☐ TB, chap. 15 (half)
- ☐ _____
- ☐ _____

Day 4
- ☐ Proverbs 11
- ☐ CCC 1581-1584
- ☐ TB, chap. 15 (finish chapter)
- ☐ _____
- ☐ _____

Day 5
- ☐ Proverbs 12
- ☐ CCC 1585-1587
- ☐ TB, chap. 16
- ☐ _____
- ☐ _____

The Eucharist is the very source of Christian marriage. The
Eucharistic sacrifice in fact represents Christ's covenant of
love with the Church, sealed with his blood on the cross.

— SAINT JOHN PAUL II, *FAMILIARIS CONSORTIO* 57

Year 3, Week 47

Day 1
- ☐ Proverbs 13
- ☐ CCC 1588-1589
- ☐ TB, chap. 17
- ☐ _____
- ☐ _____

Day 2
- ☐ Proverbs 14-15
- ☐ CCC 1590-1595
- ☐ TB, chap. 18
- ☐ _____
- ☐ _____

Day 3
- ☐ Proverbs 16
- ☐ CCC 1596-1600
- ☐ TB, chap. 19
- ☐ _____
- ☐ _____

Day 4
- ☐ Proverbs 17-18
- ☐ CCC 1601-1605
- ☐ TB, chap. 20
- ☐ _____
- ☐ _____

Day 5
- ☐ Proverbs 19
- ☐ CCC 1606-1608
- ☐ TB, chap. 21
- ☐ _____
- ☐ _____

Year 3, Week 48

Day 1
- ☐ Proverbs 20
- ☐ CCC 1609-1611
- ☐ TB, chap. 22
- ☐ _____
- ☐ _____

Day 2
- ☐ Proverbs 21
- ☐ CCC 1612-1614
- ☐ TB, chap. 23 (half)
- ☐ _____
- ☐ _____

Day 3
- ☐ Proverbs 22-23
- ☐ CCC 1615-1617
- ☐ TB, chap. 23 (finish chapter)
- ☐ _____
- ☐ _____

Day 4
- ☐ Proverbs 24
- ☐ CCC 1618-1620
- ☐ TB, chap. 24 (half)
- ☐ _____
- ☐ _____

Day 5
- ☐ Proverbs 25
- ☐ CCC 1621-1624
- ☐ TB, chap. 24 (finish chapter)
- ☐ _____
- ☐ _____

Since the priest's eyes are accustomed to look upon Christ's Body,
they must be chaste and modest, and his hands, that touch the Creator
of heaven and earth, must be pure and ever lifted toward heaven.

— THOMAS À KEMPIS, *THE IMITATION OF CHRIST*

Year 3, Week 49

Day 1
- ☐ Proverbs 26
- ☐ CCC 1625-1630
- ☐ TB, chap. 25
- ☐ _____
- ☐ _____

Day 2
- ☐ Proverbs 27
- ☐ CCC 1631-1632
- ☐ TB, chap. 26
- ☐ _____
- ☐ _____

Day 3
- ☐ Proverbs 28-29
- ☐ CCC 1633-1637
- ☐ TB, chap. 27
- ☐ _____
- ☐ _____

Day 4
- ☐ Proverbs 30
- ☐ CCC 1638-1640
- ☐ TB, chap. 28 (half)
- ☐ _____
- ☐ _____

Day 5
- ☐ Proverbs 31
- ☐ CCC 1641-1642
- ☐ TB, chap. 28 (finish chapter)
- ☐ _____
- ☐ _____

Year 3, Week 50

Day 1
- ☐ Ecclesiastes 1
- ☐ CCC 1643-1645
- ☐ TB, chap. 29
- ☐ _____
- ☐ _____

Day 2
- ☐ Ecclesiastes 2
- ☐ CCC 1646-1651
- ☐ TB, chap. 30
- ☐ _____
- ☐ _____

Day 3
- ☐ Ecclesiastes 3-4
- ☐ CCC 1652-1654
- ☐ TB, chap. 31
- ☐ _____
- ☐ _____

Day 4
- ☐ Ecclesiastes 5
- ☐ CCC 1655-1658
- ☐ TB, chap. 32 (half)
- ☐ _____
- ☐ _____

Day 5
- ☐ Ecclesiastes 6
- ☐ CCC 1659-1662
- ☐ TB, chap. 32 (finish chapter)
- ☐ _____
- ☐ _____

What makes preparation for the Sacrament of Penance a very simple and very easy process is: (1) to go frequently, so that we have not much time to go over from one confession to another; and (2) to have the habit of examining our conscience well every night and of making a good act of contrition.

— MOTHER MARY LOYOLA, *FIRST COMMUNION*

Year 3, Week 51

Day 1
- ☐ Ecclesiastes 7
- ☐ CCC 1663-1666
- ☐ TB, chap. 33 (half)
- ☐ _____
- ☐ _____

Day 2
- ☐ Ecclesiastes 8
- ☐ CCC 1667-1670
- ☐ TB, chap. 33 (finish chapter)
- ☐ _____
- ☐ _____

Day 3
- ☐ Ecclesiastes 9-10
- ☐ CCC 1671-1673
- ☐ TB, chap. 34 (half)
- ☐ _____
- ☐ _____

Day 4
- ☐ Ecclesiastes 11
- ☐ CCC 1674-1676
- ☐ TB, chap. 34 (finish chapter)
- ☐ _____
- ☐ _____

Day 5
- ☐ Ecclesiastes 12
- ☐ CCC 1677-1679
- ☐ TB, chap. 35
- ☐ _____
- ☐ _____

Year 3, Week 52

Day 1
- ☐ Song of Solomon 1-2
- ☐ CCC 1680-1683
- ☐ TB, chap. 36 (half)
- ☐ _____
- ☐ _____

Day 2
- ☐ Song of Solomon 3
- ☐ CCC 1684-1686
- ☐ TB, chap. 36 (finish chapter)
- ☐ _____
- ☐ _____

Day 3
- ☐ Song of Solomon 4-5
- ☐ CCC 1687-1688
- ☐ TB, chap. 37
- ☐ _____
- ☐ _____

Day 4
- ☐ Song of Solomon 6
- ☐ CCC 1689
- ☐ TB, chap. 38 (half)
- ☐ _____
- ☐ _____

Day 5
- ☐ Song of Solomon 7-8
- ☐ CCC 1690
- ☐ TB, chap. 38 (finish chapter)
- ☐ _____
- ☐ _____

> This same power of the word also makes the priest venerable and honorable.... Yesterday he was but one of the multitude, one of the people; suddenly he is made a guide, a president, a teacher of piety, an instructor in hidden mysteries.
>
> —ST. GREGORY OF NYSSA, *SERMON ON THE DAY OF LIGHTS*

— Year 4 —

Reading List

Sacred Scripture: Old Testament: Wisdom through 2 Maccabees

Catechism of the Catholic Church: Life in Christ

Spiritual Reading:

Something Beautiful for God by Malcolm Muggeridge (2 weeks)

The Hidden Power of Kindness by Father Lawrence G. Lovasik (4 weeks)

The Story of a Soul by Saint Thérèse of Lisieux (4 weeks)

Spiritual Combat by Lorenzo Scupoli (4 weeks)

Journal of a Soul by Saint Pope John XXIII (8 weeks)

Trustful Surrender to Divine Providence by Father Jean Baptiste Saint-Jure (2 weeks)

The Way of Perfection by Saint Teresa of Ávila (4 weeks)

The 12 Steps to Holiness and Salvation by St. Alphonsus Liguori (4 weeks)

The Privilege of Being a Woman by Alice von Hildebrand (2 weeks)

The Imitation of Christ by Thomas à Kempis (4 weeks)

Witness to Hope by George Weigel (14 weeks)

The fact alone that pride is the primal source of all moral evil clearly demonstrates the paramount importance of humility.

—Dietrich von Hildebrand, *Humility, Wellspring of Virtue*

Year 4, Week 1

Day 1
- ☐ Wisdom of Solomon 1
- ☐ CCC, 1691-1694
- ☐ *Something Beautiful for God* (SBG), "Something Beautiful for God" (one-third)
- ☐ _____
- ☐ _____

Day 2
- ☐ Wisdom of Solomon 2
- ☐ CCC 1695-1698
- ☐ SBG, "Something Beautiful for God" (one-third)
- ☐ _____
- ☐ _____

Day 3
- ☐ Wisdom of Solomon 3-4
- ☐ CCC 1699-1700
- ☐ SBG, "Something Beautiful for God" (finish chapter)
- ☐ _____
- ☐ _____

Day 4
- ☐ Wisdom of Solomon 5
- ☐ CCC 1701-1705
- ☐ SBG, "Mother Teresa's Way of Love"
- ☐ _____
- ☐ _____

Day 5
- ☐ Wisdom of Solomon 6
- ☐ CCC 1706-1709
- ☐ SBG, "Mother Teresa Speaks" (one-third)
- ☐ _____
- ☐ _____

Year 4, Week 2

Day 1
- ☐ Wisdom of Solomon 7
- ☐ CCC 1710-1715
- ☐ SBG, "Mother Teresa Speaks" (one-third)
- ☐ _____
- ☐ _____

Day 2
- ☐ Wisdom of Solomon 8-9
- ☐ CCC 1716-1717
- ☐ SBG, "Mother Teresa Speaks" (finish chapter)
- ☐ _____
- ☐ _____

Day 3
- ☐ Wisdom of Solomon 10
- ☐ CCC 1718-1719
- ☐ SBG, "A Door of Utterance" (half)
- ☐ _____
- ☐ _____

Day 4
- ☐ Wisdom of Solomon 11-12
- ☐ CCC 1720-1722
- ☐ SBG, "A Door of Utterance" (finish chapter)
- ☐ _____
- ☐ _____

Day 5
- ☐ Wisdom of Solomon 13
- ☐ CCC 1723-1724
- ☐ SBG, appendix
- ☐ _____
- ☐ _____

Year 4, Week 3

Day 1
- ☐ Wisdom of Solomon 14
- ☐ CCC 1725-1729
- ☐ *The Hidden Power of Kindness* (HPK), foreword; chap. 1 (one-third)
- ☐ _____
- ☐ _____

Day 2
- ☐ Wisdom of Solomon 15
- ☐ CCC 1730-1734
- ☐ HPK, chap. 1 (one-third)
- ☐ _____
- ☐ _____

Day 3
- ☐ Wisdom of Solomon 16-17
- ☐ CCC 1735-1738
- ☐ HPK, chap. 1 (finish chapter)
- ☐ _____
- ☐ _____

Day 4
- ☐ Wisdom of Solomon 18
- ☐ CCC 1739-1742
- ☐ HPK, chap. 2
- ☐ _____
- ☐ _____

Day 5
- ☐ Wisdom of Solomon 19
- ☐ CCC 1743-1748
- ☐ HPK, chap. 3
- ☐ _____
- ☐ _____

Year 4, Week 4

Day 1
- ☐ Sirach 1
- ☐ CCC 1749-1752
- ☐ HPK, chap. 4
- ☐ _____
- ☐ _____

Day 2
- ☐ Sirach 2-3
- ☐ CCC 1753-1756
- ☐ HPK, chaps. 5-6
- ☐ _____
- ☐ _____

Day 3
- ☐ Sirach 4
- ☐ CCC 1757-1761
- ☐ HPK, chap. 7 (half)
- ☐ _____
- ☐ _____

Day 4
- ☐ Sirach 5-6
- ☐ CCC 1762-1766
- ☐ HPK, chap. 7 (finish chapter)
- ☐ _____
- ☐ _____

Day 5
- ☐ Sirach 7
- ☐ CCC 1767-1770
- ☐ HPK, chap. 8
- ☐ _____
- ☐ _____

Be long-suffering with one another and gentle, just as God is with you.

— ST. IGNATIUS OF ANTIOCH, *LETTER TO POLYCARP*, CA. AD 110

Year 4, Week 5

Day 1
- ☐ Sirach 8
- ☐ CCC 1771-1775
- ☐ HPK, chap. 9 (half)
- ☐ _____
- ☐ _____

Day 2
- ☐ Sirach 9-10
- ☐ CCC 1776-1778
- ☐ HPK, chap. 9 (finish chapter)
- ☐ _____
- ☐ _____

Day 3
- ☐ Sirach 11
- ☐ CCC 1779-1782
- ☐ HPK, chap. 10
- ☐ _____
- ☐ _____

Day 4
- ☐ Sirach 12-13
- ☐ CCC 1783-1785
- ☐ HPK, chaps. 11-12
- ☐ _____
- ☐ _____

Day 5
- ☐ Sirach 14
- ☐ CCC 1786-1789
- ☐ HPK, chap. 13
- ☐ _____
- ☐ _____

Year 4, Week 6

Day 1
- ☐ Sirach 15
- ☐ CCC 1790-1794
- ☐ HPK, chap. 14
- ☐ _____
- ☐ _____

Day 2
- ☐ Sirach 16-17
- ☐ CCC 1795-1802
- ☐ HPK, chap. 15
- ☐ _____
- ☐ _____

Day 3
- ☐ Sirach 18
- ☐ CCC 1803-1805
- ☐ HPK, chap. 16
- ☐ _____
- ☐ _____

Day 4
- ☐ Sirach 19-20
- ☐ CCC 1806-1809
- ☐ HPK, chap. 17 (two-thirds)
- ☐ _____
- ☐ _____

Day 5
- ☐ Sirach 21
- ☐ CCC 1810-1811
- ☐ HPK, chap. 17 (finish chapter);
  appendix
- ☐ _____
- ☐ _____

> The truly humble man prefers to be despised
> and yet does not try to appear humble.
>
> —VENERABLE LOUIS OF GRANADA, *SUMMA OF THE CHRISTIAN LIFE*

Year 4, Week 7

Day 1
- ☐ Sirach 22-23
- ☐ CCC 1812-1813
- ☐ *The Story of a Soul* (SOS), chap. 1
- ☐ _____
- ☐ _____

Day 2
- ☐ Sirach 24
- ☐ CCC 1814-1816
- ☐ SOS, chap. 2 (half)
- ☐ _____
- ☐ _____

Day 3
- ☐ Sirach 25-26
- ☐ CCC 1817-1819
- ☐ SOS, chap. 2 (finish chapter)
- ☐ _____
- ☐ _____

Day 4
- ☐ Sirach 27
- ☐ CCC 1820-1821
- ☐ SOS, chap. 3
- ☐ _____
- ☐ _____

Day 5
- ☐ Sirach 28-29
- ☐ CCC 1822-1825
- ☐ SOS, chap. 4 (half)
- ☐ _____
- ☐ _____

Year 4, Week 8

Day 1
- ☐ Sirach 30
- ☐ CCC 1826-1829
- ☐ SOS, chap. 4 (finish chapter)
- ☐ _____
- ☐ _____

Day 2
- ☐ Sirach 31-32
- ☐ CCC 1830-1832
- ☐ SOS, chap. 5 (half)
- ☐ _____
- ☐ _____

Day 3
- ☐ Sirach 33
- ☐ CCC 1833-1839
- ☐ SOS, chap. 5 (finish chapter)
- ☐ _____
- ☐ _____

Day 4
- ☐ Sirach 34-35
- ☐ CCC 1840-1845
- ☐ SOS, chap. 6 (half)
- ☐ _____
- ☐ _____

Day 5
- ☐ Sirach 36
- ☐ CCC 1846-1848
- ☐ SOS, chap. 6 (finish chapter)
- ☐ _____
- ☐ _____

The peaceful soul does not seek, now, to live morally, but to live
for God; morality is only a by-product of the union with God.

—ARCHBISHOP FULTON SHEEN, *THE ANGEL'S BLACKBOARD*

Year 4, Week 9

Day 1
- ☐ Sirach 37-38
- ☐ CCC 1849-1851
- ☐ SOS, chap. 7
- ☐ _____
- ☐ _____

Day 2
- ☐ Sirach 39
- ☐ CCC 1852-1853
- ☐ SOS, chap. 8 (half)
- ☐ _____
- ☐ _____

Day 3
- ☐ Sirach 40-41
- ☐ CCC 1854-1856
- ☐ SOS, chap. 8 (finish chapter)
- ☐ _____
- ☐ _____

Day 4
- ☐ Sirach 42
- ☐ CCC 1857-1860
- ☐ SOS, chap. 9 (half)
- ☐ _____
- ☐ _____

Day 5
- ☐ Sirach 43-44
- ☐ CCC 1861-1864
- ☐ SOS, chap. 9 (finish chapter)
- ☐ _____
- ☐ _____

Year 4, Week 10

Day 1
- ☐ Sirach 45
- ☐ CCC 1865-1869
- ☐ SOS, chap. 10 (half)
- ☐ _____
- ☐ _____

Day 2
- ☐ Sirach 46-47
- ☐ CCC 1870-1876
- ☐ SOS, chap. 10 (finish chapter)
- ☐ _____
- ☐ _____

Day 3
- ☐ Sirach 48
- ☐ CCC 1877-1881
- ☐ SOS, chap. 11 (half)
- ☐ _____
- ☐ _____

Day 4
- ☐ Sirach 49-50
- ☐ CCC 1882-1885
- ☐ SOS, chap. 11 (finish chapter)
- ☐ _____
- ☐ _____

Day 5
- ☐ Sirach 51
- ☐ CCC 1886-1887
- ☐ SOS, epilogue
- ☐ _____
- ☐ _____

I will love him alone and not make myself unhappy by being taken up with trivialities, now that I have caught a glimpse of what He has reserved for those He loves.

— SAINT THÉRÈSE OF LISIEUX, *THE STORY OF A SOUL*

Year 4, Week 11

Day 1
- ☐ Isaiah 1
- ☐ CCC 1888-1889
- ☐ *Spiritual Combat* (SPC), part 1, chap. 1
- ☐ _____
- ☐ _____

Day 2
- ☐ Isaiah 2-3
- ☐ CCC 1890-1896
- ☐ SPC, part 1, chaps. 2-3
- ☐ _____
- ☐ _____

Day 3
- ☐ Isaiah 4
- ☐ CCC 1897-1900
- ☐ SPC, part 1, chap. 4 (one-eighth)
- ☐ _____
- ☐ _____

Day 4
- ☐ Isaiah 5-6
- ☐ CCC 1901-1904
- ☐ SPC, part 1, chap. 4 (one-eighth)
- ☐ _____
- ☐ _____

Day 5
- ☐ Isaiah 7
- ☐ CCC 1905-1909
- ☐ SPC, part 1, chap. 4 (one eighth)
- ☐ _____
- ☐ _____

Year 4, Week 12

Day 1
- ☐ Isaiah 8
- ☐ CCC 1910-1912
- ☐ SPC, part 1, chap. 4 (one-eighth)
- ☐ _____
- ☐ _____

Day 2
- ☐ Isaiah 9-10
- ☐ CCC 1913-1917
- ☐ SPC, part 1, chap. 4 (one-eighth)
- ☐ _____
- ☐ _____

Day 3
- ☐ Isaiah 11
- ☐ CCC 1918-1927
- ☐ SPC, part 1, chap. 4 (one-eighth)
- ☐ _____
- ☐ _____

Day 4
- ☐ Isaiah 12-13
- ☐ CCC 1928-1930
- ☐ SPC, part 1, chap. 4 (one-eighth)
- ☐ _____
- ☐ _____

Day 5
- ☐ Isaiah 14
- ☐ CCC 1931-1933
- ☐ SPC, part 1, chap. 4 (finish chapter)
- ☐ _____
- ☐ _____

Strive to enter by the narrow gate, fear no difficulties, do
battle against thy evil desires, vanquish thy bad habits, count
for nothing the scoffs of the foolish and the weak.

— SAINT CLAUDE DE LA COLOMBIÈRE, *THE SPIRITUAL RETREAT*

Year 4, Week 13

Day 1
- ☐ Isaiah 15-16
- ☐ CCC 1934-1936
- ☐ SPC, part 1, chap. 5 (half)
- ☐ _____
- ☐ _____

Day 2
- ☐ Isaiah 17
- ☐ CCC 1937-1938
- ☐ SPC, part 1, chap. 5 (finish chapter)
- ☐ _____
- ☐ _____

Day 3
- ☐ Isaiah 18-19
- ☐ CCC 1939-1942
- ☐ SPC, part 1, chap. 6 (half)
- ☐ _____
- ☐ _____

Day 4
- ☐ Isaiah 20
- ☐ CCC 1943-1948
- ☐ SPC, part 1, chap. 6 (finish chapter)
- ☐ _____
- ☐ _____

Day 5
- ☐ Isaiah 21-22
- ☐ CCC 1949-1953
- ☐ SPC, part 1, chap. 7
- ☐ _____
- ☐ _____

Year 4, Week 14

Day 1
- ☐ Isaiah 23
- ☐ CCC 1954-1957
- ☐ SPC, part 2, chap. 1 (half)
- ☐ _____
- ☐ _____

Day 2
- ☐ Isaiah 24-25
- ☐ CCC 1958-1960
- ☐ SPC, part 2, chap. 1 (finish chapter)
- ☐ _____
- ☐ _____

Day 3
- ☐ Isaiah 26
- ☐ CCC 1961-1962
- ☐ SPC, part 2, chap. 2
- ☐ _____
- ☐ _____

Day 4
- ☐ Isaiah 27-28
- ☐ CCC 1963-1964
- ☐ SPC, part 2, chap. 3
- ☐ _____
- ☐ _____

Day 5
- ☐ Isaiah 29
- ☐ CCC 1965-1967
- ☐ SPC, part 2, chap. 4
- ☐ _____
- ☐ _____

And remember that if you do not see, you cannot hear.
That is, the soul who does not see into my Truth with the
eye of its intellect cannot hear or know my Truth.

—JESUS TO SAINT CATHERINE OF SIENA, *LITTLE TALKS WITH GOD*

Year 4, Week 15

Day 1
☐ Isaiah 30-31
☐ CCC 1968-1970
☐ *Journal of a Soul* (JOS), 1895-1896
☐ _____
☐ _____

Day 2
☐ Isaiah 32
☐ CCC 1971-1972
☐ JOS, 1897-1898 through June 19
☐ _____
☐ _____

Day 3
☐ Isaiah 33-34
☐ CCC 1973-1974
☐ JOS, 1898, June 21-August 8
☐ _____
☐ _____

Day 4
☐ Isaiah 35
☐ CCC 1975-1986
☐ JOS, 1898, August 9-September 20
☐ _____
☐ _____

Day 5
☐ Isaiah 36-37
☐ CCC 1987-1991
☐ JOS, 1898, September 21-end
☐ _____
☐ _____

Year 4, Week 16

Day 1
☐ Isaiah 38
☐ CCC 1992-1995
☐ JOS, 1899-1900
☐ _____
☐ _____

Day 2
☐ Isaiah 39-40
☐ CCC 1996-1999
☐ JOS, 1901-1902 (half)
☐ _____
☐ _____

Day 3
☐ Isaiah 41
☐ CCC 2000-2002
☐ JOS, 1902 (finish)
☐ _____
☐ _____

Day 4
☐ Isaiah 42-43
☐ CCC 2003-2005
☐ JOS, 1903 (one-fourth)
☐ _____
☐ _____

Day 5
☐ Isaiah 44
☐ CCC 2006-2008
☐ JOS, 1903 (one-fourth)
☐ _____
☐ _____

In the cross alone do we find the soul's eternal salvation
and hope of everlasting life. Take up your cross, therefore,
and follow Jesus and you will pass into unending life.

—THOMAS À KEMPIS, *THE IMITATION OF CHRIST*

Year 4, Week 17

Day 1
- ☐ Isaiah 45-46
- ☐ CCC 2009-2011
- ☐ JOS, 1903 (one-fourth)
- ☐ _____
- ☐ _____

Day 2
- ☐ Isaiah 47
- ☐ CCC 2012-2014
- ☐ JOS, 1903 (finish)
- ☐ _____
- ☐ _____

Day 3
- ☐ Isaiah 48-49
- ☐ CCC 2015-2016
- ☐ JOS, 1904
- ☐ _____
- ☐ _____

Day 4
- ☐ Isaiah 50
- ☐ CCC 2017-2023
- ☐ JOS, 1905-1909
- ☐ _____
- ☐ _____

Day 5
- ☐ Isaiah 51-52
- ☐ CCC 2024-2029
- ☐ JOS, 1910-1914
- ☐ _____
- ☐ _____

Year 4, Week 18

Day 1
- ☐ Isaiah 53
- ☐ CCC 2030-2031
- ☐ JOS, 1915-1924
- ☐ _____
- ☐ _____

Day 2
- ☐ Isaiah 54-55
- ☐ CCC 2032-2036
- ☐ JOS, 1925-1929
- ☐ _____
- ☐ _____

Day 3
- ☐ Isaiah 56
- ☐ CCC 2037-2040
- ☐ JOS, 1930-1934
- ☐ _____
- ☐ _____

Day 4
- ☐ Isaiah 57-58
- ☐ CCC 2041-2043
- ☐ JOS, 1935-1939
- ☐ _____
- ☐ _____

Day 5
- ☐ Isaiah 59
- ☐ CCC 2044-2046
- ☐ JOS, 1940 (half)
- ☐ _____
- ☐ _____

This day, like all the days of my life, came from his hands and served a purpose in his providence. I had to learn to believe that, no matter what the circumstances, and to act accordingly—with complete trust and confidence in his will, his wisdom, and his grace.

— FATHER WALTER CISZEK, *HE LEADETH ME*

Year 4, Week 19

Day 1
- ☐ Isaiah 60
- ☐ CCC 2047-2051
- ☐ JOS, 1940 (finish chapter)
- ☐ _____
- ☐ _____

Day 2
- ☐ Isaiah 61-62
- ☐ CCC, The Ten Commandments
- ☐ JOS, 1942-1945
- ☐ _____
- ☐ _____

Day 3
- ☐ Isaiah 63
- ☐ CCC 2052-2053
- ☐ JOS, 1947-1948
- ☐ _____
- ☐ _____

Day 4
- ☐ Isaiah 64-65
- ☐ CCC 2054-2055
- ☐ JOS, 1950-1953
- ☐ _____
- ☐ _____

Day 5
- ☐ Isaiah 66
- ☐ CCC 2056-2057
- ☐ JOS, 1954-1957
- ☐ _____
- ☐ _____

Year 4, Week 20

Day 1
- ☐ Jeremiah 1-2
- ☐ CCC 2058-2060
- ☐ JOS, 1958-1960
- ☐ _____
- ☐ _____

Day 2
- ☐ Jeremiah 3
- ☐ CCC 2061-2063
- ☐ JOS, 1961 (half)
- ☐ _____
- ☐ _____

Day 3
- ☐ Jeremiah 4-5
- ☐ CCC 2064-2066
- ☐ JOS, 1961 (finish chapter)
- ☐ _____
- ☐ _____

Day 4
- ☐ Jeremiah 6
- ☐ CCC 2067-2069
- ☐ JOS, 1962
- ☐ _____
- ☐ _____

Day 5
- ☐ Jeremiah 7-8
- ☐ CCC 2070-2071
- ☐ JOS, "Four Letters"
- ☐ _____
- ☐ _____

Another paradox of the spiritual way: the soul which has less
need to reform its behavior is the more anxious to do so, and does
not stop until it has succeeded. And the contrary is also true.

— SAINT JOSEMARÍA ESCRIVÁ, *FURROW*

Year 4, Week 21

Day 1
- ☐ Jeremiah 9
- ☐ CCC 2072-2074
- ☐ JOS, "Spiritual Testament"
- ☐ _____
- ☐ _____

Day 2
- ☐ Jeremiah 10-11
- ☐ CCC 2075-2082
- ☐ JOS, "The Holy Rosary" (half)
- ☐ _____
- ☐ _____

Day 3
- ☐ Jeremiah 12
- ☐ CCC 2083
- ☐ JOS, "The Holy Rosary" (finish chapter)
- ☐ _____
- ☐ _____

Day 4
- ☐ Jeremiah 13-14
- ☐ CCC 2084-2086
- ☐ JOS, "Some Prayers" (1929-1955)
- ☐ _____
- ☐ _____

Day 5
- ☐ Jeremiah 15
- ☐ CCC 2087-2089
- ☐ JOS, "Some Prayers" (1956-1960)
- ☐ _____
- ☐ _____

Year 4, Week 22

Day 1
- ☐ Jeremiah 16-17
- ☐ CCC 2090-2092
- ☐ JOS, "Some Prayers" (1961-end of chapter)
- ☐ _____
- ☐ _____

Day 2
- ☐ Jeremiah 18
- ☐ CCC 2093-2094
- ☐ JOS, appendix 1
- ☐ _____
- ☐ _____

Day 3
- ☐ Jeremiah 19-20
- ☐ CCC 2095-2097
- ☐ JOS, appendix 2
- ☐ _____
- ☐ _____

Day 4
- ☐ Jeremiah 21
- ☐ CCC 2098-2100
- ☐ JOS, appendices 3-4
- ☐ _____
- ☐ _____

Day 5
- ☐ Jeremiah 22-23
- ☐ CCC 2101-2103
- ☐ JOS, appendices 5-7
- ☐ _____
- ☐ _____

I am a pilgrim here on earth. I look to heaven as my goal, my homeland, my dwelling place. O heaven, you are so beautiful, and you are for me!

— SAINT JOHN XXIII, *JOURNAL OF A SOUL*

Year 4, Week 23

Day 1
- ☐ Jeremiah 24
- ☐ CCC 2104-2105
- ☐ *Trustful Surrender to Divine Providence* (TSD), part 1 (half)
- ☐ _____
- ☐ _____

Day 2
- ☐ Jeremiah 25-26
- ☐ CCC 2106-2109
- ☐ TSD, part 1 (finish chapter)
- ☐ _____
- ☐ _____

Day 3
- ☐ Jeremiah 27
- ☐ CCC 2110-2114
- ☐ TSD, part 2
- ☐ _____
- ☐ _____

Day 4
- ☐ Jeremiah 28-29
- ☐ CCC 2115-2117
- ☐ TSD, part 3 (one-fourth)
- ☐ _____
- ☐ _____

Day 5
- ☐ Jeremiah 30
- ☐ CCC 2118-2120
- ☐ TSD, part 3 (one-fourth)
- ☐ _____
- ☐ _____

Year 4, Week 24

Day 1
- ☐ Jeremiah 31-32
- ☐ CCC 2121-2122
- ☐ TSD, part 3 (one-fourth)
- ☐ _____
- ☐ _____

Day 2
- ☐ Jeremiah 33
- ☐ CCC 2123-2124
- ☐ TSD, part 3 (finish chapter)
- ☐ _____
- ☐ _____

Day 3
- ☐ Exodus 34-35
- ☐ CCC 2125-2126
- ☐ TSD, part 4 (half)
- ☐ _____
- ☐ _____

Day 4
- ☐ Jeremiah 36
- ☐ CCC 2127-2128
- ☐ TSD, part 4 (finish chapter)
- ☐ _____
- ☐ _____

Day 5
- ☐ Jeremiah 37-38
- ☐ CCC 2129-2132
- ☐ TSD, part 5
- ☐ _____
- ☐ _____

We have the power to let the current pass through us, use us, produce the light of the world. Or we can refuse to be used and allow darkness to spread.

— SAINT TERESA OF CALCUTTA, *NO GREATER LOVE*

Year 4, Week 25

Day 1
☐ Jeremiah 39
☐ CCC 2133-2141
☐ *The Way of Perfection* (WOP), chaps. 1-2
☐ _____
☐ _____

Day 2
☐ Jeremiah 40-41
☐ CCC 2142-2144
☐ WOP, chaps. 4, 6 (Some versions of WOP omit chapters 3 and 5, as they deal directly with living in a religious order, so they are omitted here.)
☐ _____
☐ _____

Day 3
☐ Jeremiah 42
☐ CCC 2145-2149
☐ WOP, chaps. 7-9
☐ _____
☐ _____

Day 4
☐ Jeremiah 43-44
☐ CCC 2150-2152
☐ WOP, chaps. 10-12
☐ _____
☐ _____

Day 5
☐ Jeremiah 45
☐ CCC 2153-2155
☐ WOP, chaps. 13-15
☐ _____
☐ _____

Year 4, Week 26

Day 1
☐ Jeremiah 46
☐ CCC 2156-2159
☐ WOP, chap. 16
☐ _____
☐ _____

Day 2
☐ Jeremiah 47-48
☐ CCC 2160-2167
☐ WOP, chaps. 17-18
☐ _____
☐ _____

Day 3
☐ Jeremiah 49
☐ CCC 2168-2170
☐ WOP, chap. 19
☐ _____
☐ _____

Day 4
☐ Jeremiah 50-51
☐ CCC 2171-2173
☐ WOP, chap. 20
☐ _____
☐ _____

Day 5
☐ Jeremiah 52
☐ CCC 2174-2176
☐ WOP, chap. 21
☐ _____
☐ _____

Year 4, Week 27

Day 1
- ☐ Lamentations 1
- ☐ CCC 2177-2179
- ☐ WOP, chaps. 22-23
- ☐ _____
- ☐ _____

Day 2
- ☐ Lamentations 2
- ☐ CCC 2180-2183
- ☐ WOP, chaps. 24-26
- ☐ _____
- ☐ _____

Day 3
- ☐ Lamentations 3
- ☐ CCC 2184-2186
- ☐ WOP, chaps. 27-28
- ☐ _____
- ☐ _____

Day 4
- ☐ Lamentations 4
- ☐ CCC 2187-2188
- ☐ WOP, chap. 29
- ☐ _____
- ☐ _____

Day 5
- ☐ Lamentations 5
- ☐ CCC 2189-2195
- ☐ WOP, chaps. 30-31
- ☐ _____
- ☐ _____

Year 4, Week 28

Day 1
- ☐ Baruch 1
- ☐ CCC 2196
- ☐ WOP, chaps. 32-33
- ☐ _____
- ☐ _____

Day 2
- ☐ Baruch 2
- ☐ CCC 2197-2198
- ☐ WOP, chap. 34
- ☐ _____
- ☐ _____

Day 3
- ☐ Baruch 3-4
- ☐ CCC 2199-2200
- ☐ WOP, chaps. 35-36
- ☐ _____
- ☐ _____

Day 4
- ☐ Baruch 5
- ☐ CCC 2201-2203
- ☐ WOP, chaps. 37-39
- ☐ _____
- ☐ _____

Day 5
- ☐ Baruch 6
- ☐ CCC 2204-2206
- ☐ WOP, chaps. 40-42
- ☐ _____
- ☐ _____

Of all the temptations to which the Christian is
exposed, there is none more subtle, more dangerous, and
more difficult to recognize than that of pride.

—VENERABLE LOUIS OF GRANADA, *SUMMA OF THE CHRISTIAN LIFE*

Year 4, Week 29

Day 1
- ☐ Ezekiel 1
- ☐ CCC 2207-2210
- ☐ *The 12 Steps to Holiness and Salvation* (12ST), chap. 1 (half)
- ☐ _____
- ☐ _____

Day 2
- ☐ Ezekiel 2-3
- ☐ CCC 2211-2213
- ☐ 12ST, chap. 1 (finish chapter)
- ☐ _____
- ☐ _____

Day 3
- ☐ Ezekiel 4
- ☐ CCC 2214-2217
- ☐ 12ST, chap. 2 (half)
- ☐ _____
- ☐ _____

Day 4
- ☐ Ezekiel 5-6
- ☐ CCC 2218-2220
- ☐ 12ST, chap. 2 (finish chapter)
- ☐ _____
- ☐ _____

Day 5
- ☐ Ezekiel 7
- ☐ CCC 2221-2223
- ☐ 12ST, chap. 3 (half)
- ☐ _____
- ☐ _____

Year 4, Week 30

Day 1
- ☐ Ezekiel 8
- ☐ CCC 2224-2227
- ☐ 12ST, chap. 3 (finish chapter)
- ☐ _____
- ☐ _____

Day 2
- ☐ Ezekiel 9-10
- ☐ CCC 2228-2231
- ☐ 12ST, chap. 4
- ☐ _____
- ☐ _____

Day 3
- ☐ Ezekiel 11
- ☐ CCC 2232-2233
- ☐ 12ST, chap. 5 (half)
- ☐ _____
- ☐ _____

Day 4
- ☐ Ezekiel 12-13
- ☐ CCC 2234-2237
- ☐ 12ST, chap. 5 (finish chapter)
- ☐ _____
- ☐ _____

Day 5
- ☐ Ezekiel 14
- ☐ CCC 2238-2239
- ☐ 12ST, chap. 6 (half)
- ☐ _____
- ☐ _____

> The more generous you are for God, the happier you will be.
>
> — SAINT JOSEMARÍA ESCRIVÁ, *FURROW*

Year 4, Week 31

Day 1
- ☐ Ezekiel 15
- ☐ CCC 2240-2241
- ☐ 12ST, chap. 6 (finish chapter)
- ☐ _____
- ☐ _____

Day 2
- ☐ Ezekiel 16-17
- ☐ CCC 2242-2243
- ☐ 12ST, chap. 7
- ☐ _____
- ☐ _____

Day 3
- ☐ Ezekiel 18
- ☐ CCC 2244
- ☐ 12ST, chap. 8 (half)
- ☐ _____
- ☐ _____

Day 4
- ☐ Ezekiel 19-20
- ☐ CCC 2245-2246
- ☐ 12ST, chap. 8 (finish chapter)
- ☐ _____
- ☐ _____

Day 5
- ☐ Ezekiel 21
- ☐ CCC 2247-2257
- ☐ 12ST, chap. 9
- ☐ _____
- ☐ _____

Year 4, Week 32

Day 1
- ☐ Ezekiel 22
- ☐ CCC 2258-2260
- ☐ 12ST, chap. 10 (half)
- ☐ _____
- ☐ _____

Day 2
- ☐ Ezekiel 23
- ☐ CCC 2261-2262
- ☐ 12ST, chap. 10 (finish chapter)
- ☐ _____
- ☐ _____

Day 3
- ☐ Ezekiel 24-25
- ☐ CCC 2263-2264
- ☐ 12ST, chap. 11
- ☐ _____
- ☐ _____

Day 4
- ☐ Ezekiel 26
- ☐ CCC 2265-2266
- ☐ 12ST, chap. 12 (half)
- ☐ _____
- ☐ _____

Day 5
- ☐ Ezekiel 27
- ☐ CCC 2267
- ☐ 12ST, (finish chapter)
- ☐ _____
- ☐ _____

> Let us, then, continue unceasingly in our hope and in the Pledge of our justification, that is, in Christ Jesus, who bore our sins in His own body on the tree, who did no sin, nor was guile found in His mouth; yet, for our sakes that we might live in Him, He endured everything.
>
> — SAINT POLYCARP OF SMYRNA, *SECOND LETTER TO THE PHILIPPIANS*, CA. AD 135

Year 4, Week 33

Day 1
- ☐ Ezekiel 28
- ☐ CCC 2268-2269
- ☐ *The Privilege of Being a Woman* (PBW), part 1
- ☐ _____
- ☐ _____

Day 2
- ☐ Ezekiel 29-30
- ☐ CCC 2270-2271
- ☐ PBW, part 2
- ☐ _____
- ☐ _____

Day 3
- ☐ Ezekiel 31
- ☐ CCC 2272-2273
- ☐ PBW, part 3
- ☐ _____
- ☐ _____

Day 4
- ☐ Ezekiel 32-33
- ☐ CCC 2274-2275
- ☐ PBW, part 4 (half)
- ☐ _____
- ☐ _____

Day 5
- ☐ Ezekiel 34
- ☐ CCC 2276-2277
- ☐ PBW, part 4 (finish chapter)
- ☐ _____
- ☐ _____

Year 4, Week 34

Day 1
- ☐ Ezekiel 35
- ☐ CCC 2278-2279
- ☐ PBW, part 5
- ☐ _____
- ☐ _____

Day 2
- ☐ Ezekiel 36-37
- ☐ CCC 2280-2283
- ☐ PBW, part 6
- ☐ _____
- ☐ _____

Day 3
- ☐ Ezekiel 38
- ☐ CCC 2284-2285
- ☐ PBW, part 7
- ☐ _____
- ☐ _____

Day 4
- ☐ Ezekiel 39-40
- ☐ CCC 2286-2287
- ☐ PBW, part 8
- ☐ _____
- ☐ _____

Day 5
- ☐ Ezekiel 41
- ☐ CCC 2288-2291
- ☐ PBW, part 9
- ☐ _____
- ☐ _____

Realize that there is nothing more harmful
to you in this world than self-love.

—THOMAS À KEMPIS, *THE IMITATION OF CHRIST*

Year 4, Week 35

Day 1
- ☐ Ezekiel 42
- ☐ CCC 2292-2294
- ☐ *The Imitation of Christ* (IOC), book 1, chaps. 1-9
- ☐ _____
- ☐ _____

Day 2
- ☐ Ezekiel 43-44
- ☐ CCC 2295-2296
- ☐ IOC, book 1, chaps. 10-17
- ☐ _____
- ☐ _____

Day 3
- ☐ Ezekiel 45
- ☐ CCC 2297-2298
- ☐ IOC, book 1, chaps. 18-21
- ☐ _____
- ☐ _____

Day 4
- ☐ Ezekiel 46-47
- ☐ CCC 2299-2301
- ☐ IOC, book 1, chaps. 22-25
- ☐ _____
- ☐ _____

Day 5
- ☐ Ezekiel 48
- ☐ CCC 2302-2304
- ☐ IOC, book 2, chaps. 1-7
- ☐ _____
- ☐ _____

Year 4, Week 36

Day 1
- ☐ Daniel 1
- ☐ CCC 2305-2306
- ☐ IOC, book 2, chaps. 8-11
- ☐ _____
- ☐ _____

Day 2
- ☐ Daniel 2-3
- ☐ CCC 2307-2309
- ☐ IOC, book 2, chap. 12
- ☐ _____
- ☐ _____

Day 3
- ☐ Daniel 4
- ☐ CCC 2310-2314
- ☐ IOC, book 3, chaps. 1-6
- ☐ _____
- ☐ _____

Day 4
- ☐ Daniel 5-6
- ☐ CCC 2315-2317
- ☐ IOC, book 3, chaps. 7-13
- ☐ _____
- ☐ _____

Day 5
- ☐ Daniel 7
- ☐ CCC 2318-2324
- ☐ IOC, book 3, chaps. 14-20
- ☐ _____
- ☐ _____

How changed the world would be if we worked as hard at being good as we work at making ourselves comfortable or beautiful!

—ARCHBISHOP FULTON SHEEN, *THE ANGEL'S BLACKBOARD*

Year 4, Week 37

Day 1
- ☐ Daniel 8
- ☐ CCC 2325-2330
- ☐ IOC, book 3, chaps. 21-26
- ☐ _____
- ☐ _____

Day 2
- ☐ Daniel 9-10
- ☐ CCC 2331-2333
- ☐ IOC, book 3, chaps. 27-33
- ☐ _____
- ☐ _____

Day 3
- ☐ Daniel 11
- ☐ CCC 2334-2336
- ☐ IOC, book 3, chaps. 34-42
- ☐ _____
- ☐ _____

Day 4
- ☐ Daniel 12-13
- ☐ CCC 2337
- ☐ IOC, book 3, chaps. 43-48
- ☐ _____
- ☐ _____

Day 5
- ☐ Daniel 14
- ☐ CCC 2338-2339
- ☐ IOC, book 3, chaps. 49-53
- ☐ _____
- ☐ _____

Year 4, Week 38

Day 1
- ☐ Hosea 1
- ☐ CCC 2340-2342
- ☐ IOC, book 3, chaps. 54-57
- ☐ _____
- ☐ _____

Day 2
- ☐ Hosea 2-3
- ☐ CCC 2343-2345
- ☐ IOC, book 3, chaps. 58-59
- ☐ _____
- ☐ _____

Day 3
- ☐ Hosea 4
- ☐ CCC 2346-2347
- ☐ IOC, book 4, chaps. 1-5
- ☐ _____
- ☐ _____

Day 4
- ☐ Hosea 5-6
- ☐ CCC 2348-2350
- ☐ IOC, book 4, chaps. 6-11
- ☐ _____
- ☐ _____

Day 5
- ☐ Hosea 7
- ☐ CCC 2351-2352
- ☐ IOC, book 4, chaps. 12-18
- ☐ _____
- ☐ _____

What am I but an ant or grain of sand? Why do I puff
myself up so proudly? Arrogance, pride, self-esteem!
What am I set in this world to do? To serve God.

— SAINT JOHN XXIII, *JOURNAL OF A SOUL*

Year 4, Week 39

Day 1
- ☐ Hosea 8
- ☐ CCC 2353-2354
- ☐ *Witness to Hope* (WTH), preface; "Note on Pronunciation"
- ☐ _____
- ☐ _____

Day 2
- ☐ Hosea 9-10
- ☐ CCC 2355-2356
- ☐ WTH, prologue (half)
- ☐ _____
- ☐ _____

Day 3
- ☐ Hosea 11
- ☐ CCC 2357
- ☐ WTH, prologue (finish chapter)
- ☐ _____
- ☐ _____

Day 4
- ☐ Hosea 12-13
- ☐ CCC 2358-2359
- ☐ WTH, chap. 1 (half)
- ☐ _____
- ☐ _____

Day 5
- ☐ Hosea 14
- ☐ CCC 2360-2361
- ☐ WTH, chap. 1 (finish chapter)
- ☐ _____
- ☐ _____

Year 4, Week 40

Day 1
- ☐ Joel 1
- ☐ CCC 2362-2363
- ☐ WTH, chap. 2 (one-third)
- ☐ _____
- ☐ _____

Day 2
- ☐ Joel 2
- ☐ CCC 2364-2365
- ☐ WTH, chap. 2 (one-third)
- ☐ _____
- ☐ _____

Day 3
- ☐ Joel 3
- ☐ CCC 2366-2367
- ☐ WTH, chap. 2 (finish chapter)
- ☐ _____
- ☐ _____

Day 4
- ☐ Amos 1-2
- ☐ CCC 2368-2369
- ☐ WTH, chap. 3 (one-third)
- ☐ _____
- ☐ _____

Day 5
- ☐ Amos 3
- ☐ CCC 2370
- ☐ WTH, chap. 3 (one-third)
- ☐ _____
- ☐ _____

May no one read sadness or sorrow in your face, when you spread in the world around you the sweet smell of your sacrifice: the children of God should always be sowers of peace and joy.

— ST. JOSEMARÍA ESCRIVÁ, *FURROW*

Year 4, Week 41

Day 1
- ☐ Amos 4
- ☐ CCC 2371-2372
- ☐ WTH, chap. 3 (finish chapter)
- ☐ _____
- ☐ _____

Day 2
- ☐ Amos 5
- ☐ CCC 2373-2376
- ☐ WTH, chap. 4 (half)
- ☐ _____
- ☐ _____

Day 3
- ☐ Amos 6-7
- ☐ CCC 2377
- ☐ WTH, chap. 4 (finish chapter)
- ☐ _____
- ☐ _____

Day 4
- ☐ Amos 8
- ☐ CCC 2378-2379
- ☐ WTH, chap. 5 (one-third)
- ☐ _____
- ☐ _____

Day 5
- ☐ Amos 9
- ☐ CCC 2380-2381
- ☐ WTH, chap. 5 (one-third)
- ☐ _____
- ☐ _____

Year 4, Week 42

Day 1
- ☐ Obadiah
- ☐ CCC 2382-2383
- ☐ WTH, chap. 5 (finish chapter)
- ☐ _____
- ☐ _____

Day 2
- ☐ Jonah 1
- ☐ CCC 2384-2386
- ☐ WTH, chap. 6 (one-fifth)
- ☐ _____
- ☐ _____

Day 3
- ☐ Jonah 2
- ☐ CCC 2387-2389
- ☐ WTH, chap. 6 (one-fifth)
- ☐ _____
- ☐ _____

Day 4
- ☐ Jonah 3
- ☐ CCC 2390-2391
- ☐ WTH, chap. 6 (one-fifth)
- ☐ _____
- ☐ _____

Day 5
- ☐ Jonah 4
- ☐ CCC 2392-2400
- ☐ WTH, chap. 6 (one-fifth)
- ☐ _____
- ☐ _____

You must be willing, for the love of God, to endure all things, for example, labor and sorrow, temptation and annoyance, anxiety and want, illness and injury, opposition and reproach, humiliation and disgrace, censure and contempt. All these will help you to acquire virtue.

—THOMAS À KEMPIS, *THE IMITATION OF CHRIST*

Year 4, Week 43

Day 1
☐ Micah 1
☐ CCC 2401-2403
☐ WTH, chap. 6 (finish chapter)
☐ _____
☐ _____

Day 2
☐ Micah 2-3
☐ CCC 2404-2407
☐ WTH, chap. 7 (half)
☐ _____
☐ _____

Day 3
☐ Micah 4
☐ CCC 2408-2409
☐ WTH, chap. 7 (finish chapter)
☐ _____
☐ _____

Day 4
☐ Micah 5-6
☐ CCC 2410-2411
☐ WTH, chap. 8 (half)
☐ _____
☐ _____

Day 5
☐ Micah 7
☐ CCC 2412
☐ WTH, chap. 8 (finish chapter)
☐ _____
☐ _____

Year 4, Week 44

Day 1
☐ Nahum 1
☐ CCC 2413-2414
☐ WTH, chap. 9 (one-third)
☐ _____
☐ _____

Day 2
☐ Nahum 2-3
☐ CCC 2415-2416
☐ WTH, chap. 9 (one-third)
☐ _____
☐ _____

Day 3
☐ Habakkuk 1
☐ CCC 2417-2418
☐ WTH, chap. 9 (finish chapter)
☐ _____
☐ _____

Day 4
☐ Habakkuk 2
☐ CCC 2419-2421
☐ WTH, chap. 10 (half)
☐ _____
☐ _____

Day 5
☐ Habakkuk 3
☐ CCC 2422-2425
☐ WTH, chap. 10 (finish chapter)
☐ _____
☐ _____

We must not measure ourselves by anything that comes to an end, least of all life, since not a day of it is secure. Who, if she thought that each hour might be her last, would not spend it working for God?

— SAINT TERESA OF ÁVILA, *THE WAY OF PERFECTION*

Year 4, Week 45

Day 1
☐ Zephaniah 1
☐ CCC 2426-2427
☐ WTH, chap. 11 (half)
☐ _____
☐ _____

Day 2
☐ Zephaniah 2
☐ CCC 2428-2430
☐ WTH, chap. 11 (finish chapter)
☐ _____
☐ _____

Day 3
☐ Zephaniah 3
☐ CCC 2431-2433
☐ WTH, chap. 12 (one-third)
☐ _____
☐ _____

Day 4
☐ Haggai 1
☐ CCC 2434-2436
☐ WTH, chap. 12 (one-third)
☐ _____
☐ _____

Day 5
☐ Haggai 2
☐ CCC 2437-2438
☐ WTH, chap. 12 (finish chapter)
☐ _____
☐ _____

Year 4, Week 46

Day 1
☐ Zechariah 1
☐ CCC 2439-2440
☐ WTH, chap. 13 (one-third)
☐ _____
☐ _____

Day 2
☐ Zechariah 2-3
☐ CCC 2441-2442
☐ WTH, chap. 13 (one-third)
☐ _____
☐ _____

Day 3
☐ Zechariah 4
☐ CCC 2443-2445
☐ WTH, chap. 13 (finish chapter)
☐ _____
☐ _____

Day 4
☐ Zechariah 5-6
☐ CCC 2446-2447
☐ WTH, chap. 14 (one-fourth)
☐ _____
☐ _____

Day 5
☐ Zechariah 7
☐ CCC 2448-2449
☐ WTH, chap. 14 (one-fourth)
☐ _____
☐ _____

Your arms, My Jesus, are the elevator which will take me
up to Heaven. There is no need for me to grow up; on the
contrary, I must stay little, and become more and more so.

—SAINT THÉRÈSE OF LISIEUX, *THE STORY OF A SOUL*

Year 4, Week 47

Day 1
- ☐ Zechariah 8
- ☐ CCC 2450-2456
- ☐ WTH, chap. 14 (one-fourth)
- ☐ _____
- ☐ _____

Day 2
- ☐ Zechariah 9-10
- ☐ CCC 2457-2463
- ☐ WTH, chap. 14 (finish chapter)
- ☐ _____
- ☐ _____

Day 3
- ☐ Zechariah 11
- ☐ CCC 2464-2466
- ☐ WTH, chap. 15 (one-fifth)
- ☐ _____
- ☐ _____

Day 4
- ☐ Zechariah 12-13
- ☐ CCC 2467-2470
- ☐ WTH, chap. 15 (one-fifth)
- ☐ _____
- ☐ _____

Day 5
- ☐ Zechariah 14
- ☐ CCC 2471-2472
- ☐ WTH, chap. 15 (one-fifth)
- ☐ _____
- ☐ _____

Year 4, Week 48

Day 1
- ☐ Malachi 1
- ☐ CCC 2473-2474
- ☐ WTH, chap. 15 (one-fifth)
- ☐ _____
- ☐ _____

Day 2
- ☐ Malachi 2
- ☐ CCC 2475-2478
- ☐ WTH, chap. 15 (finish chapter)
- ☐ _____
- ☐ _____

Day 3
- ☐ Malachi 3
- ☐ CCC 2479-2483
- ☐ WTH, chap. 16 (one-fourth)
- ☐ _____
- ☐ _____

Day 4
- ☐ Malachi 4
- ☐ CCC 2484-2487
- ☐ WTH, chap. 16 (one-fourth)
- ☐ _____
- ☐ _____

Day 5
- ☐ 1 Maccabees 1-2
- ☐ CCC 2488-2490
- ☐ WTH, chap. 16 (one-fourth)
- ☐ _____
- ☐ _____

You shall not hate any man; but some you shall reprove, some you shall pray for, and some you shall love more than the breath of life that is in you.

— *DIDACHE*

Year 4, Week 49

Day 1
- ☐ 1 Maccabees 3-4
- ☐ CCC 2491-2492
- ☐ WTH, chap. 16 (finish chapter)
- ☐ _____
- ☐ _____

Day 2
- ☐ 1 Maccabees 5-6
- ☐ CCC 2493-2496
- ☐ WTH, chap. 17 (one-third)
- ☐ _____
- ☐ _____

Day 3
- ☐ 1 Maccabees 7-8
- ☐ CCC 2497-2499
- ☐ WTH, chap. 17 (one-third)
- ☐ _____
- ☐ _____

Day 4
- ☐ 1 Maccabees 9-10
- ☐ CCC 2500
- ☐ WTH, chap. 17 (finish chapter)
- ☐ _____
- ☐ _____

Day 5
- ☐ 1 Maccabees 11
- ☐ CCC 2501-2503
- ☐ WTH, chap. 18 (one-fifth)
- ☐ _____
- ☐ _____

Year 4, Week 50

Day 1
- ☐ 1 Maccabees 12
- ☐ CCC 2504-2508
- ☐ WTH, chap. 18 (one-fifth)
- ☐ _____
- ☐ _____

Day 2
- ☐ 1 Maccabees 13
- ☐ CCC 2509-2513
- ☐ WTH, chap. 18 (one-fifth)
- ☐ _____
- ☐ _____

Day 3
- ☐ 1 Maccabees 14
- ☐ CCC 2514-2516
- ☐ WTH, chap. 18 (one-fifth)
- ☐ _____
- ☐ _____

Day 4
- ☐ 1 Maccabees 15
- ☐ CCC 2517-2519
- ☐ WTH, chap. 18 (finish chapter)
- ☐ _____
- ☐ _____

Day 5
- ☐ 1 Maccabees 16
- ☐ CCC 2520-2521
- ☐ WTH, chap. 19 (one-third)
- ☐ _____
- ☐ _____

> When the Proconsul urged him and said, "Take the oath and I will release you; revile Christ," Polykarp answered: "Eighty-six years I have served Him, and He has never done me wrong. How, then, should I be able to blaspheme my King who has saved me?"
>
> — *THE MARTYRDOM OF SAINT POLYCARP*

Year 4, Week 51

Day 1
- ☐ 2 Maccabees 1-2
- ☐ CCC 2522-2524
- ☐ WTH, chap. 19 (one-third)
- ☐ _____
- ☐ _____

Day 2
- ☐ 2 Maccabees 3
- ☐ CCC 2525-2527
- ☐ WTH, chap. 19 (finish chapter)
- ☐ _____
- ☐ _____

Day 3
- ☐ 2 Maccabees 4-5
- ☐ CCC 2528-2533
- ☐ WTH, chap. 20 (one-fourth)
- ☐ _____
- ☐ _____

Day 4
- ☐ 2 Maccabees 6
- ☐ CCC 2534-2535
- ☐ WTH, chap. 20 (one-fourth)
- ☐ _____
- ☐ _____

Day 5
- ☐ 2 Maccabees 7-8
- ☐ CCC 2536-2537
- ☐ WTH, chap. 20 (one-fourth)
- ☐ _____
- ☐ _____

Year 4, Week 52

Day 1
- ☐ 2 Maccabees 9
- ☐ CCC 2538-2540
- ☐ WTH, chap. 20 (finish chapter)
- ☐ _____
- ☐ _____

Day 2
- ☐ 2 Maccabees 10-11
- ☐ CCC 2541-2543
- ☐ WTH, epilogue (half)
- ☐ _____
- ☐ _____

Day 3
- ☐ 2 Maccabees 12
- ☐ CCC 2544-2547
- ☐ WTH, epilogue (finish epilogue)
- ☐ _____
- ☐ _____

Day 4
- ☐ 2 Maccabees 13-14
- ☐ CCC 2548-2550
- ☐ WTH, afterword (half)
- ☐ _____
- ☐ _____

Day 5
- ☐ 2 Maccabees 15
- ☐ CCC 2551-2557
- ☐ WTH, afterword (finish afterword)
- ☐ _____
- ☐ _____

> [Paul], an able wrestler, urges us on in the struggle for
> immortality,... so that we may regard as a precious crown that
> which we acquire by our own struggle.... And because it comes
> to us in a struggle, it is therefore the more precious.
>
> — SAINT IRENAEUS, *AGAINST HERESIES*, CA. AD 180

— Year 5 —

Reading List

Sacred Scripture: The entire New Testament

Catechism of the Catholic Church: Prayer

Spiritual Reading:

Meditations from a Simple Path by Mother Teresa (1 week)

In Silence with God by Benedict Baur (4 weeks)

Interior Freedom by Jacques Philippe (3 weeks)

Conversation with Christ by Peter Thomas Rohrbach (4 weeks)

True Devotion to the Holy Spirit by Luis M. Martinez (6 weeks)

Furrow by Saint Josemaría Escrivá (3 weeks)

Interior Castle by Saint Teresa of Ávila (4 weeks)

Difficulties in Mental Prayer by Eugene Boylan (4 weeks)

Introduction to the Devout Life by Saint Francis de Sales (10 weeks)

True Devotion to Mary by Saint Louis de Montfort (3 weeks)

Soul of the Apostolate by Dom Jean-Baptiste Chautard (7 weeks)

Little Talks with God by Saint Catherine of Siena (3 weeks)

Whenever my soul is so dry that I am incapable of a
single good thought, I always say an *Our Father* or a
Hail Mary very slowly, and these prayers alone cheer
me up and nourish my soul with divine food.

— Saint Thérèse of Lisieux, *The Story of a Soul*

Year 5, Week 1

Day 1
- ☐ Matthew 1
- ☐ CCC 2558
- ☐ *Meditations from a Simple Path* (MSP), introduction; "The Fruit of Silence Is Prayer"
- ☐ _____
- ☐ _____

Day 2
- ☐ Matthew 2
- ☐ CCC 2559
- ☐ MSP, "The Fruit of Prayer Is Faith"
- ☐ _____
- ☐ _____

Day 3
- ☐ Matthew 3
- ☐ CCC 2560
- ☐ MSP, "The Fruit of Faith Is Love"
- ☐ _____
- ☐ _____

Day 4
- ☐ Matthew 4
- ☐ CCC 2561
- ☐ MSP, "The Fruit of Love Is Service"
- ☐ _____
- ☐ _____

Day 5
- ☐ Matthew 5
- ☐ CCC 2562-2564
- ☐ MSP, "The Fruit of Service Is Peace"
- ☐ _____
- ☐ _____

Year 5, Week 2

Day 1
- ☐ Matthew 6
- ☐ CCC 2565
- ☐ *In Silence with God* (ISG), chap. 1
- ☐ _____
- ☐ _____

Day 2
- ☐ Matthew 7
- ☐ CCC 2566
- ☐ ISG, chap. 2
- ☐ _____
- ☐ _____

Day 3
- ☐ Matthew 8
- ☐ CCC 2567
- ☐ ISG, chap. 3
- ☐ _____
- ☐ _____

Day 4
- ☐ Matthew 9
- ☐ CCC 2568
- ☐ ISG, chaps. 4-5
- ☐ _____
- ☐ _____

Day 5
- ☐ Matthew 10
- ☐ CCC 2569
- ☐ ISG, chap. 6
- ☐ _____
- ☐ _____

Prayer is helplessness casting itself on Power, infirmity leaning on Strength, misery reaching to Mercy, and a prisoner clamoring for Relief.

—ARCHBISHOP FULTON SHEEN, *LIFE IS WORTH LIVING*

Year 5, Week 3

Day 1
- ☐ Matthew 11
- ☐ CCC 2570
- ☐ ISG, chap. 7
- ☐ _____
- ☐ _____

Day 2
- ☐ Matthew 12
- ☐ CCC 2571
- ☐ ISG, chap. 8
- ☐ _____
- ☐ _____

Day 3
- ☐ Matthew 13
- ☐ CCC 2572
- ☐ ISG, chap. 9
- ☐ _____
- ☐ _____

Day 4
- ☐ Matthew 14
- ☐ CCC 2573
- ☐ ISG, chaps. 10-11
- ☐ _____
- ☐ _____

Day 5
- ☐ Matthew 15
- ☐ CCC 2574
- ☐ ISG, chap. 12
- ☐ _____
- ☐ _____

Year 5, Week 4

Day 1
- ☐ Matthew 16
- ☐ CCC 2575
- ☐ ISG, chap. 13
- ☐ _____
- ☐ _____

Day 2
- ☐ Matthew 17
- ☐ CCC 2576
- ☐ ISG, chap. 14
- ☐ _____
- ☐ _____

Day 3
- ☐ Matthew 18
- ☐ CCC 2577
- ☐ ISG, chap. 15
- ☐ _____
- ☐ _____

Day 4
- ☐ Matthew 19
- ☐ CCC 2578
- ☐ ISG, chap. 16
- ☐ _____
- ☐ _____

Day 5
- ☐ Matthew 20
- ☐ CCC 2579
- ☐ ISG, chap. 17
- ☐ _____
- ☐ _____

A powerful aid in preserving recollection is the
remembrance of the presence of God.

— SAINT ALPHONSUS LIGUORI, *THE 12 STEPS TO HOLINESS AND SALVATION*

Year 5, Week 5

Day 1
- ☐ Matthew 21
- ☐ CCC 2580
- ☐ ISG, chap. 18
- ☐ _____
- ☐ _____

Day 2
- ☐ Matthew 22
- ☐ CCC 2581
- ☐ ISG, chap. 19
- ☐ _____
- ☐ _____

Day 3
- ☐ Matthew 23
- ☐ CCC 2582-2583
- ☐ ISG, chap. 20
- ☐ _____
- ☐ _____

Day 4
- ☐ Matthew 24
- ☐ CCC 2584
- ☐ ISG, chap. 21
- ☐ _____
- ☐ _____

Day 5
- ☐ Matthew 25
- ☐ CCC 2585-2586
- ☐ ISG, chap. 22
- ☐ _____
- ☐ _____

Year 5, Week 6

Day 1
- ☐ Matthew 26
- ☐ CCC 2587
- ☐ _Interior Freedom_ (IF), introduction; part 1, chap. 1 (one-third)
- ☐ _____
- ☐ _____

Day 2
- ☐ Matthew 27
- ☐ CCC 2588
- ☐ IF, part 1, chap. 1 (one-third)
- ☐ _____
- ☐ _____

Day 3
- ☐ Matthew 28
- ☐ CCC 2589
- ☐ IF, part 1, chap. 1 (finish chapter)
- ☐ _____
- ☐ _____

Day 4
- ☐ Mark 1
- ☐ CCC 2590-2593
- ☐ IF, part 1, chap. 2
- ☐ _____
- ☐ _____

Day 5
- ☐ Mark 2
- ☐ CCC 2594-2597
- ☐ IF, part 1, chap. 3 (half)
- ☐ _____
- ☐ _____

Millions and millions of favors are hanging from heaven
on silken cords, and prayer is the sword that cuts them.

—ARCHBISHOP FULTON SHEEN, _THE ANGEL'S BLACKBOARD_

Year 5, Week 7

Day 1
☐ Mark 3
☐ CCC 2598
☐ IF, part 1, chap. 3 (finish chapter)
☐ _____
☐ _____

Day 2
☐ Mark 4
☐ CCC 2599
☐ IF, part 1, chap. 4 (half)
☐ _____
☐ _____

Day 3
☐ Mark 5
☐ CCC 2600
☐ IF, part 1, chap. 4 (finish chapter)
☐ _____
☐ _____

Day 4
☐ Mark 6
☐ CCC 2601
☐ IF, part 2, chaps. 1-4
☐ _____
☐ _____

Day 5
☐ Mark 7
☐ CCC 2602
☐ IF, part 2, chaps. 5-8
☐ _____
☐ _____

Year 5, Week 8

Day 1
☐ Mark 8
☐ CCC 2603
☐ IF, part 3, chaps. 1-6
☐ _____
☐ _____

Day 2
☐ Mark 9
☐ CCC 2604
☐ IF, part 3, chaps. 7-11
☐ _____
☐ _____

Day 3
☐ Mark 10
☐ CCC 2605
☐ IF, part 4
☐ _____
☐ _____

Day 4
☐ Mark 11
☐ CCC 2606
☐ IF, part 5, chaps. 1-3
☐ _____
☐ _____

Day 5
☐ Mark 12
☐ CCC 2607
☐ IF, part 5, chaps. 4-6
☐ _____
☐ _____

Prayer, for me, is simply a raising of the heart, a simple glance towards Heaven, an expression of love and gratitude in the midst of trial, as well as in times of joy; in a word, it is something noble and supernatural expanding my soul and uniting it to God.

—SAINT THÉRÈSE OF LISIEUX, *THE STORY OF A SOUL*

Year 5, Week 9

Day 1
- ☐ Mark 13
- ☐ CCC 2608
- ☐ *Conversation with Christ* (CWC), chaps. 1-2
- ☐ _____
- ☐ _____

Day 2
- ☐ Mark 14
- ☐ CCC 2609
- ☐ CWC, chap. 3
- ☐ _____
- ☐ _____

Day 3
- ☐ Mark 15
- ☐ CCC 2610
- ☐ CWC, chap. 4
- ☐ _____
- ☐ _____

Day 4
- ☐ Mark 16
- ☐ CCC 2611
- ☐ CWC, chaps. 5-6
- ☐ _____
- ☐ _____

Day 5
- ☐ Luke 1
- ☐ CCC 2612
- ☐ CWC, chap. 7
- ☐ _____
- ☐ _____

Year 5, Week 10

Day 1
- ☐ Luke 2
- ☐ CCC 2613
- ☐ CWC, chap. 8
- ☐ _____
- ☐ _____

Day 2
- ☐ Luke 3
- ☐ CCC 2614
- ☐ CWC, chap. 9 (half)
- ☐ _____
- ☐ _____

Day 3
- ☐ Luke 4
- ☐ CCC 2615
- ☐ CWC, chap. 9 (finish chapter)
- ☐ _____
- ☐ _____

Day 4
- ☐ Luke 5
- ☐ CCC 2616
- ☐ CWC, chaps. 10-11
- ☐ _____
- ☐ _____

Day 5
- ☐ Luke 6
- ☐ CCC 2617
- ☐ CWC, chap. 12
- ☐ _____
- ☐ _____

If you abstain from unnecessary conversation and useless visiting, as well as from listening to idle news and gossip, you will find sufficient and suitable times for your meditations.

—THOMAS À KEMPIS, *THE IMITATION OF CHRIST*

Year 5, Week 11

Day 1
- ☐ Luke 7
- ☐ CCC 2618
- ☐ CWC, chap. 13
- ☐ _____
- ☐ _____

Day 2
- ☐ Luke 8
- ☐ CCC 2619
- ☐ CWC, chap. 14
- ☐ _____
- ☐ _____

Day 3
- ☐ Luke 9
- ☐ CCC 2620-2622
- ☐ CWC, chap. 15
- ☐ _____
- ☐ _____

Day 4
- ☐ Luke 10
- ☐ CCC 2623
- ☐ CWC, chap. 16
- ☐ _____
- ☐ _____

Day 5
- ☐ Luke 11
- ☐ CCC 2624
- ☐ CWC, chap. 17
- ☐ _____
- ☐ _____

Year 5, Week 12

Day 1
- ☐ Luke 12
- ☐ CCC 2625
- ☐ CWC, chap. 18
- ☐ _____
- ☐ _____

Day 2
- ☐ Luke 13
- ☐ CCC 2626-2628
- ☐ CWC, chap. 19
- ☐ _____
- ☐ _____

Day 3
- ☐ Luke 14
- ☐ CCC 2629
- ☐ CWC, chap. 20
- ☐ _____
- ☐ _____

Day 4
- ☐ Luke 15
- ☐ CCC 2630
- ☐ CWC, chap. 21
- ☐ _____
- ☐ _____

Day 5
- ☐ Luke 16
- ☐ CCC 2631
- ☐ CWC, chap. 22
- ☐ _____
- ☐ _____

A short time ago I was told by a very learned man that souls
without prayer are like people whose bodies or limbs are paralyzed:
they possess feet and hands but they cannot control them.

— SAINT TERESA OF ÁVILA, *INTERIOR CASTLE*

Year 5, Week 13

Day 1
☐ Luke 17
☐ CCC 2632-2633
☐ *True Devotion to the Holy Spirit*
  (TDHS), chap. 1
☐ _____
☐ _____

Day 2
☐ Luke 18
☐ CCC 2634
☐ TDHS, chap. 2
☐ _____
☐ _____

Day 3
☐ Luke 19
☐ CCC 2635
☐ TDHS, chap. 3
☐ _____
☐ _____

Day 4
☐ Luke 20
☐ CCC 2636
☐ TDHS, chap. 4
☐ _____
☐ _____

Day 5
☐ Luke 21
☐ CCC 2637-2638
☐ TDHS, chap. 5
☐ _____
☐ _____

Year 5, Week 14

Day 1
☐ Luke 22
☐ CCC 2639
☐ TDHS, chap. 6
☐ _____
☐ _____

Day 2
☐ Luke 23
☐ CCC 2640-2641
☐ TDHS, chaps. 7-8
☐ _____
☐ _____

Day 3
☐ Luke 24
☐ CCC 2642
☐ TDHS, chaps. 9-10
☐ _____
☐ _____

Day 4
☐ John 1
☐ CCC 2643
☐ TDHS, chap. 11
☐ _____
☐ _____

Day 5
☐ John 2
☐ CCC 2644-2646
☐ TDHS, chaps. 12-13
☐ _____
☐ _____

There are not two kinds of answers to prayer, but three:
One is "Yes." Another is "No." The third is "Wait."

—ARCHBISHOP FULTON SHEEN, *SEVEN WORDS OF JESUS AND MARY*

Year 5, Week 15

Day 1
- ☐ John 3
- ☐ CCC 2647-2649
- ☐ TDHS, chap. 14
- ☐ _____
- ☐ _____

Day 2
- ☐ John 4
- ☐ CCC 2650
- ☐ TDHS, chap. 15
- ☐ _____
- ☐ _____

Day 3
- ☐ John 5
- ☐ CCC 2651
- ☐ TDHS, chap. 16
- ☐ _____
- ☐ _____

Day 4
- ☐ John 6
- ☐ CCC 2652
- ☐ TDHS, chaps. 17-18
- ☐ _____
- ☐ _____

Day 5
- ☐ John 7
- ☐ CCC 2653-2654
- ☐ TDHS, chap. 19
- ☐ _____
- ☐ _____

Year 5, Week 16

Day 1
- ☐ John 8
- ☐ CCC 2655
- ☐ TDHS, chap. 20
- ☐ _____
- ☐ _____

Day 2
- ☐ John 9
- ☐ CCC 2656-2658
- ☐ TDHS, chap. 21
- ☐ _____
- ☐ _____

Day 3
- ☐ John 10
- ☐ CCC 2659-2660
- ☐ TDHS, chap. 22
- ☐ _____
- ☐ _____

Day 4
- ☐ John 11
- ☐ CCC 2661-2662
- ☐ TDHS, chap. 23
- ☐ _____
- ☐ _____

Day 5
- ☐ John 12
- ☐ CCC 2663
- ☐ TDHS, chap. 24
- ☐ _____
- ☐ _____

> We want so much to pray properly and then we fail. We get discouraged
> and give up. If you want to pray better, you must pray more.
>
> — SAINT TERESA OF CALCUTTA, *NO GREATER LOVE*

Year 5, Week 17

Day 1
- ☐ John 13
- ☐ CCC 2664
- ☐ TDHS, chap. 25
- ☐ _____
- ☐ _____

Day 2
- ☐ John 14
- ☐ CCC 2665
- ☐ TDHS, chap. 26
- ☐ _____
- ☐ _____

Day 3
- ☐ John 15
- ☐ CCC 2666
- ☐ TDHS, chap. 27
- ☐ _____
- ☐ _____

Day 4
- ☐ John 16
- ☐ CCC 2667
- ☐ TDHS, chap. 28
- ☐ _____
- ☐ _____

Day 5
- ☐ John 17
- ☐ CCC 2668
- ☐ TDHS, chap. 29
- ☐ _____
- ☐ _____

Year 5, Week 18

Day 1
- ☐ John 18
- ☐ CCC 2669
- ☐ TDHS, chap. 30
- ☐ _____
- ☐ _____

Day 2
- ☐ John 19
- ☐ CCC 2670
- ☐ TDHS, chap. 31
- ☐ _____
- ☐ _____

Day 3
- ☐ John 20
- ☐ CCC 2671
- ☐ TDHS, chap. 32
- ☐ _____
- ☐ _____

Day 4
- ☐ John 21
- ☐ CCC 2672
- ☐ TDHS, chap. 33
- ☐ _____
- ☐ _____

Day 5
- ☐ Acts 1
- ☐ CCC 2673-2674
- ☐ TDHS, chap. 34
- ☐ _____
- ☐ _____

Be daring in your prayer, and the Lord will turn you from a pessimist into an optimist; from being timid, to being daring, from being feeble-spirited to being a man of faith, an apostle!

— ST. JOSEMARÍA ESCRIVÁ, *FURROW*

Year 5, Week 19

Day 1
☐ Acts 2
☐ CCC 2675
☐ *Furrow* (FW), "Generosity"; "Human Respect"
☐ _____
☐ _____

Day 2
☐ Acts 3
☐ CCC 2676
☐ FW, "Cheerfulness"; "Daring"
☐ _____
☐ _____

Day 3
☐ Acts 4
☐ CCC 2677
☐ FW, "The Struggle"
☐ _____
☐ _____

Day 4
☐ Acts 5
☐ CCC 2678
☐ FW, "Fishers of Men"
☐ _____
☐ _____

Day 5
☐ Acts 6
☐ CCC 2679
☐ FW, "Suffering"; "Humility"
☐ _____
☐ _____

Year 5, Week 20

Day 1
☐ Acts 7
☐ CCC 2680-2682
☐ FW, "Citizenship"; "Sincerity"; "Loyalty"; "Discipline"
☐ _____
☐ _____

Day 2
☐ Acts 8
☐ CCC 2683
☐ FW, "Personality"; "Prayer"
☐ _____
☐ _____

Day 3
☐ Acts 9
☐ CCC 2684
☐ FW, "Work"
☐ _____
☐ _____

Day 4
☐ Acts 10
☐ CCC 2685
☐ FW, "Frivolity"; "Naturalness"
☐ _____
☐ _____

Day 5
☐ Acts 11
☐ CCC 2686
☐ FW, "Truthfulness"; "Ambition"; "Hypocrisy"
☐ _____
☐ _____

> A higher form of prayer than petition—and a potent remedy against the externalization of life—is meditation.
>
> —ARCHBISHOP FULTON SHEEN, *THE ANGEL'S BLACKBOARD*

Year 5, Week 21

Day 1
- ☐ Acts 12
- ☐ CCC 2687
- ☐ FW, "Interior Life"; "Pride"; "Friendship"
- ☐ _____
- ☐ _____

Day 2
- ☐ Acts 13
- ☐ CCC 2688
- ☐ FW, "The Will"; "The Heart"; "Purity"
- ☐ _____
- ☐ _____

Day 3
- ☐ Acts 14
- ☐ CCC 2689
- ☐ FW, "Peace"; "Beyond Death"
- ☐ _____
- ☐ _____

Day 4
- ☐ Acts 15
- ☐ CCC 2690
- ☐ FW, "The Tongue"; "Spreading the Faith"
- ☐ _____
- ☐ _____

Day 5
- ☐ Acts 16
- ☐ CCC 2691
- ☐ FW, "Responsibility"; "Penance"
- ☐ _____
- ☐ _____

Year 5, Week 22

Day 1
- ☐ Acts 17
- ☐ CCC 2692-2694
- ☐ *Interior Castle* (IC), IC-JHS; First Mansions, chap. 1
- ☐ _____
- ☐ _____

Day 2
- ☐ Acts 18
- ☐ CCC 2695-2696
- ☐ IC, First Mansions, chap. 2
- ☐ _____
- ☐ _____

Day 3
- ☐ Acts 19
- ☐ CCC 2697
- ☐ IC, Second Mansions
- ☐ _____
- ☐ _____

Day 4
- ☐ Acts 20
- ☐ CCC 2698
- ☐ IC, Third Mansions
- ☐ _____
- ☐ _____

Day 5
- ☐ Acts 21
- ☐ CCC 2699
- ☐ IC, Fourth Mansions, chap. 1
- ☐ _____
- ☐ _____

> Provided we do not abandon our prayer, the Lord will turn everything we do to our profit, even though we may find no one to teach us.
>
> — SAINT TERESA OF ÁVILA, *INTERIOR CASTLE*

Year 5, Week 23

Day 1
☐ Acts 22
☐ CCC 2700
☐ IC, Fourth Mansions, chap. 2
☐ _____
☐ _____

Day 2
☐ Acts 23
☐ CCC 2701
☐ IC, Fourth Mansions, chap. 3
☐ _____
☐ _____

Day 3
☐ Acts 24
☐ CCC 2702
☐ IC, Fifth Mansions, chap. 1
☐ _____
☐ _____

Day 4
☐ Acts 25
☐ CCC 2703
☐ IC, Fifth Mansions, chap. 2
☐ _____
☐ _____

Day 5
☐ Acts 26
☐ CCC 2704
☐ IC, Fifth Mansions, chaps. 3-4
☐ _____
☐ _____

Year 5, Week 24

Day 1
☐ Acts 27
☐ CCC 2705
☐ IC, Sixth Mansions, chaps. 1-2
☐ _____
☐ _____

Day 2
☐ Acts 28
☐ CCC 2706
☐ IC, Sixth Mansions, chap. 3
☐ _____
☐ _____

Day 3
☐ Romans 1
☐ CCC 2707
☐ IC, Sixth Mansions, chap. 4
☐ _____
☐ _____

Day 4
☐ Romans 2
☐ CCC 2708
☐ IC, Sixth Mansions, chaps. 5-6
☐ _____
☐ _____

Day 5
☐ Romans 3
☐ CCC 2709
☐ IC, Sixth Mansions, chap. 7
☐ _____
☐ _____

Truly, the Lord's Prayer is the beginning and end of
all prayers, the key to every other form of prayer.

— FATHER WALTER CISZEK, *HE LEADETH ME*

Year 5, Week 25

Day 1
- ☐ Romans 4
- ☐ CCC 2710
- ☐ IC, Sixth Mansions, chap. 8
- ☐ _____
- ☐ _____

Day 2
- ☐ Romans 5
- ☐ CCC 2711
- ☐ IC, Sixth Mansions, chaps. 9-10
- ☐ _____
- ☐ _____

Day 3
- ☐ Romans 6
- ☐ CCC 2712
- ☐ IC, Sixth Mansions, chap. 11
- ☐ _____
- ☐ _____

Day 4
- ☐ Romans 7
- ☐ CCC 2713
- ☐ IC, Seventh Mansions, chaps. 1-2
- ☐ _____
- ☐ _____

Day 5
- ☐ Romans 8
- ☐ CCC 2714
- ☐ IC, Seventh Mansions, chaps. 3-4; JHS
- ☐ _____
- ☐ _____

Year 5, Week 26

Day 1
- ☐ Romans 9
- ☐ CCC 2715
- ☐ _Difficulties in Mental Prayer_ (DMP), preface
- ☐ _____
- ☐ _____

Day 2
- ☐ Romans 10
- ☐ CCC 2716
- ☐ DMP, chap. 1
- ☐ _____
- ☐ _____

Day 3
- ☐ Romans 11
- ☐ CCC 2717
- ☐ DMP, chaps. 2-3
- ☐ _____
- ☐ _____

Day 4
- ☐ Romans 12
- ☐ CCC 2718
- ☐ DMP, chap. 4
- ☐ _____
- ☐ _____

Day 5
- ☐ Romans 13
- ☐ CCC 2719
- ☐ DMP, chap. 5
- ☐ _____
- ☐ _____

> Blessed are the ears that are attuned to God's quiet whisper and ignore the world's raucous sounds.
>
> —THOMAS À KEMPIS, _THE IMITATION OF CHRIST_

Year 5, Week 27

Day 1
- ☐ Romans 14
- ☐ CCC 2720-2721
- ☐ DMP, chap. 6
- ☐ _____
- ☐ _____

Day 2
- ☐ Romans 15
- ☐ CCC 2722-2724
- ☐ DMP, chap. 7
- ☐ _____
- ☐ _____

Day 3
- ☐ Romans 16
- ☐ CCC 2725
- ☐ DMP, chap. 8
- ☐ _____
- ☐ _____

Day 4
- ☐ 1 Corinthians 1
- ☐ CCC 2726
- ☐ DMP, chap. 9
- ☐ _____
- ☐ _____

Day 5
- ☐ 1 Corinthians 2
- ☐ CCC 2727
- ☐ DMP, chap. 10
- ☐ _____
- ☐ _____

Year 5, Week 28

Day 1
- ☐ 1 Corinthians 3
- ☐ CCC 2728
- ☐ DMP, chap. 11
- ☐ _____
- ☐ _____

Day 2
- ☐ 1 Corinthians 4
- ☐ CCC 2729
- ☐ DMP, chap. 12
- ☐ _____
- ☐ _____

Day 3
- ☐ 1 Corinthians 5
- ☐ CCC 2730
- ☐ DMP, chap. 13
- ☐ _____
- ☐ _____

Day 4
- ☐ 1 Corinthians 6
- ☐ CCC 2731
- ☐ DMP, chap. 14
- ☐ _____
- ☐ _____

Day 5
- ☐ 1 Corinthians 7
- ☐ CCC 2732
- ☐ DMP, chap. 15
- ☐ _____
- ☐ _____

> Apply yourself attentively to pray for all rational creatures,
> for the mystical body of the holy church, and for those friends
> whom I have given you, whom you love with particular love.
>
> — SAINT CATHERINE OF SIENA, *LITTLE TALKS WITH GOD*

Year 5, Week 29

Day 1
- ☐ 1 Corinthians 8
- ☐ CCC 2733
- ☐ DMP, chaps. 16-17
- ☐ _____
- ☐ _____

Day 2
- ☐ 1 Corinthians 9
- ☐ CCC 2734
- ☐ DMP, chap. 18
- ☐ _____
- ☐ _____

Day 3
- ☐ 1 Corinthians 10
- ☐ CCC 2735
- ☐ DMP, chap. 19
- ☐ _____
- ☐ _____

Day 4
- ☐ 1 Corinthians 11
- ☐ CCC 2736
- ☐ DMP, chap. 20
- ☐ _____
- ☐ _____

Day 5
- ☐ 1 Corinthians 12
- ☐ CCC 2737
- ☐ DMP, chap. 21; appendix
- ☐ _____
- ☐ _____

Year 5, Week 30

Day 1
- ☐ 1 Corinthians 13
- ☐ CCC 2738
- ☐ _Introduction to the Devout Life_ (IDL), part 1, chaps. 1-2
- ☐ _____
- ☐ _____

Day 2
- ☐ 1 Corinthians 14
- ☐ CCC 2739
- ☐ IDL, part 1, chaps. 3-6
- ☐ _____
- ☐ _____

Day 3
- ☐ 1 Corinthians 15
- ☐ CCC 2740
- ☐ IDL, part 1, chaps. 7-8
- ☐ _____
- ☐ _____

Day 4
- ☐ 1 Corinthians 16
- ☐ CCC 2741
- ☐ IDL, part 1, chap. 9
- ☐ _____
- ☐ _____

Day 5
- ☐ 2 Corinthians 1
- ☐ CCC 2742
- ☐ IDL, part 1, chap. 10
- ☐ _____
- ☐ _____

If we pray the gospel, we will allow Christ to grow in us.

— SAINT TERESA OF CALCUTTA, _NO GREATER LOVE_

Year 5, Week 31

Day 1
- ☐ 2 Corinthians 2
- ☐ CCC 2743
- ☐ IDL, part 1, chap. 11
- ☐ _____
- ☐ _____

Day 2
- ☐ 2 Corinthians 3
- ☐ CCC 2744
- ☐ IDL, part 1, chap. 12
- ☐ _____
- ☐ _____

Day 3
- ☐ 2 Corinthians 4
- ☐ CCC 2745
- ☐ IDL, part 1, chap. 13
- ☐ _____
- ☐ _____

Day 4
- ☐ 2 Corinthians 5
- ☐ CCC 2746
- ☐ IDL, part 1, chap. 14
- ☐ _____
- ☐ _____

Day 5
- ☐ 2 Corinthians 6
- ☐ CCC 2747
- ☐ IDL, part 1, chap. 15
- ☐ _____
- ☐ _____

Year 5, Week 32

Day 1
- ☐ 2 Corinthians 7
- ☐ CCC 2748
- ☐ IDL, part 1, chap. 16
- ☐ _____
- ☐ _____

Day 2
- ☐ 2 Corinthians 8
- ☐ CCC 2749
- ☐ IDL, part 1, chap. 17
- ☐ _____
- ☐ _____

Day 3
- ☐ 2 Corinthians 9
- ☐ CCC 2750
- ☐ IDL, part 1, chap. 18
- ☐ _____
- ☐ _____

Day 4
- ☐ 2 Corinthians 10
- ☐ CCC 2751
- ☐ IDL, part 1, chaps. 19-21
- ☐ _____
- ☐ _____

Day 5
- ☐ 2 Corinthians 11
- ☐ CCC 2752
- ☐ IDL, part 1, chaps. 22-24
- ☐ _____
- ☐ _____

If we wish, therefore, to please God we must pray
not only with the lips, but also with the heart.

—SAINT ALPHONSUS LIGUORI, *THE 12 STEPS TO HOLINESS AND SALVATION*

Year 5, Week 33

Day 1
- ☐ 2 Corinthians 12
- ☐ CCC 2753
- ☐ IDL, part 2, chaps. 1-3
- ☐ _____
- ☐ _____

Day 2
- ☐ 2 Corinthians 13
- ☐ CCC 2754
- ☐ IDL, part 2, chaps. 4-8
- ☐ _____
- ☐ _____

Day 3
- ☐ Galatians 1
- ☐ CCC 2755
- ☐ IDL, part 2, chaps. 9-12
- ☐ _____
- ☐ _____

Day 4
- ☐ Galatians 2
- ☐ CCC 2756
- ☐ IDL, part 2, chaps. 13-14
- ☐ _____
- ☐ _____

Day 5
- ☐ Galatians 3
- ☐ CCC 2757
- ☐ IDL, part 2, chaps. 15-18
- ☐ _____
- ☐ _____

Year 5, Week 34

Day 1
- ☐ Galatians 4
- ☐ CCC 2758
- ☐ IDL, part 2, chap. 19
- ☐ _____
- ☐ _____

Day 2
- ☐ Galatians 5
- ☐ CCC 2759
- ☐ IDL, part 2, chaps. 20-21
- ☐ _____
- ☐ _____

Day 3
- ☐ Galatians 6
- ☐ CCC 2760
- ☐ IDL, part 3, chaps. 1-2
- ☐ _____
- ☐ _____

Day 4
- ☐ Ephesians 1
- ☐ CCC 2761
- ☐ IDL, part 3, chaps. 3-4
- ☐ _____
- ☐ _____

Day 5
- ☐ Ephesians 2
- ☐ CCC 2762
- ☐ IDL, part 3, chaps. 5-6
- ☐ _____
- ☐ _____

> Now when we have received our Lord and have him in our body, let us not then let him alone, and get us forth about other things, and look no more unto him ... but let all our business be about him. Let us by devout prayer talk to him, by devout meditation talk with him.
>
> —SAINT THOMAS MORE, *TREATISE TO RECEIVE THE BLESSED BODY*

Year 5, Week 35

Day 1
- ☐ Ephesians 3
- ☐ CCC 2763
- ☐ IDL, part 3, chaps. 7-8
- ☐ _____
- ☐ _____

Day 2
- ☐ Ephesians 4
- ☐ CCC 2764
- ☐ IDL, part 3, chaps. 9-11
- ☐ _____
- ☐ _____

Day 3
- ☐ Ephesians 5
- ☐ CCC 2765
- ☐ IDL, part 3, chaps. 12-13
- ☐ _____
- ☐ _____

Day 4
- ☐ Ephesians 6
- ☐ CCC 2766
- ☐ IDL, part 3, chaps. 14-15
- ☐ _____
- ☐ _____

Day 5
- ☐ Philippians 1
- ☐ CCC 2767
- ☐ IDL, part 3, chaps. 16-18
- ☐ _____
- ☐ _____

Year 5, Week 36

Day 1
- ☐ Philippians 2
- ☐ CCC 2768
- ☐ IDL, part 3, chaps. 19-21
- ☐ _____
- ☐ _____

Day 2
- ☐ Philippians 3
- ☐ CCC 2769
- ☐ IDL, part 3, chaps. 22-23
- ☐ _____
- ☐ _____

Day 3
- ☐ Philippians 4
- ☐ CCC 2770
- ☐ IDL, part 3, chaps. 24-27
- ☐ _____
- ☐ _____

Day 4
- ☐ Colossians 1
- ☐ CCC 2771
- ☐ IDL, part 3, chap. 28
- ☐ _____
- ☐ _____

Day 5
- ☐ Colossians 2
- ☐ CCC 2772
- ☐ IDL, part 3, chap. 29
- ☐ _____
- ☐ _____

Prayer, true prayer, is a communication—and it occurs only when two people, two minds, are truly present to each other in some way.

—FATHER WALTER CISZEK, *HE LEADETH ME*

Year 5, Week 37

Day 1
- ☐ Colossians 3
- ☐ CCC 2773
- ☐ IDL, part 3, chaps. 30-33
- ☐ _____
- ☐ _____

Day 2
- ☐ Colossians 4
- ☐ CCC 2774
- ☐ IDL, part 3, chaps. 34-37
- ☐ _____
- ☐ _____

Day 3
- ☐ 1 Thessalonians 1
- ☐ CCC 2775
- ☐ IDL, part 3, chap. 38
- ☐ _____
- ☐ _____

Day 4
- ☐ 1 Thessalonians 2
- ☐ CCC 2776
- ☐ IDL, part 3, chap. 39
- ☐ _____
- ☐ _____

Day 5
- ☐ 1 Thessalonians 3
- ☐ CCC 2777
- ☐ IDL, part 3, chaps. 40-41
- ☐ _____
- ☐ _____

Year 5, Week 38

Day 1
- ☐ 1 Thessalonians 4
- ☐ CCC 2778
- ☐ IDL, part 4, chaps. 1-3
- ☐ _____
- ☐ _____

Day 2
- ☐ 1 Thessalonians 5
- ☐ CCC 2779
- ☐ IDL, part 4, chaps. 4-9
- ☐ _____
- ☐ _____

Day 3
- ☐ 2 Thessalonians 1
- ☐ CCC 2780
- ☐ IDL, part 4, chaps. 10-12
- ☐ _____
- ☐ _____

Day 4
- ☐ 2 Thessalonians 2
- ☐ CCC 2781
- ☐ IDL, part 4, chap. 13
- ☐ _____
- ☐ _____

Day 5
- ☐ 2 Thessalonians 3
- ☐ CCC 2782
- ☐ IDL, part 4, chap. 14
- ☐ _____
- ☐ _____

Meditation is the mother of true and solid devotion;
for it leads the will courageously and sweetly to perform
that which is pleasing in the sight of God.

— SAINT CLAUDE DE LA COLOMBIÈRE, *THE SPIRITUAL RETREAT*

Year 5, Week 39

Day 1
☐ 1 Timothy 1
☐ CCC 2783
☐ IDL, part 4, chap. 15
☐ _____
☐ _____

Day 2
☐ 1 Timothy 2
☐ CCC 2784
☐ IDL, part 5, chaps. 1-3
☐ _____
☐ _____

Day 3
☐ 1 Timothy 3
☐ CCC 2785
☐ IDL, part 5, chaps. 4-8
☐ _____
☐ _____

Day 4
☐ 1 Timothy 4
☐ CCC 2786
☐ IDL, part 5, chaps. 9-14
☐ _____
☐ _____

Day 5
☐ 1 Timothy 5
☐ CCC 2787
☐ IDL, part 5, chaps. 15-18
☐ _____
☐ _____

Year 5, Week 40

Upon completion of True Devotion to Mary, *the consecration can take place outside the context of the reading schedule.*

Day 1
☐ 1 Timothy 6
☐ CCC 2788
☐ *True Devotion to Mary* (TDM), "Preliminary Remarks"
☐ _____
☐ _____

Day 2
☐ 2 Timothy 1
☐ CCC 2789
☐ TDM, part 1, chap. 1 (half)
☐ _____
☐ _____

Day 3
☐ 2 Timothy 2
☐ CCC 2790
☐ TDM, part 1, chap. 1 (finish chapter)
☐ _____
☐ _____

Day 4
☐ 2 Timothy 3
☐ CCC 2791
☐ TDM, part 1, chap. 2 (half)
☐ _____
☐ _____

Day 5
☐ 2 Timothy 4
☐ CCC 2792
☐ TDM, part 1, chap. 2 (finish chapter)
☐ _____
☐ _____

Year 5, Week 41

Day 1
- ☐ Titus 1
- ☐ CCC 2793
- ☐ TDM, part 1, chap. 3 (half)
- ☐ _____
- ☐ _____

Day 2
- ☐ Titus 2
- ☐ CCC 2794
- ☐ TDM, part 1, chap. 3 (finish chapter)
- ☐ _____
- ☐ _____

Day 3
- ☐ Titus 3
- ☐ CCC 2795
- ☐ TDM, part 2, chap. 1
- ☐ _____
- ☐ _____

Day 4
- ☐ Philemon
- ☐ CCC 2796
- ☐ TDM, part 2, chap. 2 (one-fourth)
- ☐ _____
- ☐ _____

Day 5
- ☐ Hebrews 1
- ☐ CCC 2797
- ☐ TDM, part 2, chap. 2 (one-fourth)
- ☐ _____
- ☐ _____

Year 5, Week 42

Day 1
- ☐ Hebrews 2
- ☐ CCC 2798
- ☐ TDM, part 2, chap. 2 (one-fourth)
- ☐ _____
- ☐ _____

Day 2
- ☐ Hebrews 3
- ☐ CCC 2799
- ☐ TDM, part 2, chap. 2 (finish chapter)
- ☐ _____
- ☐ _____

Day 3
- ☐ Hebrews 4
- ☐ CCC 2800
- ☐ TDM, part 2, chap. 3
- ☐ _____
- ☐ _____

Day 4
- ☐ Hebrews 5
- ☐ CCC 2801
- ☐ TDM, part 2, chap. 4 (half)
- ☐ _____
- ☐ _____

Day 5
- ☐ Hebrews 6
- ☐ CCC 2802
- ☐ TDM, part 2, chap. 4 (finish chapter)
- ☐ _____
- ☐ _____

Have no anxiety about anything, but in everything by prayer and supplication with thanksgiving let your requests be made known to God. And the peace of God, which passes all understanding, will keep your hearts and your minds in Jesus Christ.

— PHILIPPIANS 4:6–7

Year 5, Week 43

Day 1
☐ Hebrews 7
☐ CCC 2803
☐ *The Soul of the Apostolate* (SOA), prologue; part 1, chaps. 1-2
☐ _____
☐ _____

Day 2
☐ Hebrews 8
☐ CCC 2804
☐ SOA, part 1, chap. 3
☐ _____
☐ _____

Day 3
☐ Hebrews 9
☐ CCC 2805
☐ SOA, part 1, chap. 4
☐ _____
☐ _____

Day 4
☐ Hebrews 10
☐ CCC 2806
☐ SOA, part 1, chap. 5
☐ _____
☐ _____

Day 5
☐ Hebrews 11
☐ CCC 2807
☐ SOA, part 1, chap. 6
☐ _____
☐ _____

Year 5, Week 44

Day 1
☐ Hebrews 12
☐ CCC 2808
☐ SOA, part 1, chap. 7
☐ _____
☐ _____

Day 2
☐ Hebrews 13
☐ CCC 2809
☐ SOA, part 2, chaps. 1-2
☐ _____
☐ _____

Day 3
☐ James 1
☐ CCC 2810
☐ SOA, part 2, chap. 3
☐ _____
☐ _____

Day 4
☐ James 2
☐ CCC 2811
☐ SOA, part 2, chaps. 4-5
☐ _____
☐ _____

Day 5
☐ James 3
☐ CCC 2812
☐ SOA, part 3, chap. 1
☐ _____
☐ _____

We assemble in a meeting and comprise a congregation, so that we might surround God with our prayers, as if by force of arms. Such violence is pleasing to God.

—TERTULLIAN, *APOLOGY*, AD 197

Year 5, Week 45

Day 1
- ☐ James 4
- ☐ CCC 2813
- ☐ SOA, part 3, chap. 2 (half)
- ☐ _____
- ☐ _____

Day 2
- ☐ James 5
- ☐ CCC 2814
- ☐ SOA, part 3, chap. 2 (finish chapter)
- ☐ _____
- ☐ _____

Day 3
- ☐ 1 Peter 1
- ☐ CCC 2815
- ☐ SOA, part 3, chap. 3, through c
- ☐ _____
- ☐ _____

Day 4
- ☐ 1 Peter 2
- ☐ CCC 2816
- ☐ SOA, part 3, chap. 3, d-f
- ☐ _____
- ☐ _____

Day 5
- ☐ 1 Peter 3
- ☐ CCC 2817
- ☐ SOA, part 4, through a
- ☐ _____
- ☐ _____

Year 5, Week 46

Day 1
- ☐ 1 Peter 4
- ☐ CCC 2818
- ☐ SOA, part 4, b
- ☐ _____
- ☐ _____

Day 2
- ☐ 1 Peter 5
- ☐ CCC 2819
- ☐ SOA, part 4, c (half)
- ☐ _____
- ☐ _____

Day 3
- ☐ 2 Peter 1
- ☐ CCC 2820-2821
- ☐ SOA, part 4, c (finish chapter)
- ☐ _____
- ☐ _____

Day 4
- ☐ 2 Peter 2
- ☐ CCC 2822
- ☐ SOA, part 4, d
- ☐ _____
- ☐ _____

Day 5
- ☐ 2 Peter 3
- ☐ CCC 2823
- ☐ SOA, part 4, e
- ☐ _____
- ☐ _____

Entrust yourself completely to My will saying, "Not as I want, but according to Your will, O God, let it be done unto me." These words, spoken from the depths of one's heart, can raise a soul to the summit of sanctity in a short time. In such a soul I delight.

—JESUS TO SAINT FAUSTINA, *DIARY OF SAINT MARIA FAUSTINA KOWALSKA*

Year 5, Week 47

Day 1
- ☐ 1 John 1
- ☐ CCC 2824
- ☐ SOA, part 4, f (half)
- ☐ _____
- ☐ _____

Day 2
- ☐ 1 John 2
- ☐ CCC 2825
- ☐ SOA, part 4, f (finish chapter)
- ☐ _____
- ☐ _____

Day 3
- ☐ 1 John 3
- ☐ CCC 2826
- ☐ SOA, part 4, g
- ☐ _____
- ☐ _____

Day 4
- ☐ 1 John 4
- ☐ CCC 2827
- ☐ SOA, part 5, chap. 1 through "VIDEO"
- ☐ _____
- ☐ _____

Day 5
- ☐ 1 John 5
- ☐ CCC 2828-2829
- ☐ SOA, part 5, "SITIO" through "VOLEO TECUM"
- ☐ _____
- ☐ _____

Year 5, Week 48

Day 1
- ☐ 2 John
- ☐ CCC 2830
- ☐ SOA, part 5, chap. 3 through II, "What Is Liturgical Life?"
- ☐ _____
- ☐ _____

Day 2
- ☐ 3 John
- ☐ CCC 2831
- ☐ SOA, part 5, chap. 3, III, "The Liturgical Spirit—'First Principle'"
- ☐ _____
- ☐ _____

Day 3
- ☐ Jude
- ☐ CCC 2832
- ☐ SOA, part 5, chap. 3, III, "Second Principle"
- ☐ _____
- ☐ _____

Day 4
- ☐ Revelation 1
- ☐ CCC 2833
- ☐ SOA, part 5, chap. 3, III, "Third Principle—Christus"
- ☐ _____
- ☐ _____

Day 5
- ☐ Revelation 2
- ☐ CCC 2834
- ☐ SOA, part 5, chap. 3, IV
- ☐ _____
- ☐ _____

Year 5, Week 49

Day 1
- ☐ Revelation 3
- ☐ CCC 2835
- ☐ SOA, part 5, chap. 3, V
- ☐ _____
- ☐ _____

Day 2
- ☐ Revelation 4
- ☐ CCC 2836
- ☐ SOA, part 5, chap. 4 (half)
- ☐ _____
- ☐ _____

Day 3
- ☐ Revelation 5
- ☐ CCC 2837
- ☐ SOA, part 5, chap. 4 (finish chapter)
- ☐ _____
- ☐ _____

Day 4
- ☐ Revelation 6
- ☐ CCC 2838
- ☐ SOA, part 5, chap. 5
- ☐ _____
- ☐ _____

Day 5
- ☐ Revelation 7
- ☐ CCC 2839-2841
- ☐ SOA, epilogue; appendix
- ☐ _____
- ☐ _____

Year 5, Week 50

Day 1
- ☐ Revelation 8
- ☐ CCC 2842
- ☐ _Little Talks with God_ (LTG), introduction
- ☐ _____
- ☐ _____

Day 2
- ☐ Revelation 9
- ☐ CCC 2843
- ☐ LTG, "On Divine Providence"
- ☐ _____
- ☐ _____

Day 3
- ☐ Revelation 10
- ☐ CCC 2844
- ☐ LTG, "On Discretion" (one-fifth)
- ☐ _____
- ☐ _____

Day 4
- ☐ Revelation 11
- ☐ CCC 2845
- ☐ LTG, "On Discretion" (one-fifth)
- ☐ _____
- ☐ _____

Day 5
- ☐ Revelation 12
- ☐ CCC 2846
- ☐ LTG, "On Discretion" (one-fifth)
- ☐ _____
- ☐ _____

Shut the door of your room and call Jesus, your Beloved, to you, and stay there with Him. There is no greater peace anywhere else than to be with Jesus.

— THOMAS À KEMPIS, _THE IMITATION OF CHRIST_

Year 5, Week 51

Day 1
- ☐ Revelation 13
- ☐ CCC 2847
- ☐ LTG, "On Discretion" (one-fifth)
- ☐ _____
- ☐ _____

Day 2
- ☐ Revelation 14
- ☐ CCC 2848
- ☐ LTG, "On Discretion" (finish chapter)
- ☐ _____
- ☐ _____

Day 3
- ☐ Revelation 15
- ☐ CCC 2849
- ☐ LTG, "On Prayer" (one-fifth)
- ☐ _____
- ☐ _____

Day 4
- ☐ Revelation 16
- ☐ CCC 2850-2851
- ☐ LTG, "On Prayer" (one-fifth)
- ☐ _____
- ☐ _____

Day 5
- ☐ Revelation 17
- ☐ CCC 2852
- ☐ LTG, "On Prayer" (one-fifth)
- ☐ _____
- ☐ _____

Year 5, Week 52

Day 1
- ☐ Revelation 18
- ☐ CCC 2853
- ☐ LTG, "On Prayer" (one-fifth)
- ☐ _____
- ☐ _____

Day 2
- ☐ Revelation 19
- ☐ CCC 2854
- ☐ LTG, "On Prayer" (finish chapter)
- ☐ _____
- ☐ _____

Day 3
- ☐ Revelation 20
- ☐ CCC 2855-2856
- ☐ LTG, "On Obedience" (one-third)
- ☐ _____
- ☐ _____

Day 4
- ☐ Revelation 21
- ☐ CCC 2857-2860
- ☐ LTG, "On Obedience" (one-third)
- ☐ _____
- ☐ _____

Day 5
- ☐ Revelation 22
- ☐ CCC 2861-2865
- ☐ LTG, "On Obedience" (finish chapter)
- ☐ _____
- ☐ _____

Pray at all times in the Spirit, with all prayer and supplication.

— EPHESIANS 6:18

RECOMMENDED READING LIST

Contributors

Bishop James Conley
Bishop of Lincoln, Nebraska

Charlotte Ostermann
Catholic speaker, author, blogger, educator

Dan Burke
Executive director, *National Catholic Register*; founder, Catholic Spiritual Direction

Danny Abramowicz
Former NFL football player and coach; host of EWTN's *Crossing the Goal*

Diana von Glahn
Producer and host of *The Faithful Traveler*, an EWTN travel series that explores art, architecture, history, and faith at shrines around the world

Father C. John McCloskey
Priest of the Prelature of Opus Dei and member of the Priestly Society of the Holy Cross, writer, and spiritual director (see appendix 2 for Fr. McCloskey's complete "Catholic Lifetime Reading List")

Father Mike Schmitz
Chaplain for Newman Catholic Campus Ministries at the University of Minnesota in Duluth; director of the Office of Youth Ministry for the Diocese of Duluth; popular speaker on all things Catholic

Father Timothy Gallagher
International minister of retreats, spiritual direction, and teaching about the spiritual life; author of nine books, including seven on the spiritual teaching of Saint Ignatius of Loyola

Jason Evert
Catholic author and chastity speaker; founder of Totus Tuus Press and Chastity Project

Jennifer Fulwiler
Radio host, author, speaker

Karl Keating
Founder of Catholic Answers

Lisa Hendey
Founder and editor of CatholicMom.com; bestselling author

Marcy Klatt
The Catholic Book Lady

Mike Aquilina
Award-winning author of more than forty books on Catholic history, doctrine, and devotion

Patrick Coffin
Host of *Catholic Answers Live*; speaker, author, and movie producer

Patti MacGuire Armstrong
Correspondent for *Our Sunday Visitor* and *National Catholic Register*; award-winning author

Paul McCusker
Dramatist for audio, stage, and screen; author of more than twenty-five novels

Peter Kreeft
Professor of philosophy at Boston College and the King's College; author of numerous best-selling books on Christian philosophy, theology, and apologetics

Sam Guzman
Founder and editor of *The Catholic Gentleman*

Sarah Reinhard
Catholic author, blogger, and speaker

Steve Ray
Catholic speaker, author, pilgrimage guide, and frequent guest on EWTN

Tim Gray
President of the Augustine Institute; world-renowned speaker, author, and teacher

Tim Staples
Director of Apologetics and Evangelization at Catholic Answers

Trent Beattie
Catholic author and editor

Trent Horn
Apologist and speaker for Catholic Answers

Notable Favorites of Notable Catholics
(98 Must Reads)

Several prominent Catholics were asked to share at least one favorite book from each of the four pillars of faith. Responses were compiled to create the list you have before you. You may notice that some books were suggested by more than one person. Additionally, certain titles were suggested by multiple people, but in different categories. This reflects the fact that there is some overlap between pillars. *He Leadeth Me* by Father Walter Ciszek, for example, is in invaluable addition to the "Life in Christ" pillar, because Ciszek's testimony of his time in captivity provides critical insight into what it means to live out the will of God joyfully. Additionally, it works in the prayer section because Cizsek's testimony essentially teaches the value of prayer at all times, in all places.

The Profession of Faith

Catechism of the Catholic Church (Dan Burke, Lisa Hendey)
The King's Achievement by Robert Hugh Benson (Paul McCusker)
Saints and Sinners: A History of the Popes by Eamon Duffy (Paul McCusker)
Come Rack, Come Rope by Robert Hugh Benson (Paul McCusker)
Theology and Sanity by Frank Sheed (Peter Kreeft, Trent Horn, Bishop Conley)
Practical Theology by Peter Kreeft (Sarah Reinhard)
The Ultimate Catholic Quiz: 100 Questions Most Catholics Can't Answer by Karl Keating (Jennifer Fulwiler)
Scripture Alone? by Joel Peters (Trent Beattie)
The Russian Church and the Papacy by Vladimir Soloviev (Sam Guzman)
Purgatory by Fr. F. X. Shouppe (Diana von Glahn)
Father Elijah by Michael D. O'Brien (Diana von Glahn)
Chronicles of Narnia (series) by C. S. Lewis (Diana von Glahn)

The Radiance of Being by Stratford Caldecott (Charlotte Ostermann)

The Difference God Makes by Cardinal George (Charlotte Ostermann)

The Religious Sense by Fr. Luigi Giussani (Charlotte Ostermann)

God or Nothing by Cardinal Sarah (Charlotte Ostermann)

Love and Responsibility by Karol Wojtyła (Jason Evert)

Christianity for Modern Pagans by Peter Kreeft (Fr. Mike Schmitz)

The Spirit of Early Christian Thought: Seeking the Face of God by Robert Louis Wilken (Mike Aquilina)

Difficulties by Ronald Knox and Arnold Lunn (Karl Keating)

Principles of Catholic Theology: Building Stones for a Fundamental Theology by Joseph Cardinal Ratzinger (Tim Staples)

The New Testament and the People of God by N. T. Wright (Tim Gray)

Theology for Beginners by Frank Sheed (Patrick Coffin)

To Know Christ Jesus by Frank Sheed (Fr. Timothy Gallagher)

The Lord by Romano Guardini (Danny Abramowicz)

Celebration of the Christian Mystery

Spirit of the Liturgy by Pope Benedict XVI (Dan Burke, Charlotte Ostermann, Fr. Mike Schmitz, Mike Aquilina)

Father Elijah by Michael O'Brien (Paul McCusker)

Jesus and the Jewish Roots of the Eucharist by Brant Pitre (Paul McCusker)

7 Secrets of the Eucharist by Vinny Flynn (Marcy Klatt, Jennifer Fulwiler)

The Lamb's Supper by Scott Hahn (Peter Kreeft, Charlotte Ostermann, Trent Horn)

Rebuilt: Awakening the Faithful, Reaching the Lost, and Making Church Matter by Fr. Michael White and Tom Corcoran (Lisa Hendey)

Mr. Blue by Myles Connolly (Sarah Reinhard)

Pardon and Peace by Father Alfred Wilson (not to be confused with another book with the same title from Ignatius Press) (Trent Beattie)

The Incredible Catholic Mass by Venerable Martin von Cochem (Trent Beattie)

Visits to the Blessed Sacrament by St. Alphonsus Liguori (Trent Beattie)

These Are the Sacraments by Fulton J. Sheen (Sam Guzman, Tim Staples)

In Conversation with God series by Francis Fernandez (Diana von Glahn)

The Seven Sacraments by Stratford Caldecott (Charlotte Ostermann)

This Is the Mass by Henri Daniel-Rops (Karl Keating)

The Bible and the Liturgy by Jean Danilou (Tim Gray)

Swear to God: The Promise and Power of the Sacraments by Dr. Scott Hahn (Patrick Coffin)

Christian Prayer (for praying the Liturgy of the Hours) (Fr. Timothy Gallagher)

Liturgical Piety by Louis Bouyer (Bishop Conley)

Catechism of the Catholic Church (Danny Abramowicz)

Life in Christ

I Want to See God by Fr. P. Marie Eugene (Dan Burke)

Loss and Gain by John Henry Newman (Paul McCusker)

The Lord by Romano Guardini (Paul McCusker)

The Day Christ Died by Jim Bishop (Paul McCusker)

The Greatest Story Ever Told by Fulton Oursler (Paul McCusker)

The Better Part by Fr. John Bartunek (Paul McCusker)

Trustful Surrender to Divine Providence by Fr. Jean Baptiste Saint-Jure (Patti McGuire Armstrong)

The Shadow of His Wings by Fr. Gereon Goldmann, OFM (Patti McGuire Armstrong, Jennifer Fulwiler)

When You Suffer: Biblical Keys for Hope and Understanding by Jeff Cavins (Patti McGuire Armstrong)

Mother Angelica: The Remarkable Story of a Nun, Her Nerve, and a Network of Miracles by Raymond Arroyo (Patti McGuire Armstrong)

These Beautiful Bones: An Everyday Theology of the Body by Emily Stimpson (Marcy Klatt)

Jesus of Nazareth: The Baptism in the Jordan to the Transfiguration by Pope Benedict XVI (Marcy Klatt)

The Diary of Saint Faustina (Marcy Klatt)

The Practice of the Presence of God by Brother Lawrence (Peter Kreeft)

The Imitation of Christ by Thomas à Kempis (Lisa Hendey, Diana von Glahn, Trent Horn, Danny Abramowicz)

Life of Christ by Archbishop Fulton Sheen (Sarah Reinhard, Diana von Glahn, Tim Staples)

The Screwtape Letters by C. S. Lewis (Sarah Reinhard, Diana von Glahn)

Achieving Peace of Heart by Father Narciso Irala (Trent Beattie)

The Thoughts of St. Thérèse (TAN Books) (Trent Beattie)

The Kolbe Reader by St. Maximilian Kolbe (Sam Guzman)

The Way by Saint Josemaría Escrivá (Diana von Glahn)

The Great Divorce by C. S. Lewis (Diana von Glahn)

Souls at Rest by Charlotte Ostermann (Charlotte Ostermann)

Transformation in Christ by Dietrich von Hildebrand (Charlotte Ostermann)

The Reed of God by Caryll Houselander (Charlotte Ostermann)

Bridging the Great Divide by Fr. Robert Barron (Charlotte Ostermann)

Beauty for Truth's Sake by Stratford Caldecott (Charlotte Ostermann)

God Alone by Saint Louis de Montfort (Jason Everett)

Learning the Virtues That Lead You to God by Father Romano Guardini (Fr. Mike Schmitz)

The Hidden Power of Kindness by Lawrence Lovasik (Mike Aquilina)

To Know Christ Jesus by Frank Sheed (Karl Keating)

The Cost of Discipleship by Dietrich Bonhoeffer (Tim Gray)

The Divine Romance by Fulton J. Sheen (Patrick Coffin)

He Leadeth Me by Walter Ciszek (Fr. Timothy Gallagher)

In the Likeness of Christ by Edward Leen (Bishop Conley)

Prayer

Interior Castle by St. Teresa of Ávila (Dan Burke, Tim Staples)

The Fulfillment of All Desire by Ralph Martin (Paul McCusker)

Introduction to the Devout Life by St. Francis de Sales (Paul McCusker, Lisa Hendey, Fr. Timothy Gallagher)

Time for God by Fr. Jacques Philippe (Patti McGuire Armstrong)

Worshipping a Hidden God by Archbishop Luis Martinez (Marcy Klatt)

True Devotion to the Holy Spirit by Archbishop Luis Martinez (Marcy Klatt)

Praying Scripture for a Change: An Introduction to Lectio Divina by Tim Gray (Marcy Klatt)

The Fire Within by Fr. Thomas Dubay (Marcy Klatt, Peter Kreeft, Charlotte Ostermann)

He Leadeth Me by Walter Ciszek (Jennifer Fulwiler, Mike Aquilina)

Prayer: The Great Means of Grace by an anonymous nun (Trent Beattie)

Divine Intimacy by Fr. Gabriel of St. Mary Magdalene (Sam Guzman)

The Diary of Saint Faustina (Diana von Glahn)

The Secret of the Rosary by St. Louis de Montfort (Diana von Glahn)

The Rosary of Our Lady by Romano Guardini (Charlotte Ostermann)

Praying the Rosary for Inner Healing by Dwight Longenecker (Charlotte Ostermann)

The Great Conversation by Peter Kreeft (Trent Horn)

The Soul of the Apostolate by Jean-Baptiste Chautard (Jason Evert)

Abandonment to Divine Providence by Jean-Pierre de Caussade (Fr. Mike Schmitz, Danny Abramowicz)

Prayers, Verses, and Devotions by John Henry Newman (Karl Keating)

A Ladder for Monks by Guigo the Carthusian (Tim Gray)

Confessions by St. Augustine (Tim Gray)

The Bible, particularly *The Ignatius Study Bible, Second Catholic Edition* (Patrick Coffin)

Deep Conversion, Deep Prayer Thomas Dubay (Bishop Conley)

A CATHOLIC LIFETIME READING PLAN

by Father C. John McCloskey

Catechism of the Catholic Church (Catholicism Explained/Theology)

Karl Adam, *The Spirit of Catholicism* (Catholicism Explained/Theology)

Augustine, *City of God* (Spiritual Classics)

Augustine, *Confessions* (Spiritual Classics)

Jordan Aumann, *Spiritual Theology* (Spiritual Reading)

Benedict Baur, *Frequent Confession* (Spiritual Reading)

Benedict Baur, *In Silence with God* (Spiritual Reading)

Hilaire Belloc, *The Great Heresies* (History and Culture)

Hilaire Belloc, *How The Reformation Happened* (History and Culture)

Hilaire Belloc, *Survivals and New Arrivals* (History and Culture)

Benedict XVI, *Opera Omnia* (Misc.)

Benedict XVI, *Day by Day with the Pope* (Misc.)

Art and Laraine Bennett, *The Temperament God Gave You* (Misc.)

Art and Laraine Bennett, *The Emotions God Gave You* (Misc.)

Robert Hugh Benson, *Lord of the World* (Literary Classics)

George Bernanos, *The Diary of a Country Priest* (Literary Classics)

Louis Bouyer, *The Spirit and Forms of Protestantism* (Catholicism Explained/Theology)

Eugene Boylan, *Difficulties in Mental Prayer* (Spiritual Reading)

Eugene Boylan, *Tremendous Lover* (Spiritual Reading)

Cormac Burke, *Covenanted Happiness* (Spiritual Reading)

Warren Carroll, *History of Christendom* (all volumes) (History and Culture)

St. Catherine of Siena, *Little Talks with God* (modernized version of *The Dialogues*) (Spiritual Classics)

Miguel de Cervantes, *Don Quixote* (Literary Classics)

Jean-Baptiste Chautard, *Soul of Apostolate* (Spiritual Reading)

G. K. Chesterton, *The Everlasting Man* (Spiritual Classics)

G. K. Chesterton, *Orthodoxy* (Spiritual Classics)

G. K. Chesterton, *St. Thomas Aquinas* (Holy Men and Women)

G. K. Chesterton, *St. Francis of Assisi* (Holy Men and Women)

Georges Chevrot, *Simon Peter* (Holy Men and Women)

Walter Ciszek, *He Leadeth Me* (Spiritual Reading)

H. W. Crocker III, *Triumph* (History and Culture)

Jean-Pierre de Caussaude, *Abandonment to Divine Providence* (Spiritual Reading)

Dante, *Divine Comedy* (Literary Classics)

Christopher Dawson, *Christianity and European Culture* (edited by Gerald J. Russello; History and Culture)

Dorothy Day, *Long Loneliness* (Holy Men and Women)

Luis de la Palma, *The Sacred Passion* (Spiritual Reading)

Francis de Sales, *Introduction to Devout Life* (Spiritual Reading)

Francis de Sales, *Treatise on the Love of God* (Spiritual Reading)

Jean C. J. d'Elbée, *I Believe in Love* (Spiritual Reading)

T. S. Eliot, *Christianity and Culture* (Literary Classics)

Shusaku Endo, *Silence* (Literary Classics)

Clarence J. Enzler, *My Other Self* (Misc.)

Josemaría Escrivá, *Christ Is Passing By* (Spiritual Reading)

Josemaría Escrivá, *The Way, Furrow, The Forge* (Spiritual Reading)

Josemaría Escrivá, *The Way of the Cross* (Spiritual Reading)

Frederick William Faber, *All for Jesus* (Spiritual Reading)

Fr. Walter Farrell, *My Way of Life* (Spiritual Classics)

Réginald Garrigou-Lagrange, *Three Ages of Interior Life*, I (Spiritual Reading)

Réginald Garrigou-Lagrange, *Three Ages of Interior Life*, II (Spiritual Reading)

Louis Granada, *The Sinner's Guide* (Spiritual Reading)

Romano Guardini, *The Lord*

Romano Guardini, *The End of the Modern World* (History and Culture)

Scott and Kimberly Hahn, *Rome Sweet Home* (Catholicism Explained/Theology)

James Hannam, *God's Philosophers* (History)

Alice von Hildebrand, *The Privilege of Being a Woman*

Dietrich von Hildebrand, *Transformation in Christ*

Joseph Holzner, *Paul of Tarsus* (Spiritual Reading)

Gerard Manley Hopkins, *Hopkins: Poetry and Prose* (Literary Classics)

John XXIII, *Journal of a Soul* (Holy Men and Women)

John of the Cross, *Dark Night of the Soul* (Spiritual Classics)

John Paul II, all works (Misc.)

Matthew Kelly, *Rediscovering Catholicism* (Spiritual Reading)

Thomas à Kempis, *The Imitation of Christ* (Spiritual Reading)

Ronald Knox, *Enthusiasm* (History and Culture)

Peter Kreeft, *Christianity for Modern Pagans* (Catholicism Explained/Theology)

Jean Leclercq, *Love of Learning and the Desire for God* (History and Culture)

C. S. Lewis, *Mere Christianity* (Spiritual Classics)

C. S. Lewis, *The Problem of Pain* (Spiritual Classics)

C. S. Lewis, *The Screwtape Letters* (Spiritual Classics)

Alphonsus Liguori, *The Practice of the Love of God* (Spiritual Reading)

Alphonsus Liguori, The *12 Steps to Holiness and Salvation* (Spiritual Reading)

Alphonsus Liguori, *Uniformity with God's Will* (Spiritual Reading)

Luiz Martinez, *True Devotion to the Holy Spirit* (Spiritual Reading)

Louis de Montfort, *True Devotion to Mary* (Spiritual Reading)

Lawrence Lovasik, *The Hidden Power of Kindness* (Spiritual Reading)

Alessandro Manzoni, *The Betrothed* (Spiritual Reading)

Georgina Masson, *The Companion Guide to Rome* (Misc.)

Thomas Merton, *The Seven Storey Mountain* (Holy Men and Women)

James Monti, *The King's Good Servant but God's First* (Holy Men and Women)

Thomas More, *The Sadness of Christ* (Spiritual Reading)

Malcolm Muggeridge, *Something Beautiful for God* (Holy Men and Women)

Richard John Neuhaus, *Catholic Matters* (Misc.)

John Henry Newman, *Apologia Pro Vita Sua* (Holy Men and Women)

John Henry Newman, *Essay on Development of Christian Doctrine* (Catholicism Explained/Theology)

John Henry Newman, *The Idea of a University* (Literary Classics)

John Henry Newman, *The Rule of Our Warfare*

Flannery O'Connor, *Flannery O'Connor: Complete Stories* (Literary Classics)

Ludwig Ott, *Fundamentals of Catholic Dogma* (Catholicism Explained/Theology)

Fulton Oursler, *The Greatest Story Ever Told* (Spiritual Classics)

Walker Percy, *Lost in the Cosmos* (Literary Classics)

Walker Percy, *Love in the Ruins* (Literary Classics)

Bonaventure Perquin, *Abba Father* (Spiritual Reading)

Josef Pieper, *The Four Cardinal Virtues* (Catholicism Explained/Theology)

Fr. Jacques Phillipe, all works

Raoul Plus, *Winning Souls for Christ* (Spiritual Reading)

Charles Rice, *50 Questions on the Natural Law* (Misc.).

Peter Thomas Rohrbach, *Conversation with Christ* (Spiritual Reading)

Lorenzo Scupoli, *Spiritual Combat* (Spiritual Reading)

A. G. Sertillanges, *The Intellectual Life* (Misc.)

Frank Sheed, *Theology for Beginners* (Spiritual Reading)

Frank Sheed, *To Know Christ Jesus* (Spiritual Reading)

Fulton Sheen, *Life of Christ* (Spiritual Reading)
Fulton Sheen, *Three to Get Married* (Spiritual Reading)
Henryk Sienkiewicz, *Quo Vadis* (Literary Classics)
Edith Stein, *Essays on Woman* (Misc.)
Federico Suarez, *Mary of Nazareth* (Holy Men and Women)
Adolphe Tanqueray, *The Spiritual Life* (Spiritual Reading)
Mother Teresa, *Meditations from a Simple Path* (Spiritual Classics)
Teresa of Ávila, *Interior Castle* (Spiritual Classics)
Teresa of Ávila, *The Way of Perfection* (Spiritual Classics)
Thérèse of Lisieux, *The Story of a Soul* (Spiritual Classics)
J. R. R. Tolkien, *The Lord of Rings* (Literary Classics)
Francis Trochu, *The Curé d'Ars* (Holy Men and Women)
Sigrid Undset, *Kristen Lavransdatter* 1 (Literary Classics)
Sigrid Undset, *Kristen Lavransdatter* 2 (Literary Classics)
Sigrid Undset, *Kristen Lavransdatter* 3 (Literary Classics)
Gerald Vann, *The Divine Pity*
William T. Walsh, *Our Lady of Fátima* (History and Culture)
Evelyn Waugh, *Brideshead Revisited* (Literary Classics)
Gerard B. Wegemer, *Thomas More* (Holy Men and Women)
George Weigel, *Witness to Hope* (Holy Men and Women)

VICKI BURBACH

As a wife and busy mother of six children, Vicki Burbach relishes the calm inspiration of spiritual reading amidst the roller coaster of life. A passionate convert to the Faith, Vicki is an avid reader who moderates an international book club at SpiritualDirection.com. She feels blessed to journey with thousands of like-minded pilgrims through some of the greatest Catholic books ever written. Her writing has been featured online at *National Catholic Register*, Big Pulpit, and *Catholic Exchange*. You can also find her at PelicansBreast.com.

SPIRITUAL DIRECTION
≈ SERIES ≈

SOPHIA INSTITUTE PRESS

If this book has caused a stir in your heart to continue to pursue your relationship with God, we invite you to explore two extraordinary resources, SpiritualDirection.com and the Avila Institute for Spiritual Formation.

The readers of SpiritualDirection.com reside in almost every country of the world where hearts yearn for God. It is the world's most popular English site dedicated to authentic Catholic spirituality.

The Students of the Avila Institute for Spiritual Formation sit at the feet of the rich and deep well of the wisdom of the saints.

You can find more about the Avila Institute at
WWW.AVILA-INSTITUTE.COM.

Sophia Institute

Sophia Institute is a nonprofit institution that seeks to nurture the spiritual, moral, and cultural life of souls and to spread the Gospel of Christ in conformity with the authentic teachings of the Roman Catholic Church.

Sophia Institute Press fulfills this mission by offering translations, reprints, and new publications that afford readers a rich source of the enduring wisdom of mankind.

Sophia Institute also operates two popular online Catholic resources: CrisisMagazine.com and CatholicExchange.com.

Crisis Magazine provides insightful cultural analysis that arms readers with the arguments necessary for navigating the ideological and theological minefields of the day. *Catholic Exchange* provides world news from a Catholic perspective as well as daily devotionals and articles that will help you to grow in holiness and live a life consistent with the teachings of the Church.

In 2013, Sophia Institute launched Sophia Institute for Teachers to renew and rebuild Catholic culture through service to Catholic education. With the goal of nurturing the spiritual, moral, and cultural life of souls, and an abiding respect for the role and work of teachers, we strive to provide materials and programs that are at once enlightening to the mind and ennobling to the heart; faithful and complete, as well as useful and practical.

Sophia Institute gratefully recognizes the Solidarity Association for preserving and encouraging the growth of our apostolate over the course of many years. Without their generous and timely support, this book would not be in your hands.

www.SophiaInstitute.com
www.CatholicExchange.com
www.CrisisMagazine.com
www.SophiaInstituteforTeachers.org

Sophia Institute Press® is a registered trademark of Sophia Institute. Sophia Institute is a tax-exempt institution as defined by the Internal Revenue Code, Section 501(c)(3). Tax I.D. 22-2548708.